My Lord and My God

By Theodore Pitcairn

The Book Sealed With Seven Seals
(The Bible or Word of God Unfolded and Explained)

The Ten Commandments

The Seven Days of Creation

My Lord and My God

MY LORD
AND
MY GOD

ESSAYS ON
MODERN RELIGION,
THE BIBLE
AND
EMANUEL SWEDENBORG

by

Theodore Pitcairn

Exposition Press • *New York*

First Printing, March 1967
Second Printing, March 1967
Third Printing, April 1967
Fourth Printing, August 1967
Fifth Printing, September 1967

EXPOSITION PRESS INC.

386 Park Avenue South   New York, N.Y. 10016

FIRST   EDITION

© 1967 by Theodore Pitcairn. *All rights reserved, including the right of reproduction in whole or in part in any form except for short quotations in critical essays and reviews.* Manufactured in the United States of America.

EP 45677

CONTENTS

PART TWO

*An Explication of Genesis and
Certain Other Chapters of the Bible
Based on the Work "Arcana Coelestia"
by Emanuel Swedenborg*

Contents   vii

PROLOGUE

With the exception of the chapter on atheists and agnostics, this book is addressed not to the sophisticated nor to the naïve or credulous, but to those who believe there is a God and that it is likely that He has revealed Himself to man, and who desire carefully to weigh the evidence with an open mind.

This book will not appeal to those whose ambition is to belong to the avant-garde, or the wave of the future. We believe that there are few who are willing to give up much of their worldly ambitions for the sake of finding the truth and living according to it. On the other hand, there are many who are curious about the latest novelties, and who are eager to appear modern and in tune with the times.

A religious belief which demands profound study and effort, which has no prospect of becoming popular, which is and will be despised by the learned sophisticates, and which therefore will be accepted by few, has little appeal, except to those who desire to find and follow the truth even if it causes them to be despised or ridiculed.

The great majority of people say that they believe in God. But in modern times, particularly in America and Europe, the idea of God has become more and more vague and uncertain, so that to many, God has become an unknown God. It is the hope of this book that for some the following expression of Paul may be fulfilled: "For as I passed by, and beheld your devotions, I found an altar with this inscription, TO THE UNKNOWN GOD. Whom therefore ye ignorantly worship, Him declare I unto you." (Acts 17:23.)

When Abraham Lincoln was running for President,

some of the clergy, who knew that he was not a member of
any denomination, came to him and asked him what was his
religion. To this question he replied: "Thou shalt love the
Lord thy God with all thy heart, and with all thy soul, and
with all thy mind, and with all thy strength: this is the
First and Great Commandment. And the Second is like
unto it; thou shalt love thy neighbor as thyself." (Lincoln
combined Matthew 22:37-39 and Mark 12:30,31.)

Most Christians would say that they agree with Lincoln,
but there is scarcely one in a hundred who seriously attempts actually to carry out such a belief in his life.

In past centuries many made faith, or the contemplation of God, the only thing of importance and neglected the
things having to do with our love and duty to our neighbor.
At the present day most, even in the churches, looking to
the good of society—or social gospel, as it is called—which
they identify with love toward their neighbor, neglect the
words of the greatest Commandment, "Thou shalt love the
Lord thy God ... with all thy *mind.*"

They regard theology, which is loving God with the
mind, as of little importance.

Is it not a primary saying of the Lord, "Ye shall know
the truth and the truth shall make you free"? (John 8:32.)
If a person does not believe it is possible to know the truth
for certain, can he honestly think he is a Christian?

Yet love of one's neighbor is merely an earthly love akin
to the animal feeling if it is not united to loving God with
all one's heart, soul, mind, and strength, which idea includes a wholehearted desire to understand God, or, what is
the same, to have a theology. On the other hand, the love
of God, apart from loving and doing one's duty to one's
neighbor, is not a love of God at all; for the Lord said, "He
who hath My commandments and keepeth them, he it is that
loveth Me" (John 14:21), and He said, "This is My Commandment, that ye love one another, as I have loved you."
(John 15:12.)

Many eagerly give much time and effort to solving a

business problem or to a study of economics, a foreign language, literature, philosophy, or other subjects; but when it comes to theology, they feel an aversion to any serious study. With many the very thought of making a serious effort to understand the nature of the Trinity, even the thought that it is a primary duty to try to understand this subject, causes a feeling of annoyance. Yet how can one love God with all one's understanding if one does not know for sure whether God is one person or three persons? Thus, although the First and Great Commandment is subscribed to in theory by nearly all, in practice it is rejected: a sign that there is very little real love of God.

How many strive with all their might to understand and know God, and to live according to their understanding with all their heart and soul? Are they not few? If this is so, why is it so?

There are many reasons why there is an aversion to a serious study of theology; one of them is spiritual laziness. To many the pursuit of the things of this world appears real, bringing concrete results, whereas the pursuit of the knowledge and wisdom of God appears vague and unreal, with no likelihood of arriving at any certainty or any definite concept. Even in the churches it has been taught that the mysteries of faith are above human comprehension, and that therefore "the understanding must be kept in obedience to faith"—which necessarily implies a blind faith. Such an idea certainly discourages anyone from seriously trying to obey the First and Great Commandment.

Another reason is that many doubt that there is any definite source of truth concerning God. Many doubt that the Bible is the Word of God, and see no way by which they can come to a sure knowledge of God; they therefore turn to science or other subjects where they feel they can deal with facts and actual experiences, or they seek to understand the meaning of life in their subjective experiences.

Nowadays most people think theology is unimportant; they think that they can have a kind of intuition of God,

apart from any definite idea. If a person thinks he loves
his father and mother and is uninterested in the character
and quality of his parents, in the history of their life, in
their goals, their ideals, and their thoughts, his love is a
sentimental love of no value. In the same way, if a man
thinks he loves God and is uninterested in theology, or does
not hope to find a true theology, his love is a sentimental
love of no value; for theology is nothing but the knowledge
of God, and to pretend to love without wishing to know
God is a fantasy. In a word, if one says he loves God and is
uninterested in theology, his love is not genuine.

In ancient Greece there were two classes of intellectual
leaders: the philosophers and the sophists. The true philosopher was the one who loved wisdom, who placed the
pursuit of wisdom above all personal advantage, who was
willing to sacrifice himself for the truth. The true philosopher exposed sham goodness and fallacious opinions without regard to person. He searched for the basic causes of
things. He was therefore at times persecuted—even put to
death. Socrates, before taking hemlock, said, "I would
rather die having spoken after my manner than to speak
in your manner and live." The sophist was one who, as in
modern times, taught "how to make friends and influence
people." He taught the art of becoming a demagogue. His
art consisted of the striking phrase, the superficial appearance of learnedness, the advocacy of the latest novelty—
the show, without the substance, of philosophy.

History teaches us that civilizations grow and flourish,
and then degenerate and fall. It is the same with religions.
There are those who feel that the present civilization shows
signs of decay. Prominent men and women have pointed
this out, but what causes the decay is not clearly seen. The
fall of civilizations and religions is the result of false attitudes or a false religious philosophy—that is, of sophistry
—arising out of wrong motives.

We especially address ourselves to those who are distressed at the signs of the times and desire to consider the

basic causes of the confusion of our day: causes which are on the plane of ideas but which have their effect in the life of people. We shall examine the cause of what we see as the decline of Christian civilization and consider remedies for it.

Certain remedies have indeed been proposed by those who recognize the decline. But these are based on unwarranted optimism or wishful thinking. They are based on the idea that if one is optimistic—has self-confidence and desire for change—a change for the better will take place. Now such an attitude can produce apparent or temporary improvement, but it is a palliative cure, having no inner or lasting effect. The only real cure demands a new understanding of and faith in the Lord, a new understanding of the relation of God to man and of man to God; and a new repentance out of a humble heart. This must be accompanied by a hope—but a realistic hope, not an optimistic idea that all things will turn quickly for the better; a hope that there will be a sufficient number of people who will come to a new repentance so that there can be established a true Christian civilization which can endure.

PART ONE

Problems in Today's World and Their Solution

[1]

The Doubting Thomas

If we are to make the First and Great Commandment —to love the Lord our God with all our heart, soul, mind, and strength—the center of our life, the first question is, Who is God? For if we do not know who He is, we certainly cannot love Him with all our heart, soul, mind, and strength.

When the Lord appeared to Thomas, after His resurrection, Thomas said, "My Lord and my God." (John 20: 28.) Thomas is called "the doubting Thomas," yet Thomas was the only one of the Apostles who called Jesus "my Lord and my God."

To these words of Thomas, Jesus replied, "Thomas, because thou hast seen me, thou hast believed: blessed are they that have not seen, and yet have believed." (John 20: 29.)

It is important not only to know, if possible, who our Lord and God is, but also to know the nature, attributes, or qualities of God. A false idea of God necessarily leads to a false idea of man, and, vice versa, a false idea of man leads to a false idea of God, and this, to a false idea of life.

A man who was speaking to one of a certain religion in a distant land asked him why he was honest while so many of his co-religionists were not. The other replied that in their religions the gods often did dishonest things, and that they saw no reason for being more honest than their gods. As to the question why he was honest, he replied only that he liked honesty. Many in Christian churches think

God has human weaknesses, such as becoming angry, changing His mind, loving praise for its own sake, and showing
special favors to some when solicited to do so by those
close to Him. This subject will be set forth more fully in a
later section of this book. A man can become an image of
God if he has a living faith and desire, but he can strive
intelligently toward this goal only if he has a clear idea of
God and His relation to man—something which few have.

If the Gospels are a true account, Jesus said He was
God, yet relatively few in Christian lands, particularly relatively few Protestants, believe this. If it is denied that the
Lord is God, then it is evident that the account given in the
Gospels is inaccurate, and that the Bible is not the Word of
God. Most who do not believe that the Lord is God do not
believe that the Lord was born of a virgin, that He was
resurrected as to the body, or that he performed miracles.
If the account of the Lord's life given in the Bible is so inaccurate as to the facts and some of the teachings, how can
one know what is true or what is not true in Christian teaching? One person in this case guesses this is true and another
that; one more and another less. Christianity is reduced to
mere opinions or guesses, and there is no faith, no clear seeing of the truth. If the Gospels are true, Jesus is the light,
as He said: "I am the light of the world." But if all of religion is guesswork, where is the light? Do not men then
walk in darkness? Christianity then becomes not a religion,
but a supposition that there are certain moral and social
principles, any of which may be questioned. There is no resemblance between such an idea of Christianity and the
faith of the early Christians as expressed by the early Christian fathers. Such an idea of Christianity cannot properly
be called Christian, for similar moral and social principles
were held by the Stoics and are held by Buddhists, Confu-
cians, and others.

Why It Is Difficult to Believe That Jesus Is God

It is difficult for modern man to believe that the Lord Jesus Christ is God. Let us consider some of these difficulties and how they can be met.

The first reason given for not believing is, as some say, "How is it possible, if we consider the size of the universe with its millions of galaxies, to believe that a man who lived on the little speck we call our earth is the God of the universe?" If we regard this question from a materialistic point of view, that is, from a spatial point of view, it does indeed appear impossible; but if we view it from the point of view of spirit, it does not appear impossible. The universe we live in is a marvelous thing, but the mind of man, which can marvel at the universe and to a degree comprehend it, is much more marvelous than the material universe itself; for the whole material universe is relatively insignificant spiritually as compared to the mind of man.

What could be more marvelous than that man, in spite of the small size of his brain compared to the universe, can choose what he will do, can change and modify not only his environment, but also his character or mind, and can discipline himself? This is the greatest of marvels, which no science can explain.

Has Creation a Purpose?

Either the universe was created for the sake of man, or it really makes no sense. What sense would a lifeless universe make? Certainly a lifeless universe would have no purpose that could possibly be conceived; and if the universe has no sense or purpose, we cannot conceive of a God Who would create such a useless thing. Nor would a universe

which contained animals make much more sense. Either
God created the universe in order that there might be men
and women whom He could love and who could know and
love Him in return, or the whole of creation is meaningless.

There can be nothing which does not have some source;
there can be no activity of which there is not a source. This
applies to the material realm as well as to the mental. If
there were no electrons as a source, there could be no elec-
tricity. If there were no source of life, of love, and of wisdom, there could be no life, no love, and no wisdom. To think
that a dead mechanical force is the source of life, of love, and
of wisdom is absurd. Indeed, life, to be intelligible to us, must
be united to an organic form. In recent times it has been discovered that heredity, which gives the characteristics to
living forms, is based on certain molecules, called DNA (de-
oxyribonucleic acid), and that these molecules are ordered
in a remarkable chain. The materialist thinks that if he can
understand the composition and order of these molecules, he
will know what life is. But molecules are not life. The molecules upon which life is based are indeed remarkable, but it
is still more wonderful that such molecules exist in creation.
Is it not absurd to think that such molecules exist by mere
chance, and that the whole of creation is a thing of chance?
Suppose that civilization were wiped out by bombs, except
for a few primitive people, and that these, as they explored,
came to discover books. The books to them would appear
mere pieces of paper, having on them certain shapes we call
letters, consisting of a few straight and curved lines put
together in different ways. Later, if they ever learned to
read, would they not be astonished? The whole of the mind
of a Shakespeare, even the mind of God as revealed in the
Bible, is in these few letters composed of a few lines. Yet
these lines are not the mind of Shakespeare, and still less
are they the Divine Mind. Again, if we play a phonograph
record, we may be moved to tears by the words or by the
song, or we may be affected by the profundity of the thought
expressed; yet the record is nothing but a wiggly line on

wax. Although the mind is dependent on the brain as a book is dependent on paper, ink, and letters, the mind is no more the organic form than the wisdom in a book is the letters.

How Can We Know God?

If we can see that the purpose of creation is a world of men and women who can be loved by God and who can know Him and love Him, we come to the next step. How can we know God? We cannot comprehend or contemplate infinite love and wisdom as it is in itself. As the Lord said: "No man hath seen God at any time." (John 1:18.) We can indeed see that there is an Infinite Source of all things, but that is all. If, therefore, the purpose of creation is that we may fulfill the First and Great Commandment, to love the Lord our God with all the heart, soul, mind, and strength, the Lord must reveal Himself to man. That is, God must clothe Himself and accommodate Himself to man in such a way that man can have some idea of Him.

God Willed to Be Conjoined With Man

The Lord said: "That they all may be one: as thou, Father, art in Me, and I in thee, that they also may be one in us: . . . I in them, and thou in Me, that they may be made perfect in one." (John 17:21, 23.)

It is the nature of love to give itself to others. It is the very nature of the Divine Love to give its life, its love, and its wisdom to man. If man reciprocates the Lord's love, then the Lord conjoins Himself to man and man to the Lord.

Between the Divine, called the Father, and the Human, called the Son, there was a perfect union, so that the Human was not only a receptacle of life but became the very Divine

life, and thus became God. As the Lord said: "I am the
resurrection and the life." (John 11:25.) "I am the way, the
~~truth, and the life." (John 14:6.) Man can never become~~
life itself, for if he did he would be a god. But man can receive the life of love and faith from the Lord. As the Lord
cannot give the life of Divine Love and Wisdom to man, to
be man's own and thus to enable him to become a god, and
as the Lord longs to communicate His love and wisdom to
man, out of His love He gives His love and wisdom to man,
so that man may feel it entirely as if it were his own; although man should then acknowledge that he has nothing
that is not given him from the Lord out of heaven. If man
receives the life of love and wisdom from the Lord, and
acknowledges that it is the Lord's in him, then the Lord is
conjoined with man in the love and wisdom that man has
received from the Lord. Then are fulfilled the words of the
Lord, "I in them, and Thou in Me, that they may be made
perfect in one." (John 17:23.)

Pride and Conceit

The first reason why man does not believe that Jesus
is God is, as we have indicated, that man thinks materially
about creation; he does not understand the purpose of creation; he does not see how we can know God; and he does
not realize that God wills the conjunction of Himself with
man and of man with Himself.

The second reason for not believing that Jesus Christ
is our Lord and God is pride, conceit, or ambition. We read
in the Psalms, "The fool hath said in his heart, There is no
God." (Psalm 53:1.) Most people imagine that their opinions are the result of their thinking. They think they have
come to their conclusions from an objective viewing of the
questions under consideration, but in this they often deceive themselves. Most form their opinions from a subjective

point of view, that is, from their desires or loves, or from wishful thinking. A proud, conceited, vain, ambitious man may think he believes in God because he belongs to a church which is large and powerful, and the power of the church is reflected upon him. Another may think he believes in God because the church he belongs to has a high intellectual standing; its leaders are learned and highly educated, and its members have a higher than average social standing. Is it not obvious that such a faith or belief is not a real faith or belief in God?

A proud and conceited man feels no aversion to believing in an invisible and unknowable something which he may call God, a God who is something behind the order of creation, a God who is not a Divine Man of Infinite love and wisdom. When in the Psalms it says, "The fool hath said in his heart, There is no God," it does not refer to an inhuman God, a God of mere energy, or the source of the order of the physical universe. Many fools believe in such a God, which in reality is no God. When it says, "The fool hath said in his heart, There is no God," the fool is more often a highly learned man who has made quite a reputation for himself as an intellectual.

The reason why a proud, conceited, and vain man does not like to believe in a God who is a Divine Man of Infinite love and wisdom is that such a belief demands submission, obedience, a humbling of oneself before such a God; and this the vain and proud man does not like. This aversion or dislike becomes still greater when he is faced with the idea that the Infinite God of love and wisdom descended and clothed Himself with a human nature in the world in order to approach and save mankind. This is the real reason why so many so-called Christians do not believe in their hearts the words Jesus used when Thomas said to Him, "My Lord and my God": "Blessed are they that have not seen, and yet have believed." (John 20:28, 29.)

Jesus said, "I am the light of the world." (John 8:12.) "And this is the condemnation, that light is come into the

world, and men loved darkness rather than light, because
their deeds were evil." (John 3:19.)

As we have said, the primary evil of the world, which
causes men to deny in their hearts that Jesus Christ is their
Lord and their God, is the love of self, pride, and vanity.
Pride cannot fall before the Lord Jesus Christ saying, "My
Lord and my God."

A proud man wishes in his heart to be above all, yea,
even, if it were possible, to be God Himself. Such a man
feels himself the supreme thing in the universe. Man appears to be the supreme thing of the universe, and a proud
man wants to be the supreme man; he does not like the
idea of a God-Man infinitely above him. Such a one may
feel no aversion to acknowledging a so-called God which is
an impersonal force within nature, for as a man he can feel
in a sense superior to this; but to bow down to a God who
is an Infinite Man, this his pride prevents him from doing.
He then invents many arguments to confirm his aversion
and finally ends up by believing that he has come to his
negative conclusion from an objective point of view. Not
having a pure and humble heart, he cannot see God; for we
read, "Blessed are the pure in heart: for they shall see God"
(Matthew 5:8), and, being unable to see God, he concludes
that there is no Infinite Divine Man who can make Himself
visible to man by clothing His Infinite in an appearance
that man can see, know, love, and obey.

If one thinks of "the ground of being," or some such
entity which may be called God, in place of "Our Father who
art in Heaven," can one love such an entity with all one's
heart, with all one's soul, with all one's mind, and with all
one's strength? And if those of the church begin to make
the First and Great Commandment of no effect by their
traditions, what of Christianity is left?

The Lord said, "Except ye be converted, and become as
little children, ye shall not enter into the kingdom of heaven.
Whosoever therefore shall humble himself as this little child,
the same is greatest in the kingdom of heaven." (Mat-

thew 18:3,4.) No one who does not humble himself as a little child can really say from the heart, "My Lord and my God."

Innocence and Sophistication

But what is it to become as a little child? It does not mean to become childish, nor even naïve, although such may appear naïve to the sophisticated. To become as a little child is to become wise, not stupid. To become sophisticated is to become stupid.

In the Writings of Swedenborg it is said that to become again a little child is to come to a state of innocence, and a state of innocence is to acknowledge from the heart that we are dependent on the Lord as a child feels dependent on his parents; and that a child is in the innocence of ignorance, but a wise man is in the innocence of wisdom. The innocence of wisdom consists in acknowledging that, apart from the influx of love and wisdom from the Lord, we have no love, wisdom, or spiritual life, and that what we know compared to what we do not know is like a cup of water to the ocean. A wise man therefore acknowledges his great ignorance and is in humility although he knows more than others.

In the modern world, for the most part, sophistication has taken the place of wisdom. Men are even proud of being called sophisticated; and not knowing what wisdom is, they think that there is no other alternative to being sophisticated than to be naïve or credulous. Especially the learned are apt to be sophisticated, for their pride is in their great learning. Great learning can be of service to the wise; but for the most part the learned, on account of their pride in their learning, seldom become wise, but only sophisticated. A learned man can become a wise child beyond others if he overcomes the conceit of his own intelligence.

The sophisticated man cannot comprehend and cannot but despise such words of the Lord as "Ye must be born again" (John 3:7), and "Whosoever shall not receive the Kingdom of God as a little child." (Luke 18:17.)

Observe how in all things of life the sophisticated say, like the witches in *Macbeth*, that "Fair is foul and foul is fair," calling evil things good and good things evil. For example, many learned critics in the arts call the ugly, the clever, or the sick by the name of art, and the beautiful they call sentimental or "corny." It is indeed true that most religious art of the past century or two, and most popular art which the superficial art lovers call beautiful, is of no value, but it is not so bad as the sophisticated, perverse, and ugly that is today called art.

The sophisticated tend to hide their real feelings behind high-sounding words; but in the arts the real spirit of the age appears, just as the expression of a man's face often reveals more than his words.

The arts are a most reliable sign of the times, revealing the spirit of the age. If anyone doubts the reality of hell, he needs only to regard what is called modern in all the arts in order to be convinced.

To illustrate the above, consider the comment on a painting by Picasso reproduced in a museum bulletin and here also reproduced: "Picasso was a man of extraordinary humanity." One having any sensitivity would agree that to paint one's wife and children as Picasso did in this picture is diabolically inhuman and cruel, having nothing to do with "humanity." This is obvious; but a similar sophistication in other fields, particularly theology and philosophy, although equally present, may not be so obvious. See last illustration.

Not only in all the arts but also in religious literature much of the popular things remind one of honey sweetened with saccharin, whereas most of the highly sophisticated productions appear to be made for people with plastic hearts and electronic brains, and to have been produced by the same, the difference being that the production of computers is more orderly and useful and never offends one's intelligence or sensibilities.

The sophisticated have gained the dominant power not only in theological schools, but in most of the leading universities, art schools, magazines, and museums and in the government, so that one scarcely finds a proportion of one wise man to twenty sophisticated persons in places of prominence or power.

The sophisticated, by continually repeating clever arguments to prove that the ugly is beautiful and the false is true, have succeeded in either brainwashing a large part of the general public into accepting the ugly as art or intimidating them into saying or even believing that they do not understand the insanities which the sophisticated praise so highly.

The sophisticated continually repeat the statement that the great artists were not understood or recognized for a long time, as if this were the one thing in the history of art that is most important. But they do not emphasize that it was the highly sophisticated establishments—those who were considered the most learned, the leading critics, the so-called experts—who refused to recognize the great artists, and instead set up false idols for the people to follow and thus misled them. Part of the public was more frequently right in their judgment than were the experts, the renowned critics. The great artists were first recognized, as a rule, by those who were not considered experts in the arts.

That this is true in other fields is evident. The Messiah, who was expected, was first recognized by fishermen. It was the Sophists who were instrumental in forcing Socrates to drink hemlock.

It was not only the church, but the leading learned societies and universities, who opposed Copernicus and Galileo. Francis Bacon, considered the most learned man of his day and the father of the scientific method, and who has been called the first modern man, opposed the Copernican idea that the sun is the center of the solar system and that the planets revolve around it. I have read that Harvard University one hundred years after the publication of the system of Copernicus was still contending in favor of the Ptolemaic system of astronomy, namely, that the heavenly bodies were circling the earth.

The sophisticated may say, yes, all this may be true, but times have changed, and we do not repeat the mistakes of the past. This reminds us of what the Lord said: "Ye build the tombs of the prophets, and garnish the sepulchres of the righteous, and say, If we had been in the days of our fathers we would not have been partakers with them in the blood of the prophets. Wherefore ye be witnesses unto yourselves, that ye are the children of them which killed the prophets. Fill ye up then the measure of your fathers." (Matthew 23:29–32.)

Atheists and Agnostics

In this essay by "atheists" we mean those who firmly maintain that there is no God. By "agnostics" we mean those who do not know whether there is a God or a life after death, and who do not know whether there is such a thing as inspiration from heaven, and consequently do not see clearly, or for certain, truths which are above the plane of that which can be scientifically demonstrated.

The atheist maintains his position of atheism on the grounds that, on the basis of sensual experience or scientific evidence, it cannot be proved that there is a God; but his position is illogical and irrational, for it is equally true that on the basis of sensual experience or scientific evidence it cannot be proved that there is not a God.

In the created universe there are things which are orderly, useful, and beautiful and others which are disorderly, harmful, and ugly. As to men and women, there are some who are noble, good, and truthful and others who are ignoble, wicked, and liars. It appears to us axiomatic that everything must have an origin. What is the origin of the noble, the good, and the truthful, if there is no God? And what is the origin of the ignoble, the wicked, and the untruthful, if man has not free choice that enables him to pervert order?

The atheist and the agnostic usually maintain that those who have a faith in God, in the Word of God, and in life after death, especially if they are ministers, hold their faith out of bias or prejudice, and with respect to this we would agree that they are often right; but we maintain that the atheist and the agnostic are even more strongly affected in their thinking by prejudice and bias.

First as to the bias of those who claim to have faith. With many, what is called faith is merely habit acquired from childhood and its environment. If one's faith is merely such, and he becomes a minister or religious teacher, his so-called faith is strengthened by the self-interest of his profession.

Many have a blind faith, based on emotional reaction to the environment in which they have been brought up, particularly in relation to their parents and those by whom they have been taught. Such faith in childhood has its use; but if it is carried on into life, instead of becoming an adult one comes immediately into a premature spiritual dotage, which is something entirely different from what the Lord meant when he said, "Except ye be converted and become as little children, ye shall not enter into the Kingdom of Heaven." (Matthew 18:3.) The child which a man is again to become is a wise child, and it is not meant that he should become childish in the ordinary sense of the word. Socrates, according to our idea, is an example of a man who in his old age becomes a wise child. In the Writings of Emanuel Swedenborg, faith is defined as the seeing of truth in spiritual light or in the light of heaven, and to come to such a light involves an independent struggle.

As to the bias of the atheist and agnostic, whereas some men, out of an emotional blind clinging to the things of their childhood, maintain a kind of faith, others, because of various circumstances and their emotional reactions thereto, become rebellious. This emotional rebelliousness with some takes the form of atheism or agnosticism. Still others, who have been brought up in an atheistic or agnostic atmosphere and therefore cling to atheism or agnosticism out of childish habit just as those brought up in a religious atmosphere cling to the things of their early belief, if they are active in an atheistical movement have their negative faith strengthened by self-interest.

This is most obviously the case with communism, which is a kind of negative religion. In the communistic environment, if one considers the possibility of God, he is considered a heretic. It is evident that the atheism of communism is the result of an irrational emotionalism, as is clear from the writings of Karl Marx, although, like the emotional Christian, the emotional atheist and agnostic bring forth reasonings to support their position. The Writings of Swedenborg describe an argument in the other world between a group of ministers and a group of politicians: the ministers argued that all things which occur are the result of Divine Providence, and the politicians argued that all things are the result of mere human prudence. Both groups were then told to change their clothes, the ministers putting on the garments of the politicians and the politicians, the garments of the ministers. ("Garments" stands for the external attitude; here, the attitude of a function.) The ministers then argued in favor of human prudence and the politicians in favor of Divine Providence. This about-face would not have taken place if the ministers had loved the truth more than the honors which came to them as a result of their profession.

Some accept atheism or agnosticism because they wish to give free rein to their desires, apart from any restraint of conscience. Others become agnostics or atheists because

they see so many so-called Christians live hypocritical lives
—going to church and putting on an appearance of piety,
whereas in business and sexual conduct they are worse
than those of many who make little pretense of having
any faith. Such judge from a narrow, personal point of view
and not from a regard for whether the thing is in itself true.

In America the irrationality of atheism is apparent, and
atheists are relatively few in number, but agnosticism is
widespread. There is a certain truth in the idea that man
should become agnostic as defined at the commencement of
this chapter; for until a man feels his ignorance, he cannot
learn in such a way as to become independent, or, what is
the same, he cannot become spiritually an adult but, like a
child, remains dependent on others for his thinking. This
kind of agnostic is rare.

If a man realizes that he has no clear idea of what he
believes and is aware of his ignorance and lack of independent thinking in regard to matters of faith, if he is a real
man, he will search for the truth—or at least will strive
to see whether truth is discoverable.

Most confirmed agnostics strongly maintain that truth
above the plane of the scientific, or truth which is not de-
monstrable on the basis of physical sensation, cannot be
ascertained. Some might admit that certain moral principles
are beyond doubt. For example, there is a small section of
the human race which regards head-hunting as a normal
activity, yet there are very few who are not certain, beyond
any doubt, that head-hunting is an abnormality. But when
it comes to the things of God, many so-called agnostics
firmly maintain that such knowledge is unobtainable and
tend to regard those who are certain of such knowledge as
arrogant, and to resent such an atitude of certainty. In this
they are inconsistent, for, if they were agnostic in the sense
of not knowing, and if they maintain, as most do, that a
man has a right to his opinion and may possibly be right,
then if they were logical, they would admit that another
might see clearly and certainly a thing which they them-

selves could not see. A man who is blind and at the same time is envious and resentful because he cannot see, and thus lacks the abilities of others, might prefer to have all other men blind so that they would not be superior to himself. If there is a spiritual light and yet many, being spiritually blind, cannot see spiritual things, if they are both vain and blind, they bitterly resent the possibility that others can see clearly the things which to them are in the dark. Such emotional resentment is manifested by most confirmed agnostics, a fact which shows that agnosticism with them has become a kind of negative faith; for, if they were openminded agnostics, they would acknowledge without resentment that another could see and be in a light which they do not have. As they claim to be agnostics, and still firmly maintain this negative belief, their position is contradictory and illogical. That this is so is evident from the position they commonly take. They say that everyone has a right to his opinion; they admit that the one having faith may be right and they may be wrong, but they demand that the one having faith also should admit that he might be wrong. The fallacy of this argument will be illustrated by the following.

A blind man, if it could not be physically proved that he could not see, might say to one who had normal sight that he would admit that he was blind and the other could see provided the one who could see would admit the possibility that he might be blind. And because the one who could see would not admit that he might be blind, the blind man would accuse him of narrow-mindedness, prejudice, and arrogance.

Anyone who refuses to consider the posibility that there can take place a spiritual enlightenment by which a man can be certain of the spiritual verities he sees, as clearly and certainly as a man sees objects with his bodily eyes, is not an open-minded agnostic but a narrow-minded dogmatist.

Conservatives and Progressives

Every intelligent man is in favor of progress; but many who call themselves progressive mistake change for progress. The modern, the up-to-date, they consider an improvement on the past. History teaches that civilizations rise and decline. When a civilization is rising, those called progressive are more apt to be right; when a civilization is declining, the conservatives are more apt to be right; but few have the judgment to know when a civilization is rising or when it is declining. Much so-called progress is a delusion, temporarily appearing to be an advance but in the long run hastening a decline.

Those who tore out one of the famous twelfth-century windows in Chartres Cathedral and replaced it with an ornate fifteenth-century window undoubtedly did this in the name of progress.

A wise man never accepts the name of a conservative or a progressive. He looks for what is genuine in the present and in the past, and he is opposed to the false, the counterfeit, whether it be in the present or in the past. As the Lord said: "Every scribe instructed unto the Kingdom of Heaven is likened unto a man . . . that bringeth forth out of his treasure things new and old." (Matthew 13:52.) But few have the judgment to know whether a thing is a treasure or a counterfeit. Especially are those belonging to what is called the "establishment" nearly always wrong.

Further Reason for Obscurity as to Who Jesus Was

As we have said, modern man for the most part is so sophisticated that it is difficult for him to believe that Jesus Christ is God. Some believe that Jesus is the Son of God; as Peter said, "Thou art the Christ, the Son of the living God." (Matthew 16:16.) As long as Jesus was living among His disciples as a man, they could not believe fully in Him as God; and there was a certain truthfulness in this attitude, for, as long as He was in the world, Jesus had two natures, one from His Divine conception and the other inherited from Mary. It was only after He was fully glorified or made Divine and had put off all merely human limitations from His maternal heredity that Thomas could rightly call Him "my Lord and my God."

Another reason why modern man finds it difficult to believe that the Lord Jesus Christ, who walked on earth with man, is God, is that such an idea is totally contrary to the prevailing modern atmosphere of thought. Let us consider further why this is so.

The first reason is that modern education and the thinking it engenders have been concentrated on the sciences— have been preoccupied with things of the material world, those things that a man knows by means of the five senses of the body and the deductions therefrom. From this point of view, the universe is immensely great and man is an insignificant part of it. But, as we have said, what would all the marvels of creation amount to if there were not a man who could marvel?

In recent years many thinkers have given more emphasis to the human—to man and his subjective mind—as the all-important existing thing. The world of the mind is a world above time and space, above all scientific knowledge which comes by means of the five senses of the body. A man can be conscious of and reflect on this wonderful world of the mind; and it is only out of this world of the mind that he can reflect upon the world around him of which he is made aware by the five bodily senses.

Whereas the developing and ordering of the mind for the reception of the love and wisdom of God are the end in view, and this requires a reflection on the mind itself, such reflection is not possible apart from objective truth which is outside us. God has therefore given us a revelation in His Word as objective truth. Yet the objective truth of the Word of God becomes a living thing in man only as he works with it, applies it to his life, reflects on it in his mind and struggles to order it.

The existentialists for the most part, in placing the emphasis on the subjective, have gone to the opposite extreme from the materialists and do not see the importance of the objective Word of God.

If we think scientifically of God, we think of Him as the order or origin of the material universe, an unknown something or a thing of reasoned conclusions, but not as a Divine Person—as our Father who is in heaven. If we turn away from the idea of God as a philosophical-scientific idea, a thing of mere reason, to the idea of a Divine Person, we may come into the opposite danger of thinking of God as a limited human being on a throne out in an unknown region. As was said above, many of those called "fundamentalists" think of Him as having merely human emotions, such as in becoming angry or changing His mind, or as creating men for the sake of His own glory—and there are passages in the Bible which, if not genuinely understood, present such an appearance.

On the other hand, we can think of God as being an Infinite Divine Mind, having Infinite Love and Wisdom, a God who is above time, space, or change of state. Love and wisdom are the human itself above the plane of time and space; as they exist in the material universe, they are the human form itself which is clothed with a body. As is said in the Writings of Swedenborg, the true idea of God is to think of

Him as "Divine Love in Human form." If we are to love God, we must think of Him as a Divine man appearing in Human form; yet we must not think of Him as being large, or small, or as being here or there in space; God is not material. He dwells in the Kingdom of Heaven, which may be within us, a Kingdom which, like the mind, is not bounded by the things of space which pertain to the material world. If we think of God in this way, we can understand that man can become an image and likeness of God.

Again, the body is an image of the soul on a lower plane, the plane of space and matter. The body is soul and mind clothed with a material covering which serves it for life in this world. Everything of the body corresponds to something of the soul: the smile of the face corresponds to the joy of the mind, the sight of the body corresponds to the sight of the mind, the ear of the body to the hearing of the mind, the sense of touch to the feeling of the mind, the hands and feet to the practical working of the mind, the heart to the love of the mind, the lungs to the thinking, and so with everything of the body. If we see the material world and the body of man as having their source in the Divine things of God and as phenomena of the Kingdom of Heaven brought down to the plane of space and fixed matter, it is not so difficult to see that God Himself could take on a body in the world by birth, if in accordance with His Divine Love and Wisdom there was a reason for doing so. Such an idea is contrary to a materialist's idea of reason, but it is not contrary to enlightened human reason—a reason of the spirit elevated above all material things.

Why God Became Incarnate

If a king were the ruler of a province at a great distance, he might rule it by dictating to scribes, who would send letters to the governors of the province. But if the province were to come into such great disorder that it was in danger of being destroyed or overrun by enemies, the king would go himself to save the province and to establish law and order.

If there is a God of Infinite Love and Wisdom, when the writings He gave to mankind to guide them were insufficient for their salvation, could He do otherwise than come to them to save them?

A man with common sense can see that God could not do otherwise. But the sophisticated, who lack and often despise common sense, can never see this.

The reason for the Lord's coming into the world was this, that from His Love He desired to be conjoined with those in the human race, and because the human race had removed itself so far from the influx of the Divine Itself that they could no longer be saved, He took on a Human nature by birth in the world and made it purely Divine in order that He might accommodate and again conjoin Himself with those in the human race in their fallen state, if they would receive Him.

The teaching that the Lord Jesus Christ is God is also in agreement with the teaching of the Gospels and the prophets, for we read that not only did the Lord bless the man who called Him "my Lord and my God," but He said: "I and My Father are one" (John 10:30) ; and when Philip asked Him to show them the Father, He said: "Have I been so long time with you, and yet hast thou not known Me, Philip? he that hath seen Me hath seen the Father; . . . I am in the Father, and the Father in Me." (John 14:9, 11.) John said of Jesus Christ, "This is the true God, and eternal life." (I John 5:20.) And Paul wrote, "In him [Jesus Christ] dwelleth all the fulness of the Godhead bodily." (Colossians 2:9.)

The Old Testament plainly teaches that Jehovah was to come as the Savior. In the Prophets we read: "And it shall be said in that day, Lo, this is our God; we have waited for Him, and He will save us; this is Jehovah; we have waited for Him; we will be glad and rejoice in His salvation." (Isaiah 25:9.) "The voice of him that crieth in the wilderness, Prepare ye the way of Jehovah, make straight in the desert a highway for our God. . . . Behold, the Lord God will come with strong hand." (Isaiah 40: 3, 10.)

There are many passages in the Prophets which say that God is one, that there is no God beside Jehovah, that Jehovah would become the Savior and Redeemer, and that there is no Savior and Redeemer besides Jehovah.

All the creeds of the early Christian church say that Jesus Christ is Lord and God.

Bishop Fulton J. Sheen, in his book *Go To Heaven*, points out forcibly that if the account given in the Bible of the life of Christ is the truth, then if Jesus was not God but only man, He could not have been a good man but was the worst of impostors and utterly arrogant in claiming to be something which He was not.

Abraham Joshua Heschel, a prominent Jewish writer on religious topics, in *God in Search of Man* says that the Jewish leaders were so against Jesus primarily because He made Himself God. This is in agreement with the Gospel:

> Jesus said: I and my Father are one. Then the Jews took up stones . . . to stone Him. Jesus answered them, Many good works have I shewed you from my Father: for which of these works do ye stone me? The Jews answered him, saying, For a good work we stone thee not; but for blasphemy; and because that thou, being a man, makest thyself God. (John 10:30–33.)

There is no greater blasphemy possible than for a man

to make himself God. Wherefore, if Jesus was not God, then the Jews were right in their accusation.

Three Possibilities for an Idea as to Who Jesus Was

There are only three possibilities: (1) Jesus Christ is our Lord and God, "Jehovah come in strength"; or (2) Jesus was a blasphemer who, as the Jews said, being a man, made himself God; or (3) the Bible is a totally unreliable and falsified book which gives a false picture of the life of Jesus, or in any case is so unreliable that we can have no certain idea of what Jesus was like or of what He said.

If the latter case is true, then the Christian religion is a temple with a foundation of sand; everyone with such an idea thinks according to his own opinion, and one's own opinion takes the place of faith. This lack of faith in the Bible is what causes the faith of so many Christians to be weak. By this we do not mean that faith should be a blind faith, based merely on the authority of men. A living faith is a spiritual seeing that a thing is true; a man believes it because he sees clearly that it is true. But to see in the light of heaven that a thing of faith is true requires a right attitude of mind and heart. As we read in the Ten Blessings, "Blessed are the pure in heart, for they shall see God." (Matthew 5:8.)

In contrast we read in the Psalms, "The fool hath said in his heart, There is no God. They are corrupt, they have done abominable works, there is none that doeth good." (Psalm 14:1.)

To see God and to see the Word of God, one must be sincere and modest, shun evil, and do good. The vain man, the proud, the sophisticated, is the fool who says in his heart, "There is no God," or, "There is no Word of God," which amounts to the same thing. He says this from his heart, not primarily from his thinking, for he does not want the Word

of God. If he believed in the Word of God as Divine
Revelation, it would hurt his pride, vanity, and feeling of
superiority; he would have to humble himself. He therefore
eagerly searches out and finds ingenious arguments to prove
that the Bible is not the Word of God and presents them as
if they were scientific proofs. He poses as a man who views
religious questions objectively, whereas his denials and his
arguments against the Word of God come forth from the
proudness of his heart.

The sincere man, however, although he may at first be in
doubt and troubled by many things he reads in the Bible
which appear unreasonable or unjust, keeps an open mind.
He acknowledges that there may be an explanation which
will make the matter clear and dissipate his doubts; he has
a feeling that God, if He loves man, must desire to reveal
Himself to man. Such earnestly seek for the truth. They
are not, however, like those who so pride themselves on
being seekers for the truth that they would be disappointed
if they ever found the truth (for this would hurt the proud
seekers' feeling of superiority in being seekers after truth).
There are many such persons who would never recognize the
truth if they found it, for they are blinded by the feeling of
their own self-importance.

God Is Ever Seeking Man

Man can seek God because God is seeking man; the Lord
stands at the door and knocks. "But the hour cometh and
now is when the true worshipers shall worship the Father
in spirit and in truth; for the Father seeketh such to worship him." (John 4:23.)

On the other hand, we read: "The wicked, through the
pride of his countenance, will not seek after God: God is
not in all his thoughts." (Psalm 10:4.) It is not man's intellectual limitations which prevent him from finding the Di-

vine Truth in which God manifests Himself, but the pride of man's stony heart, man's love of himself, with its conceit, which blinds him to God and to His Word. This is man's primary sin which hides the presence of God in His Word from him.

As said in Isaiah: "Behold, Jehovah's hand is not shortened, that it cannot save; neither his ear heavy, that it cannot hear: but your iniquities have separated between you and your God, and your sins have hid his face from you." (Isaiah 59:1,2.)

Every man by his very nature loves himself in the first place, and from this love wishes in his heart to be as God, knowing from himself good and evil. He does not want a Divine Human God above himself, before whom he is to kneel and bow down. He does not want a Divine Revelation of the Word of God. If, therefore, a man is really to seek God where He can be found, it is not in the first place an intellectual question, but it is a matter of wrestling with one's own pride and the conceit of one's own intelligence, for it is these that hide the face of God, and no seeking after God will enable man to find Him as long as these hide His face.

If a man does not find his Lord and his God, he ascribes this to his understanding and not to the real cause, namely, that not having a pure heart, he cannot see God—he cannot find Him.

Adam and Eve, the Serpent and the Cherubim

As we shall explain more fully in a later chapter of this book, the Old Testament treats of the history of man—both the spiritual history of mankind and the spiritual development of the individual—and, in the supreme sense, the life of our Lord while on earth, to the extent that the things of His Spirit are concerned. The first eleven chapters of Genesis are not an historical account of persons, but a representative or symbolic description of the spiritual development of the Ancient Churches. This is explained fully in the *Arcana Coelestia*, by Emanuel Swedenborg.

The third chapter of Genesis describes the fall of the first church on earth.

The fall had its origin in the serpent. The serpent stands for trust in the bodily senses and for thinking out of such a trust—thus, for scientific or philosophic thinking about the truth of faith. Scientific and philosophic thinking on its own plane is in order; but when one tries to think of God, and the Word of God, or the Kingdom of Heaven, from a philosophy based on the sensing of the things of the material universe, this is a different thing. If one's faith is founded on the evidences of the bodily senses, one comes easily first into doubt and finally to a denial of the Kingdom of Heaven, both a denial of the Kingdom of Heaven within one and the Kingdom of Heaven that one enters through the portal of death. One who trusts more in the philosophy based on reasonings from things in the material world than in Divine Revelation is deceived by the serpent.

The woman in this chapter stands for one's own will, the desire to be independent, to know truth from one's self and not be dependent on the influx and revelation from God; the desire to be like God—knowing good and evil, to be independent of the Word of God and independent of enlightenment from God; in a word, to trust in one's self. As we read in the *Arcana Coelestia* by Emanuel Swedenborg, "Who have a stronger belief that their eyes are opened and that as God they know good and evil, than those who love themselves, and at the same time excel in worldly learning? and yet who are more blind?" (Number 206.)

The man to whom the woman gave the fruit stands for the rational faculty. The man who in the conceit of his own intelligence trusts solely to his rational faculty, more than anyone else thinks that he views all things objectively. But in this he greatly deceives himself, for it is his ambition and conceit that govern his rational thinking and cause him to come to the conclusions he arrives at; then, after confirming it by many rational considerations, he believes the conclusion to be the result of viewing the matter objectively, whereas in fact it is the result of his wishful thinking.

The tree of life stands for the perception that a man receives his life from God—not only his life in general, but especially the life of his love and wisdom. The tree of the science (usually translated "knowledge") of good and evil is the feeling that man can know what is good and evil by means of the bodily senses—by science or philosophy apart from the Word of God and apart from inspiration from God.

It is the nature of self-love and its conceit not to believe anything it cannot apprehend by the bodily senses, science, or philosophy, and it is this love of self which persuades the rational faculty to agree with its desires.

In explication of the words, "The serpent was more subtle than any wild animal of the field which Jehovah God had made," we read in the *Arcana Coelestia* by Emanuel Swedenborg as follows:

A desire to investigate the mysteries of faith by

sensuous and scientific things was not only the cause of the fall of the Most Ancient Church, but is also the cause of the fall of every church, for hence come not only falsities, but also evils of life. (Number 127.)

In ancient times those were called serpents who had more confidence in sensuous things than in revealed ones. But it is still worse at the present day, for now there are persons who not only disbelieve everything they do not see and feel, but also confirm themselves in such incredulity by sciences unknown to the ancients, and thus occasion in themselves a far greater degree of blindness. In order that it may be known how these blind themselves, so as afterwards to see and know nothing, who form their conclusions concerning heavenly matters from the things of sense, science, and philosophy, and who are not only "deaf serpents" but also the "flying serpents" frequently spoken of in the Word, which are much more pernicious, we will take as an example what they believe about the spirit. The sensual man, or he who believes only in the evidence of his senses, denies the existence of the spirit because he cannot see it, saying, "It is nothing because I do not feel it; that which I see and touch I know exists." The man of science, or he who forms his conclusions from the sciences, says, "What is the spirit, except perhaps vapor or heat, or some other entity of science that presently vanishes into thin air? Have not the animals also a body, senses and something analogous to reason? and yet it is asserted that these will die, while the spirit of man will live." Thus they deny the existence of the spirit. Philosophers also, who would be more acute than the rest of mankind, speak of the spirit in terms which they themselves do not understand, for they dispute about them. . . . All who reason from the things of sense, science, and philosophy, deny the existence of the spirit, and therefore believe nothing of what is said about the spirit and spiritual things. Not so the simple in heart;

if they are questioned about the existence of spirit, they say they know it exists, because the Lord has said they will live after death; thus instead of extinguishing their rational they vivify it by the Word of the Lord. (Number 196.)

It may be observed that all things which God created, including the serpent, were at first good. The bodily senses are good and useful, the sciences are good and useful, the love of self, if it serves and does not rule in man, is good and useful, and the rational faculty is good and useful. Thus it is said that all that God created was very good. Evil has its origin in this, that what is lower begins to rule over what is higher. For example, all the bodily appetites which man is born with are good; but when man makes his life to consist in the gratification of bodily appetites and neglects that which is nobler, he falls into evil.

Why God Permits Evil

It is often wondered: Why, if He is omnipotent, did God permit evil to arise in the world? The answer to this question is as follows. God wishes above all else to have those He can love and who, out of free choice, love Him in return. If man were not free to choose to love or not to love, he would not be man; a compelled love is not a genuine human love—it is scarcely even an animal love. Therefore, because He loved mankind, God necessarily had to let man choose, first between what was higher and what was lower—between what was more noble and what was less noble. It was owing to man's choosing the less noble that evil arose. God looks in the first place to the preservation of man's freedom, including his freedom of choice, for He prefers having evil men and devils to having automatons, compelled to love Him. He also turns all evil to some useful purpose, just as dung and urine are used to fertilize the soil.

Anyone who reflects rejoices that this is so; for who would wish to be compelled to love? Who would wish to be without freedom of choice? Who does not feel that a compulsory love of God and his neighbor is an inhuman and worthless love? It is therefore the first law of the Divine Providence that man shall be held in a free state, and that he shall be free to choose between faith in God and faith solely in himself; between loving the Word of God and the Kingdom of Heaven above all else and loving his own intelligence, his own will, and the things of this world above all else. This is the reason why the Word of God is written in such a way as not to compel belief, but is of such a nature that those who desire to believe can find reasons for their faith, and those who do not desire to believe can find reasons in favor of their doubts or denials.

By choosing to trust in their own intelligence rather than in the Word of God, men were cast out of Paradise— that is, they could no longer perceive that which the Lord called the Kingdom of Heaven within man—and cherubim were set to guard the way of the tree of life.

The Cherubim

The cherubim are guards which prevent men from entering into the arcana, the inner truths of faith, from their own intelligence. It is the spirit of truth proceeding from the Lord that enlightens man and gives him to see clearly the inner truth in the Word of God.

If man desires to enter into the mysteries or secret things of faith from himself and his own intelligence, and not from the Lord Who is the door, he is led away by bodily and earthly loves, represented by the "flame of a sword turning itself." This is of the mercy of the Lord, for if a man were to enter the inner truth of the Kingdom of God out of self-love and its conceit, he would profane it, and his later state would be worse than his former state. As the Lord said: "For this people's heart is waxed gross, and their ears are dull of hearing, and their eyes have they closed; lest at any time they should see with their eyes, and hear with their ears, and should understand with their heart, and should be converted and I should heal them." (Matthew 13:15.)

Not that the Lord does not will to convert all, but that he would prevent those who are converted, but not with their whole heart, from later turning away and profaning the holy truths of the Kingdom of God.

The cherubim are also guards in the letter of the Word of God which prevent the unprepared from entering into the inner sanctuary of truth. There are many things in the letter of the Word which are "hard sayings," many things which cause those who do not penetrate to the things of the spirit to say to themselves, "How can this be the Word of God?"

These guards are of the mercy of the Lord lest those entering without a wedding garment should violate the holy things within. The Word of the Lord is therefore written in such a way that those who are not enlightened from heaven say, "How can this be the Word of God?" For there are many things in the letter which appear not only unimportant, but also unworthy of God's Word; and so it is that the spirit of the Word "is hidden from the wise and prudent" in the things of this world and is revealed to babes—that is, to those who are in innocence.

Our Lord called Himself the door, the Way, the Truth, and the Life; the Stone which the builders rejected. It is this door which admits to Paradise, or, what is the same, into the Kingdom of Heaven which is within man. There are also guards or cherubim, which hide the Divinity of the Lord from the sophisticated, lest, seeing, they should profane.

The Lord said: "For verily I say unto you, Till heaven and earth shall pass, one jot or one tittle shall in no wise pass from the law, till all be fulfilled." (Matthew 5:18.)

The teaching of the Lord was therefore that He would fulfill every least thing of every letter of the Old Testament: thus the Old Testament as to every least thing is the Word of God. The sophisticated either do not believe the words of the Lord quoted above or do not believe that the Lord said them.

In a column by Louis Cassels in various newspapers we read under the title "Protestant Split":

> Protestantism is heading into the sharpest theological controversy since the fundamentalist-modernist clash of the 1920's.
>
> The issue is whether the Christian message needs to be radically recast to make it plausible to modern man.
>
> Among those calling for drastic overhaul of the conceptual package in which the Gospel is presented are theologians Rudolf Bultmann in Germany and Paul Tillich in the United States.
>
> Their views have been given wide circulation by English Bishop John A. T. Robinson in his book, *Honest to God*, and Episcopal Bishop James A. Pike of California in his book, *A Time for Christian Candor*.
>
> Robinson contends that many educated people today reject Christianity "because they cannot accept certain traditional beliefs which were really the envelope in which the message was sent, rather than the message itself." Pike agrees.
>
> The solution, says the California Bishop, is to "rethink and restate the unchanging Gospel in terms which are relevant to our day and meaningful to the people we would have hear it."
>
> Few theologians or church leaders would argue with that objective. The point in dispute is how far the church can go in "restating" the Gospel before it finds itself offering something besides authentic Christianity.
>
> The Bultmann-Tillich-Robinson-Pike school is not in agreement on which parts of the New Testament

are to be retained as "kernel" and which may be jettisoned as out-of-date "husk."

But there is a tacit understanding among most of the reinterpreters that any Biblical account of a physical miracle must automatically be labeled mythical. Even the supreme miracle which gave birth to the church—the Resurrection—is regarded as a subjective experience of the disciples rather than an objective historical event.

There also is a general tendency to move away from the concept of a personal God toward more abstract and impersonal terminology, such as Tillich's "Ground of Being."

The "New Theology" remains Christian at least in the sense of asserting that God is revealed to men uniquely and supremely in the life of Jesus Christ. But this belief is often expressed in language which suggests that Jesus was a man who was so good and unselfish that God's love shone through his humanity, rather than in Biblical terms of the Word of God becoming flesh and dwelling among men.

But critics are now saying that the reinterpreters have gone too far in the attempt to "demythologize" the New Testament and that they have needlessly abandoned many things which are both historically credible and essential to Christian faith.

The giant of European theology, Dr. Karl Barth, makes no secret of his feeling that the demythologizers have thrown out the baby with the bath water. There may be no scandal in a "modernized" Christianity which has no place for a personal God, an incarnation or a resurrection; but there's not much hope in it, either.

On this side of the Atlantic, also, theologians and church leaders are beginning to voice concern about attempts to reduce the Christian gospel to an inoffensive proclamation that Jesus was a nice man.

Dr. Roland Mushat Frye, writing in the scholarly journal *Theology Today*, said that the greatest threat to contemporary Christianity comes from "pseudo-sophisticates" so eager to accommodate the Gospel to the presuppositions of modern culture that they have emptied it of all "distinctively Christian content."

As soon as we deny the words of the Lord concerning the Scriptures, "For verily I say unto you, Till heaven and earth pass away, one jot or one tittle shall in no wise pass from the law, till all be fulfilled" (Matthew 5:18), the "baby" is already thrown out with the bath water. A baby or little child stands for innocence.

To the modern sophisticated theologian may we not apply the words of the Lord: "Jesus answered and said, I thank thee, O Father, Lord of heaven and earth, because thou hast hid these things from the wise and prudent, and hast revealed them unto babes." (Matthew 11:25.)

But lest we should fall into the other extreme of naïveté and over-credulousness, the Lord also said: "Be ye therefore wise as serpents, and harmless as doves." (Matthew 10:16.)

As various writers have said, some ministers use double talk, that is, they speak in such a way about the Lord that the sophisticated understand it in one way and the unsophisticated in another, giving the impression to the sophisticated that they look on Jesus as an exceptional man, and to the unsophisticated that they see him as the Son of God. Such dishonesty is common.

Although for a Christian, faith in the Lord as his Lord and God and in the Bible as the Word of God is the only door, still every man, including the Gentile, is admitted into the Kingdom of Heaven if he chooses to look to God, as best he can according to the light he has, and lives the best he can according to his lights. For such have in their hearts a willingness to be instructed; and if they were in ignorance of the Lord and the Word of God when in the world, they gladly receive faith in Jesus Christ as their Lord and God when instructed by the angels. But a Christian is faced with this choice here on earth; and if he rejects the blessing promised to those who say to the Lord Jesus Christ, "My Lord and my God," and confirms this rejection out of the hardness of his heart, he will not listen to the angelic instructors.

3

The Two Gates

It is the sophisticated who choose the broad way; it is those who are made wise by the spirit of God who choose the strait gate and the narrow way which leadeth unto life. (Matthew 7:14.)

There was a time when it was especially the learned who were sophisticated, but now the majority are more or less sophisticated and are proud of it.

In the work *Heaven and Hell*, by Swedenborg, we read:

The way that leads to heaven and the way that leads to hell were once represented to me. There was a broad way tending toward the left or to the north; and many spirits [those who had recently died] were seen going in it; but at a distance a large stone was seen where the broad way came to an end. From that stone two ways branched off, one to the left and one in the opposite direction to the right. The way that went to the left was narrow or straitened, leading through the west to the south, and thus into the light of heaven; and the way leading to the right was broad and spacious, leading obliquely downwards towards hell. [The quarters referred to here are not spatial quarters, but indicate different states of mind, having to do with the path of life, which appear like spatial quarters.] All at first seemed to be going the same way until they came to the large stone at the head of the two ways. When they reached that point, they divided; the good turned to the left and entered the straitened way that led to heaven; while the evil, not seeing the stone at the fork in the ways, fell upon it and were hurt; and when they rose up they ran on the broad way to the right which went down towards hell.

What all this meant was afterwards explained to me. The first way that was broad, wherein many good and evil went together and talked with each other as friends, because there was no visible difference between them, represented those who externally live alike honestly and justly, and between whom seemingly there is no difference. The stone at the head of the two ways, . . . upon which the evil fell and from which they ran into the way leading to hell, represented the Divine truth, which is rejected by those who look towards hell; and in the highest sense, this stone signified the Lord's Divine Human. But those who acknowledged the Divine truth and also the Divine of the Lord went by the way that led to heaven. By this again it was shown that in externals the evil lead the same kind of life as the good, or go the same way, that is, the one as readily as the other; and yet those who from the heart acknowledge the Divine, especially those within the church who acknowledge the Divine of the Lord, are led to heaven; while those who do not are led to hell. The thoughts of man which proceed from his intentions are represented in the other life by ways. (Number 534.)

Let us give an illustration of the above. A minister or priest serves his congregation, he labors long hours, he visits those who need his care, he conducts the services of the church with reverence, he preaches earnestly. Yet one minister or priest has in view his own advancement, his popularity, his desire to be liked by his congregation; in all his preaching and actions he is thinking of his own position or of increasing the prestige and wealth of his church, and thereby of himself. With his mouth he worships the Lord, but in his heart he worships himself.

Another minister or priest loves the truth in his heart. He prays to Jesus Christ, saying, "My Lord and my God," and he has a feeling that the Lord Jesus Christ is the visible God, in whom is the invisible God as the body in which is the soul—the Father in the Son, as expressed in the Gospels. He loves the Lord with all his soul and heart, and he will gladly sacrifice position, wealth, popularity, success, and friendship, if it is necessary, to uphold the truth. He would rather die than be unfaithful to the truth.

Both the good and the evil minister may appear so similar in outward speech and act that few can distinguish the one from the other. This is the meaning of the words of the Lord: "Many shall say to me in that day, Lord, Lord, have we not prophesied in Thy name? and in Thy name have cast out devils? and in Thy name done many wonderful works? And then will I profess unto them, I never knew you: depart from Me, ye that work iniquity." (Matthew 7:22,23.) Note that the iniquity may be hidden in the heart so that it is recognized by scarcely anyone—and usually not by the man himself, who regards himself as honest and sincere. What is said above about a minister or priest applies in a different way also to the politician, the businessman, the professional man, and the laborer.

4

The Logos

We read in the first chapter of John: "In the beginning was the Word [Logos] and the Word was with God, and God was the Word." Not as in the King James translation: "the Word was God."

The Word or Logos evidently is the Divine Truth, for words, if they genuinely express anything, express the truth. God here is the Divine Love, for God is Infinite Divine Love. To express itself or communicate itself, love uses words, which are truths speaking. Truths, or thoughts which are of truth, are the manifestation of love or are love in a form accommodated to the one with whom one is communicating. Wherefore God was the Word; that is, Divine Truth is the Divine Love, going forth, or proceeding.

This Divine Truth proceeding went forth from the beginning of creation; wherefore the Lord, Who was, as He said, "the Way, the truth, and the life," declared: "Before Abraham was, I am." (John 8:58.)

As all things were made from Divine Love, by means of the Divine Wisdom, or, what is the same, from the Divine Good by means of the Divine Truth, it is said, "All things were made by Him; and without Him was not anything made that was made." (John 1:3.) Now, although God indeed created the material universe from His Divine Love by means of His Divine Wisdom, the essential thing which God made is man and the spirit of man, material creation being only a means to this end. When therefore it says, "All things were made by Him," it is especially the Kingdom of Heaven within man that is created from God's love by means of His Divine Wisdom, the Divine Light or Logos. Wherefore it is said, "That was the true Light, which lighteth every man that cometh into the world. . . . And the Word was made flesh, and dwelt among us, and we beheld His glory." (John 1:9,14.)

If we see that God is Divine Love Itself, and He wishes to communicate His Divine Love to man, and that to do this He must do so through the Divine Truth accommodated and clothed in such form that man can receive and reciprocate His love, the story of the incarnation, of the Lord as the Divine Truth becoming flesh, appears natural and reasonable. But if we think materialistically or scientifically, we cannot accept such an idea.

As was stated above, the Word which was in the beginning not only was the Divine Truth in the act of creating the world, but it is, moreover, the Divine Truth communicated to man. Now, for Divine Truth to be communicated to man, it had to be spoken and written. As we shall show more fully in the latter part of this book, the Word of God, which is the Divine Truth, is contained in what is called the Bible.

The Lord said concerning the Scriptures, that is, the Law and the Prophets: "For verily I say unto you, Till heaven and earth pass, one jot or one tittle shall in no wise pass from the law, till all be fulfilled." (Matthew 5:18.)

The internal or spirit of the Law and the Prophets was also represented by Moses and Elias as they were seen in vision with Jesus when He appeared on the mount in glory, while His face did shine as the sun. (Matthew 17:2,3.)

The Divine Truth in heaven and in the church, which was the Word or Logos, formed a Divine seed, from which the virgin Mary conceived.

If we think on the plane of the spirit, this miracle is not hard to believe, for if God from His Divine Love wished to clothe Himself with the seed of the Divine Truth and come to commune with men, this is no more incredible than the first creation of life, which is an event which, as far as science knows, has not occurred in hundreds of centuries.

The Negative Attitude

In spite of the statements in the New Testament that God was the Word that became flesh, that he who saw the Lord saw the Father, that He and the Father are one, that blessed are they who say to the Lord "my Lord and my God," and He is the true God and eternal life (I John 5:20), there are those who say that the New Testament does not teach that Jesus Christ is God. Is it not evident that those who make such statements do not view what is written objectively but with a desire to find what they wish to find, with a negative attitude toward faith in the Lord Jesus Christ as a personal God? This negative attitude of the sophisticated, as we have said, exists because they do not desire to have a Divine Man, one who is God and Man, above themselves, for they themselves wish to be supreme.

Augustine

In this connection we shall quote the words of Augustine:

That the Son is very God . . . They who have said that our Lord Jesus Christ is not very God or not within the Father the One and only God, are proved wrong by the plain and unanimous voice of the Divine testimonies: as for instance, "In the beginning was the Word and the Word was with God, and the Word was God" . . . He is not only God, but also very God. And the same John most expressively affirms this in his epistle: "For we know that the Son of God is come, and hath given us understanding, that we may know the true God, and that we may be in His true Son Jesus Christ, He is the true God, and eternal life." (Book I, 9.)

The equality of the trinity are intimate to our faith. But because on account of the incarnation of the Word of God for the working of our salvation, that the man Jesus Christ might be Mediator between God and man, many things are said in the Sacred books as to signify or even expressly declare, the Father to be greater than the Son, men have erred through a want of careful examination on the whole tenor of the Scripture, and have endeavored to transfer those things which are said of Jesus Christ according to the flesh, to that substance of His which is eternal before the incarnation and is eternal.

And not therefore without cause the Scripture says both the one and the other, both that the Son is equal to the Father, and that the Father is greater than the Son. For there is no confusion when the former is understood on account of the form of God, and the latter on account of the form of a servant . . . and in truth this rule for clearing the question through all the Sacred Scripture is set forth in one chapter of the epistle of Paul when this distinction is commented to us plainly enough. For he says: "Who being in the form of God, thought it not robbery to be equal with God; but emptied Himself, and took upon Himself the form of a servant and was made in the likeness of men, and was found in the fashion of a man." (Philippians 2:6,7.) For in the form of a servant He took, He is less than the Father, but in the form of God, in which He also was before He took the form of a servant, He is equal to the Father. (Book I, 14.)

Two States of the Lord While on Earth

The Lord Jesus Christ when in the world had two states, a state of Glorification, and a state of exinanition or pouring out of His soul. When in the state of Glorification, He said, "I and the Father are one. He that seeth Me seeth the Father, I am in My Father, and the Father is in Me"; but when in states of exinanition in which He underwent temptation, He prayed to the Father as if separated from Himself. But now that He is fully glorified or made Divine, He is totally one with the Father as body and soul are one person. After His resurrection He said: "All power is given unto me in heaven and in earth." (Matthew 28:18.) That is, He is now omnipotent in His power to save mankind. As He said, "I came forth from the Father, and . . . I leave the world, and go to the Father." (John 16:28,30.) After the resurrection there can be no question of two persons. If we think of the Father and the Son as being two persons, we cannot help thinking that there are two or three Gods no matter how much we say with our mouths that there is one God.

Few now ever think about the Trinity. They feel an aversion to even considering the matter. It appears to most as old-fashioned to consider such matters of doctrine, and they regard the consideration of doctrine and creeds to be doctrinaire, abstract, and having no relation to life.

Such an idea is contrary to the attitude of the early Christians, and has come about with a decline of faith— especially with a decline of faith in the Bible as being the Word of God and a decline in the faith that the Lord Jesus Christ is God.

The Trinity

With this decline of faith no real heed is given to the First and Great Commandment: "The Lord our God is one Lord, and thou shalt love the Lord thy God with all thy heart, and with all thy soul, and with all thy mind and with all thy strength."

If a man were not sure whether his father was one person or three, and he was uninterested in finding out or considering the matter, could it be said that the man loved his father? If a man were in such a predicament, would it not affect his life—his point of view? Would it not disturb him profoundly? The fact that so few are disturbed by not comprehending the Trinity in God indicates a great indifference, a total concentration on the things of this world, and an irritation at even being asked to consider anything above this world. Is it this indifference that is not only the cause of a lack of spirituality, but also a cause of the decline of standards of morality and honesty, of the vulgarization of life that is so evident? Man, in considering himself to be essentially an animal, sinks lower than the animals.

Other-Worldliness

In the Middle Ages, other-worldliness was considered an ideal. The Kingdom of Heaven was considered the only thing of importance—at least theoretically; and the importance of life in this world was theoretically disregarded. This led to monasticism and contempt for pleasures.

If we really believe in a life after death, we recognize that life in this world is scarcely a moment in comparison to eternal life, and therefore in itself is of relatively no importance. But if we regard life in this world as a school in preparation for eternal life, then it is of great importance. A school has little importance if it does not look to a life after leaving school. Yet a school which does not have its own delights and pleasures is not a good preparation for life afterward. All kinds of healthy delights, including pleasures, are gifts of God and not to be despised. Yet things like wealth and bodily pleasures, including the appreciation of the arts, are of no use—are even a hindrance—if they are loved for their own sake and not for the sake of giving thanks to God and as of use for His praise and for showing forth the things of His Kingdom.

Bodily pleasures and worldly knowledge should not be despised or rejected, but still they should hold the lowest place of importance if man really believes in the Kingdom of Heaven.

The great fallacy of monasticism is that it is an escape, an attempt to find an easy way out of the struggle of life through placing oneself in a kind of prison, or army, in which one gives over one's problems to one's superiors and follows the commands and orders of others. This is a far easier thing to do than to lead a normal life, disciplining one's mind to regard the things of this world as relatively insignificant in comparison to the things of the Kingdom of Heaven.

To acquire a spiritually well-disciplined normal natural life, as a servant to the ruling love of the Kingdom of Heaven, is a much more difficult thing than in a moment of enthusiasm to enter a monastery, and is therefore a better preparation for the Kingdom of Heaven. How many in their business—in their family and social life—place the eternal Kingdom of God in the first place?

Could God Become Angry?

In the Christian churches an idea of salvation grew up which is frequently called "medieval" theology. The idea is that God the Father became angry with the human race on account of the sin of Adam and Eve and placed a curse on the human race. The Son agreed to come on earth, took upon Himself the curse, and by dying upon the cross He satisfied the Divine Justice and propitiated the Father, so that the Father agreed to save those who had faith that the Son had died for their sins. Does this agree with the oft-repeated words, "For His mercy is for ever"? (Psalm 136.)

Many ministers nowadays have come to see that such an idea makes God the Father a cruel God. It can also be seen that no one can hold the idea that because of the Son's suffering the Father forgave those who believed in the Son, and at the same time really think of God as one God instead of two or three Gods, no matter how much he may say with his mouth that there is one God.

In the orthodox idea the idea of justice also is totally distorted. Suppose that there was a man who had a servant who disobeyed him, and the man said that he would punish the servant, the servant's children, grandchildren, and great-grandchildren, and that the son of the man offered to take the punishment due to the servant upon himself, and the man then forgave the children, the grandchildren, and the great-grandchildren as long as they believed that the son had appeased the man. Could anyone regard this as justice?

Has not this cruel idea of God something to do with the cruelties perpetrated by the church in the Middle Ages?

Why There Is a Hell

Bishop Fulton J. Sheen in his book *Go To Heaven*, in speaking of the mercy of the Lord, says that the Lord forgives man as He commanded man to do: seventy times seven times; that He will forgive man every sin but one, namely, that of not loving the Lord. If a man said he would forgive another every evil he did, no matter how atrocious, except the sin of not loving him, everyone would agree that a man who took such an attitude was a supreme example of egotism.

The truth is that the Lord is infinitely forgiving. There is nothing He does not forgive, for He is Mercy itself, He is Infinite Divine Love. How, then, is it that there is a hell?

Strange as it may sound, we cannot believe in a hell which is not in agreement with the Lord's Infinite Love, Mercy, and Forgiveness. The Lord's love is a love of mankind. As we have said, for there to be mankind, man must be free; for the Lord cannot love men who are not free and are therefore little more than robots. The Lord therefore loves man's freedom above everything else. Now, if man is free, he can either love God and his neighbor, or he can love himself and the world in preference to God and the Kingdom of Heaven.

When a man dies, he has the same character he had while on earth—otherwise he would not be the same man. It is a law of the life after death that a man is among his like, where he naturally tends. Now hell is nothing but the gathering together of those who love themselves and their own pleasures more than God and their neighbor.

This is of the Mercy of the Lord, for were the good to be with the evil, the evil would harm or distress the good; and were the evil to be taken into heaven where all things of the heart manifestly appear, they would be in the greatest distress, for their ugliness would be manifest not only to

others but also to themselves—just as hypocrites, or those
with filthy minds, if their hypocrisy and filth become manifest, cannot stand the company of the innocent and the
chaste but flee away to their own kind. So the evil, when
they approach heaven, flee away of their own accord; for
they are far less unhappy in hell than they would be in
heaven.

As to the punishments of hell, these the inhabitants in-
flict on each other; just like any society of egotists, they
make each other miserable and come into conflict with one
another.

As God is Love and Mercy itself, He moderates the punishment in hell as far as possible. As is stated in the Writings of Swedenborg, God does not permit any punishment
more than is necessary to preserve a certain order in hell,
and He gives even the devils as much happiness as is possible in their miserable condition.

There is no vindictive punishment by God in Hell. To
think that God inflicts such punishment is a horrible idea.

As all intelligent men know, punishment for crime
should never be vindictive; the only purpose of punishment
is to protect society, and to lead, if it is possible, to the
reform or the betterment of the one being punished. As this
is true of those on earth who are just, it is infinitely true
of God. When those in hell have been brought into a certain
order, their punishments become milder and less frequent
and they are brought into the best state possible, without
taking away their freedom. But as their ruling love is their
egotism, they remain in hell. Hell-fire, like heavenly fire,
represents love, and at a distance it may appear as fire. Hell-
fire consists of lusts, anger, the desire for revenge, and so on.

God Is Infinitely Merciful

As we have said, many have come to see that God is a God of love, that in Him there can be no vindictive justice, that vindictive justice is injustice, and that therefore the idea of God's cursing mankind on account of the disobedience of Adam and Eve and of salvation by appeasement of the Father through the death on the cross is wrong.

To replace the orthodox idea of redemption, a new idea of redemption has arisen and has been accepted by many. This new idea is based on the statement of Paul: "And all things are of God, who hath reconciled us unto Himself by Jesus Christ, and hath given to us the ministry of reconciliation; to wit, that God was in Christ, reconciling the world unto Himself." (II Corinthians 5:18,19.)

The new idea is expressed in a syndicated column by Dr. Louis Cassels as follows:

They depict Christ as standing in man's stead, accepting the punishment which man deserves for his willful wrongdoing. They speak of man as being saved, ransomed, redeemed, or delivered from his just fate because of Christ's intervention on his behalf.

In attempting to capture a great mystery within the dry language of dogma, theologians have sometimes made it sound as though God were some kind of vengeful ogre who had to be appeased by a sacrificial offering of innocent blood.

This is exactly the opposite of the Bible teaching, which points to the Cross of Christ as the ultimate proof and supreme demonstration of God's forgiving love for all His human creatures.

How can this be? The teaching makes sense only if it was God Himself acting in and through Christ. And this, of course, is precisely what Christians believe. As usual, St. Paul put it more succinctly than anyone else has managed to do: "God was in Christ, reconciling the world unto Himself."

Dr. Cassels in another article writes:

Christian theology has always asserted that Jesus Christ accomplished a "reconciliation" between God and man. This is the heart of the Gospel. But what exactly does it mean?

To many people, it means something like this: "God was angry with men because of their sins. But Jesus became humanity's champion. On the Cross, He suffered in our stead, accepting the punishment we deserved. God was placated by Jesus' sacrifice, and now is prepared to love any human being who appears before His throne of judgment pleading the name of Jesus."

The doctrine of atonement, so formulated, has become one of the greatest stumbling blocks for modern seekers after faith. They just can't work up much enthusiasm for the kind of faith it describes—a vindictive God whose wrath could be appeased by the sacrifice of an innocent life.

Those who are repelled by the notion that Jesus was a sort of scapegoat for human misdeeds may find it helpful to read a new book, *The Man for Others*. . . . The author is Reverend Erik Routley, a British theologian who formerly taught in Oxford, and is now a Congregationalist pastor.

This remarkable little book is every bit as modern, courageous and open-minded as Bishop John Robinson's *Honest to God*.

And it is considerably less muddled in its theology than the sensational best-seller.

Dr. Routley feels that it is nothing short of blasphemy to suggest that what Jesus did for mankind was "to placate a tyrant God who was waiting to punish His people with death."

Actually he says, He came to reassure men that God is not hostile towards them.

Man has a natural tendency to think of God as being unfriendly and unfair. Everything that goes wrong in life is another justification for nursing a "grievance" against God. This "settled attitude of grievance" is what the Bible means by sin. It is the antithesis of faith, and the ultimate source of particular sin.

To liberate man from this attitude, God sent Jesus into the world. Jesus was a human person who bore "the stamp of God's very being." His mission was not to reconcile God to man, but rather to reconcile men to God—from one of grievance to one of reciprocal confidence.

"Jesus did not come to stand up for us against God, to vindicate mankind against a God who disbelieved in man's worthiness to be saved," says Dr. Routley. Where men were saying that "God must be caused to love the world," Jesus said "God is love"—meaning "God loves the world and has always loved it."

In the above we read that "Jesus was a human person who bore the stamp of God"; that is, He was not God but was a human person who in a remarkable way above other men was in the likeness and image of God in which men were originally created. As we showed earlier, this is not the teaching of the Gospels. Although it is true that the Lord taught that God is love, there are far more reasons for the coming of the Lord on earth than just this, some of which we shall consider in the following chapter.

[6]

Redemption

On the subject of redemption, two hundred years ago Emanuel Swedenborg wrote, in *The True Christian Religion,* as follows:

Jehovah God descended and assumed a Human that He might redeem men and save them. In the Christian churches at this day it is believed that God the Creator of the universe begat a Son from eternity, and that this Son descended and assumed a Human in order to redeem and save men. But this is an error, and of itself falls to the ground as soon as it is considered that God is one, and that it is worse than incredible in the sight of reason to say that one God begat a Son from eternity, and that God the Father, together with the Son, and Holy Spirit, each of whom singly is God, is one God. This incredible notion is wholly dissipated, . . . when it is shown from the Word that Jehovah God Himself descended and became Man and also Redeemer.

The first statement, that it was Jehovah God Himself who descended and became Man, is made clear in the following passages:

"Behold a virgin shall conceive and shall bear a Son, who shall be called God with us." (Isaiah 7:14; Matthew 1:22,23)

"Unto us a child is born, unto us a Son is given, and the government shall be upon His shoulder, and His name shall be called Wonderful, God, Mighty, Father of Eternity, the Prince of Peace." (Isaiah 9:6)

"It shall be said in that day, Lo this is our God, we have waited for Him that He may deliver us; this is Jehovah." (Isaiah 25:9)

"The voice of one crying in the wilderness, Prepare ye the way of Jehovah." (Isaiah 40:3,5) . . .

That it was Jehovah Himself who descended and assumed the Human is especially evident in Luke, where it is said:

"Mary said to the angel, How shall this come to pass, seeing I know not a man? And the angel answered her, the Holy Spirit shall come upon thee, and the power of the Most High shall overshadow thee; therefore also that holy thing which shall be born of thee shall be called the Son of God." (1:34,35) . . .

That a Son born from eternity descended and assumed the human is a total error which falls to the ground and is dissipated in the light of those passages in the Word where Jehovah Himself says that He Himself is the Savior and Redeemer, as in the following:

"Am I not Jehovah, and there is no God else beside Me? A just God and a Savior, there is none beside Me." (Isaiah 45:21,22.)

"I am Jehovah and beside Me there is no Savior." (Isaiah 43:11)

"I am Jehovah thy God . . . and thou shalt acknowledge no God beside Me; and there is no Savior beside Me." (Hosea 13:4) . . .

"Thou, O Jehovah, art our Father, our Redeemer; from everlasting is Thy name." (Isaiah 63:16) . . .

"Jehovah of Hosts is His name; and thy Redeemer the Holy One of Israel; the God of the whole earth shall He be called." (Isaiah 54:5)

From these and many similar passages it can be seen by every man who has eyes, and a mind that has been opened by means of them, that God, who is one, descended and became Man, in order to effect Redemption. Who cannot see this in the light of morning when he gives any attention to these Divine declarations

themselves which have been presented? But those who
are in the shades of night, owing to a confirmed belief
in the birth of another God from eternity, and in His
descent and work of Redemption; shut their eyes to
these Divine declarations, and in that state study how
to apply them to their own falsities and pervert them.
(*True Christian Religion*, Numbers 82 and 83)

As we have said, the sophisticated will never accept
this, for the reason that they have no real faith in the
Bible as the Word of God, no faith in the virgin birth, and
no faith in the Lord Jesus Christ as their Lord and God.

The Lord said to the sophisticated among the Jews,
"Thus have ye made the commandments of God of none
effect by your tradition." (Matthew 15:6.) With many, even
in the Christian church, this is more true than it was with
the Jews at the time when the Lord was on earth.

Most people consider atheism and communism to be the
greatest danger to the church. But the greatest danger is
not from without, but from the sophisticated leaders within
the church, who have no living faith in the Word of God
or in the Lord as God, and who often undermine the faith
of the simple. With the increase of worldly education, nearly
everyone is becoming sophisticated, so that spiritual wisdom
is becoming rare.

The Lord came on earth to re-establish the Church.

Nowadays, many ministers are taking part in, or are
actively supporting, various political movements instead of
concentrating on preaching against the sins which are declared to be sins against God in the Word. This is contrary
to what the Lord did when in the world. The Lord did not
mention the evils and disorders of the Roman Empire, although they were many, nor did He encourage anyone to
take part in any political movement for freedom, but quite
the reverse. Such activities do not properly belong to
churches. The Lord's words were directed against the sophisticated and hypocrites in the Church. If sophistication

and hypocrisy in the Church can be overcome in the Church, the Church can enter upon its true function or enter into its true usefulness to the world; but so long as sophistication and hypocrisy rule in the Church, no political attempts at betterment of the world can have any lasting good effect.

The chapter on Redemption in *The True Christian Religion* continues:

> There are many reasons why God could redeem men, that is, could deliver them from . . . hell, only by means of an assumed Human. . . . Redemption consisted in subjugating the hells, restoring the heavens to order, and after this re-establishing the church; and this redemption God with His omnipotence could effect only by means of the Human, as it is only by means of an arm that one can work. In the Word this Human is called "the arm of Jehovah"—or as one can attack a fortified town and destroy temples of idols therein only by means of intervening agencies. That it was by means of His Human that God had omnipotence in this Divine work, is also evident from the Word. For in no other way would it be possible for God, who is in the inmost and thus in the purest things, to pass over to outmost things, in which the hells are, and in which the men of that time were; just as the soul can do nothing without the body, or no one can conquer an enemy without coming in sight of him, or approaching him with proper equipment. (*True Christian Religion*, Number 84)

That the Lord came to overcome the power of hell is taught in the Gospels as follows:

> Now is the judgment of this world; now shall the prince of this world be cast out. (John 12:31)
> Of judgment, because the prince of this world is judged. (John 16:11)
> And the seventy returned again with joy, saying,

Lord, even the devils are subject unto us in Thy name.
And He said unto them, I beheld Satan as lightning fall
from heaven. (Luke 10:17,18)

It may be asked, How did the Lord combat the power
of evil or the hells before He came into the world; and if
He did it before, why did He have to come into the world
to do this?

The answer is that God overcame the power of evil or
the hells through the ministry of angels, all of whom were
once men, and also through men on earth whom He inspired
to teach the truth and to fight against evil; but the time
came when the power of evil, or of the hells, had so increased that angels and inspired men had not sufficient
power to accomplish this task, and God had to take it upon
Himself. To overcome the power of evil, or the hells, He
could not descend in Glory, for no one could have stood
before the naked glory of God; and if they did indeed do so,
their free choice would have been taken away. Therefore
He had to clothe His glory by taking on a Human nature
by birth in the world, so as to be able to approach both
the good and the evil: the good, to lead them into the path
of life, and the evil, to deprive them of power so dominating
that men were no longer free. Thus the Lord came to re-
store man's freedom, so that he could choose the way of
salvation, provided he was willing.

This is involved in the parable of the Lord: "And when
the time of the fruit drew near, he sent servants to the
husbandmen, . . . and the husbandmen took his servants,
and beat one, and killed another, and stoned another. Again,
he sent other servants more than the first: and they did
to them likewise. But last of all he sent unto them his son."
(Matthew 21:34–37.)

The same is signified by the words "The scepter shall
not depart from Judah, nor a lawgiver from between his
feet until Shiloh come; and unto him shall the gathering
of the people be." (Genesis 49:10.)

Hell, the devil, and Satan are scarcely believed in by

modern man, yet the evidence of their influence is very great. The Lord's being tempted by the devil on the mountain signifies His combats with the power of evil and the hells which inspire evil. Such things appear unreal to modern man because, for the most part, he has lost a living faith in the Kingdom of Heaven, and therefore in its opposite, the kingdom of hell. The devil stands for the hells, and all in heaven and hell were once men on earth.

To continue the subject of redemption from *The True Christian Religion*:

Jehovah God descended as the Divine Truth . . . although He did not separate it from the Divine Good. There are two things that constitute the essence of God, the Divine Love and the Divine Wisdom, or what is the same, the Divine Good and the Divine Truth. . . .

That Jehovah descended as the Divine Truth is shown in John as follows:

"In the beginning was the Word, and the Word was with God and God was the Word. . . . And the Word became flesh and dwelt among us." (1:1,3,14)

By the Word here the Divine Truth is meant, because the Word, which is in the church, is the Divine Truth itself, because it was dictated by Jehovah Himself. . . . But inasmuch as the Divine Truth passed down through the heavens even to the world, it became adapted to angels in heaven and also to men in the world. For this reason there is in the Word a spiritual sense in which Divine Truth is seen in clear light, and a natural sense in which it is seen obscurely. Thus it is the Divine Truth in our Word that is here meant in John. This is made still clearer by the fact that the Lord came into the world to fulfill all things of the Word; and this is why it is so often said that this or that was done to Him "that the scriptures might be fulfilled." Nor is anything but the Divine Truth meant by the Messiah or the Christ. . . .

All strength, virtue and power of God belong to the

Divine Truth from the Divine Good. . . . Therefore
it is said in David:

"Gird thy sword upon thy thigh, O Mighty One,
and in thy majesty mount up; ride upon the Word of
Truth; thy right hand shall teach thee wonderful
things. Thine arrows are sharp, thine enemies shall
fall under thee." (Psalm 45:3–5)

This is said of the Lord, and . . . His victories over
the hells. (*The True Christian Religion*, Numbers 85
and 86)

That God, although He descended as the Divine
Truth, did not separate therefrom from the Divine
Good, is evident from the conception; of which it is
said: "That the power of the Most High overshadowed
Mary." (Luke 1:35) "The power of the most High"
meaning the Divine Good. This is evident from the
passages where He says that the Father is in Him, and
He in the Father, that all things that the Father hath
are His, and that the Father and He are one. By "the
Father" the Divine Good is meant. (*The True Christian
Religion*, Number 88)

That the Lord in the world was the Divine Truth is
evident from His own words:

I am the way, the truth, and the life. (John 14:6)

We know that the Son of God is come, and hath
given us understanding that we may know him that
is true: and we are in him that is true, in his Son
Jesus Christ. This is the true God and eternal life.
(I John 5:20)

This was the true Light that lighteth every man
coming into the world. (John 1:9)

I am the light of the world. (John 9:5)

"Light" means the Divine Truth.

That God Himself should be born of a virgin indeed

seems incredible to most people. Yet if we accept the idea that God is Divine Love and the nature of love is to wish to communicate one's love to another and to have the love returned, it can be seen that it is in agreement with sound reason. No one can love someone whom one does not know; and the better one knows another, the more one can love him or her. Certainly there was no better way for God to make Himself known to men and so make it possible for men to love Him in the fullest way, than by coming and living among them.

As we have said, it is the first law of the Divine Love that man shall be free and not compelled to believe or love, for compelled faith or love is valueless. It was therefore necessary for God to come among men in such a way as not to compel faith in Him. If the Lord had come in Divine Glory such as He appeared to Peter, James, and John on the mountain when His face shone as the sun, all would have been compelled to believe on Him. If evil persons were compelled to believe on Him, their state would be far worse than when they had no faith, for they would make a profane mixture of faith with their evil life.

This is what the Lord taught:

And their eyes they have closed; lest at any time they should see with their eyes, and hear with their ears. (Matthew 13:15)

Jesus said, For judgment I am come into this world, that they which see not might see, and that they which see might be made blind. . . . If ye were blind, ye should have no sin; but now ye say, We see; therefore your sin remaineth. (John 9:39,41)

This was said to the Jews. But now in what is called the Christian Church there is a far greater blindness, for although the churches have grown, there are fewer and fewer who believe in the Bible as the Word of God and in Jesus as their Lord and God.

Why the Lord Was Born of a Virgin

If the Lord was to come into the world, He could come only by being born of a virgin in such a way that men would not have to believe in Him. It is also of the Divine Providence that there are so many arguments against the Lord's birth of a virgin that those in the Christian Church whose hearts are not turned to God can find many excuses for not believing, for to have a faith in Jesus as our Lord and God and live a life centered in oneself and the world is a more terrible thing than to have no real faith.

The Lord also had to be born of a virgin not only that He might clothe Himself with a body of this world according to order, but also in order that He might take on a human heredity, in which was a tendency toward all the evils of the human race.

If He had not clothed Himself with such a human, He could not have been tempted. No devil could approach Him in His states of glory, nor could evil men stand in His presence. He could therefore not have effected the judgment for which He came; as He said, "For judgment I am come into this world." (John 9:39.)

The reason for His coming into the world was judgment, for by judgment He cast out the prince of this world (John 12:31) and He ordered heaven and the church anew, and thus made possible the salvation of those in the human race who love Him and keep His commandments. His love and salvation also go forth to the Gentiles, who, while not knowing Him, receive indirectly of His life and light if they live according to the truths which they have.

Although the Lord took on a human heredity from Mary, as He glorified His Human He entirely put this off, so that He was no longer her son.

The Two Great Commandments

And Jesus answered him, The first of all the commandments is, Hear, O Israel; the Lord our God is one Lord: and thou shalt love the Lord thy God with all thy heart, and with all thy soul, and with all thy mind, and with all thy strength: this is the first commandment. And the second is like, namely this, Thou shalt love thy neighbor as thyself. (Mark 12:29–31)

THE WORD "LOVE" is a much-abused word. No one can have a real idea of what love is unless he distinguishes a true from a false idea of love. The world is full of a false, sentimental idea of love. In the first place, there is animal love and there is genuine human love. Animals love their young and love their kind, and they may love other kinds of animals and may love human beings; all men, by instinct, love others, whereas animal love is proper to animals. If human love remains on the plane of animal love, it is not the love that the Lord commanded. The Lord indeed spoke of a merely animal kind of love in human beings when He said: "For if ye love them which love you, what thank have ye? for sinners also love those that love them." (Luke 6:32.)

The Lord also taught how we should truly love, saying: "This is My commandment, That ye love one another, as I have loved you." (John 15:12.) But how does the Lord love us? The Lord's love looks to our eternal welfare. He does not regard any temporal thing—things of this world only— as of any significance, unless it looks to our welfare in the

Kingdom of Heaven. The things of this world last less than
a moment compared to eternal life. Wherefore suffering or
joy, miseries or happiness, are regarded by the Lord's Divine Providence or loving care only insofar as they are
useful in preparing us for our eternal welfare. The animal
kind of love in a man, which is very far removed from the
love of others as the Lord loves us, regards only one's happiness, pleasures, and welfare here on earth.

Miseries, sadness, and sufferings of all kinds are often
useful in helping to bring us to the real significance and
values of life and thus to prepare us for eternal life;
whereas too easy a time is often the worst thing possible
for the development of character. Yet not only politicians
but even the churches in recent times have tended to concentrate on making life in this world as easy and painless
as possible, and this is considered Christian charity—forgetting completely the primary teaching so oft repeated,
"Seek ye first the kingdom of God, and His righteousness."
(Matthew 6:33.)

When churches center their attention on improving the
material condition of those in this world and not on preparing men for a life in the Kingdom of Heaven, they are
no longer Christian churches except in name only, for they
have totally left the teaching of our Lord.

This does not mean that we should not help others in
regard to material things when we are able to do so, and
when our help may be useful to another and does not take
away his responsibility or tend to make him lazy. But a wise
man recognizes that such material aid is of relatively no
significance in comparison to helping one in his preparation
for eternal life.

An indication of the prevailing materialistic point of
view is this. Many are distressed on account of the hunger
of millions of people in the world, particularly when children are near to starving. Yet few are distressed that hundreds of millions of children are spiritually starving for
that food which is the love and truths which lead to eternal

life. Especially sad is it that children are growing up without any instruction in religion. The above does not mean that we should not be distressed by the fact that there are many people hungry in the world. But if a man is truly a Christian, he will be much more distressed that there are so many millions who are being spiritually starved. This illustrates the fact that, although there are millions who have a membership in a church, this is no longer a Christian nation, and that the best characteristic, or highest good, with most people is a kind of animal sympathy with their fellow human beings.

But how are we to love the Lord? This the Lord taught us as follows:

If ye love me, keep my commandments.

He that hath my commandments, and keepeth them, he it is that loveth me, . . . and I will love him. (John 14:15,21)

If ye keep my commandments, ye shall abide in my love; even as I have kept my Father's commandments, and abide in his love. (John 15:10)

The Lord's Father, the Infinite Divine Itself, was His soul, called the "power of the Highest," which overshadowed Mary and was in Him from conception. As to His Human which is called the Son, the Lord completely followed the dictates of His soul. Thus He glorified His Human until His Human also became purely Divine. He and His Father were one, one in essence and one in person.

We can be conjoined with the Lord, in His love, only if we obey His commandments.

Anyone will admit that a child who likes to kiss and hug its mother and be kissed and hugged in return but disobeys her and does all kinds of things which distress her and make her sad, and is indifferent to the distress it causes her, does not reveal real love. Or that a friend who is most cordial and hearty to another and yet acts contrary to the other's best interests does not show love. Yet there are many who think they can have faith in the Lord, and even love Him, and still disobey His commandments.

But consider further: what are the Lord's commandments?

As we have said, one of the Lord's commandments was, "A new commandment I give unto you, That ye love one another; as I have loved you." (John 13:34.) The Lord had already said that the commandment, "Thou shalt love thy neighbor as thyself," was one of the two Great Commandments. This was not a new commandment, for it had been written by Moses. But to love one another as the Lord had loved them, this was "a new commandment," for the Lord loved them as no one had loved his neighbor before. If we can come to an understanding of how the Lord loves us, then we can keep this new commandment.

There can be no genuine love of the Lord or one's neighbor unless one shuns sins which are against his neighbor, for what kind of love is it if one says he loves God and his neighbor while he sins against them?

The Lord's Command to the Young Man

Again we read:

And behold, one came and said unto him, Good Master, what good thing shall I do, that I may have eternal life? And he said unto him . . . If thou wilt enter into life, keep the commandments. He saith unto him, Which? Jesus said, Thou shalt do no murder, Thou shalt not steal, Thou shalt not bear false witness, Honor thy father and thy mother, Thou shalt love thy neighbor as thyself. (Matthew 19:16–19)

The Lord therefore made the keeping of the Ten Commandments the means of inheriting eternal life. But He taught that it was not enough to keep them according to the letter, but that they must be kept according to the spirit as well, saying: "Ye have heard, . . . Thou shalt not kill. . . . But I say unto you, whosoever is angry with his brother shall be in danger of the judgment." (Matthew 5:21,22.)

And again: "But I say unto you, That whosoever looketh on a woman to lust after her hath committed adultery with her already in his heart." (Matthew 5:28.)

The Lord, after telling the young man that the means of inheriting eternal life was to keep the commandments, added one thing more: "Sell whatsoever thou hast, and give to the poor, and thou shalt have treasure in heaven; and come, take up the cross, and follow Me." (Mark 10:21.)

Whereas the Lord in parable apparently spoke of things of this world, still all His words refer to the Kingdom of Heaven, to the things of the spirit. When He spoke of the poor, the "poor in spirit" are especially meant, as He declared in the Ten Blessings: "Blessed are the poor in spirit, for theirs is the Kingdom of Heaven." Also, when He spoke of the rich, He referred to the "rich in spirit." Spiritual riches are knowledges, especially the knowledge of the Word of God and of the church. That this is the meaning is evident from the book of Revelation, where, using the rich in a favorable sense, it is said, when addressing the church of Smyrna, "I know thy . . . poverty, (but thou art rich)." (2:9.) And in Luke: "So is he that layeth up treasure for himself, and is not rich toward God." (12:21.)

The rich in the unfavorable sense are the sophisticated, the learned doctors, the scribes, both in the Jewish Church and in the Christian Church, who have a great knowledge of the Bible, of doctrine, and of philosophy but misuse it and make it serve their own honor and power, their status, and their reputation, instead of in humility serving the Kingdom of God.

All the wealth of knowledge with them is interpreted in such a way as to favor themselves and their own glory. This is the wealth with which, unless he sells it, a man cannot enter the Kingdom of God. The poor in the favorable sense are those who acknowledge that they of themselves are ignorant of the spirit of the Word, and who are therefore willing to be instructed. Such know that what they know of the Word of God, whether it be relatively much or little, is only like a cup of water compared to the ocean, relative to the Infinite Truth contained in the Word of God, and they know that they can understand nothing of the spirit of the Word of God unless it is given them from the Lord out of heaven. They are therefore modest and regard themselves as poor, although they are rich toward God.

The final thing required to enter into life, according to the Lord's command, was to "take up the cross, and follow Me." (Mark 10:21.)

To take up the cross is to undergo trials or temptations, to sacrifice oneself, to give up one's own will, in order to live according to the will of God—but to do these things not before the world, but before God.

The Lord commanded, "Do not your alms before men, to be seen of them," ". . . let not thy left hand know what thy right hand doeth," pray not "standing in the synagogues or in the corners of the streets that they may be seen of men," "use not vain repetitions . . . much speaking"; not "to fast with a sad countenance" that "they may appear unto men to fast," but to do all things "in secret." Matthew 6:13, 5,16–18.)

All these commands of the Lord have gone unheeded in the Christian church. Men and women went into monasteries and convents where they prayed endlessly. Some courted martyrdom, and many desired their contributions to churches, hospitals, the poor, and other charities to be noised about so that they might receive credit and influence on account of good works, if not in heaven, then at least on earth.

To do something spectacularly good, especially if there is danger involved, or what appears like a great sacrifice, is not difficult. Evil people are often more eager to be recognized as heroes than are the good people. It is the fashion of the day to want to appear "committed." Now no "commitment," no dedication to accomplishing a good or useful work, is of any use unless evils are first shunned as sins against God. To do good before repentance is like adding pure water to contaminated water; no matter how much is added, the whole continues to be contaminated.

Observe the order of the commandments of the Lord on how to obtain eternal life.

"Thou shalt do no murder, Thou shalt not commit adultery, Thou shalt not steal, defraud not, Thou shalt not bear false witness, Honor thy father and thy mother, Thou shalt love thy neighbor as thyself." (Matthew 19:18,19; Mark 10:19.) Love toward one's neighbor follows the keeping of the other commandments.

As it is said in Isaiah: "Wash you, make you clean; put away the evil of your doings from before mine eyes; cease to do evil; learn to do well." (1:16,17.)

Most people want to love, they want to do good, but without keeping the commandments; therefore their offering is unacceptable to God.

Luther taught salvation by faith alone, ignoring the teaching of the Lord. Luther did, indeed, say that love to the Lord is essential for salvation, but he ignored the words of the Lord, "He that hath my commandments, and keepeth them, he it is that loveth me." (John 14:21.)

Naaman the Leper

This whole principle is illustrated by the story of Naaman, captain of the Syrian army, who was a leper, though a great man in Syria and a friend of the king.

Hearing of the powers of a prophet in Israel, he came with a letter and great treasure to Elisha, to ask to be cured of his leprosy.

Elisha did not receive him into his house but sent a messenger to tell him to go wash seven times in Jordan and he would be cured. At this Naaman was very angry and went away saying that he expected the prophet to come to him, call on the name of Jehovah, strike his hand over the place of the leprosy, and cure him.

Naaman's servant said to him, if the prophet had bid him to do some great deed, would he not have done it? Was it not much easier to wash and be clean? So Naaman did as he was commanded and was cured.

Leprosy signifies an unclean state of the spirit in which one has a kind of faith but does not live according to it. Such a man may wish to do some heroic deeds to cleanse his spirit; he may, under powerful emotion, wish to do some great deed to be saved—to become "committed."

The Jordan river signifies the first simple truths of life, the keeping of the Commandments in their obvious meaning. It is obedience to these simple truths that first enables a man to cross over to the heavenly Canaan, the Kingdom of God. To wash seven times in the river Jordan is to repent and cleanse oneself by shunning evils as sins against God, in obedience to the Commandments.

If this idea had been regarded as the first thing of the Christian religion and had been obeyed, how much better a world this would be! Keeping the Commandments, in a broader sense, includes shunning pride, vanity, arrogance, conceit, and sophistication, which sins are all included in the spirit of the Ten Commandments, as will be illustrated in a later chapter.

PART TWO

An Explication of Genesis and Certain Other Chapters of the Bible

Based On the Work *The Arcana Coelestia,*
by Emanuel Swedenborg

INTRODUCTION

Fulfilling the Law

It is known that the Lord fulfilled the Law. But what is meant by the Lord fulfilling the Law?

By "the Law" in its narrowest sense is meant the Ten Commandments. In a broader sense, by "the Law" is meant the five books of Moses, as when it is said concerning Mary's purification, "Purification according to the Law of Moses." (Luke 2:22.)

"Moses and the Prophets" are often spoken of, as when it is said of the Lord: "And beginning at Moses and all the prophets, He expounded unto them in all the scriptures the things concerning Himself." (Luke 24:27.)

In the broadest sense, the whole of the Word of the Lord is the Law. In general, by the Lord fulfilling the Law is understood either that He fulfilled all the prophecies concerning Himself, particularly the prophecy concerning His crucifixion, or that He obeyed the moral Law, in particular the Ten Commandments, and thus that He was without sin. Yet far more than this is involved in His fulfilling the Law.

But before continuing, it may be noted that orthodox Protestants think that man cannot fulfill the Law, and that the fulfilling of the Law is not the means of salvation, because it is not possible for man to fulfill the Law. They base this idea on the statement of Paul, "Therefore we conclude that a man is justified by faith without the deeds of the law." (Romans 3:28.)

By "the Law" here is meant the ceremonial law, not
the Ten Commandments, as is evident from the two preceding chapters, where we read:

> Being filled with all unrighteousness, fornication,
> wickedness, covetousness, maliciousness; full of envy,
> murder, debate, deceit, malignity . . . who knowing the
> judgment of God, that they who commit such things
> are worthy of death, not only do the same, but have
> pleasure in them that do them . . .
> But we are sure that the judgment of God is accord-
> ing to truth against them which commit such things.
> . . . But after thy hardness and impenitent heart treas-
> urest up unto thyself wrath against the day of wrath
> and revelation of the righteous judgment of God; who
> will render to every man according to his deeds.
> (Romans 1:29,32; 2:2,5,6)

The question that was disturbing the Apostles at the
time was the question of circumcision and the eating of
meat, such as pork, which was forbidden in the Mosaic Law.
It was these laws that were abrogated for Christians, and
not the Ten Commandments.

It is acknowledged by Christians that the Lord's life is an
example that we should follow, a model. Why, then, if the
Lord fulfilled the Law, must not man fulfill the Law? There
are many who obey the Law of the Ten Commandments for
the sake of their own reputation, even though they have no
faith; that is, they go to church to worship God, they honor
father and mother, they do not kill, steal, commit adultery,
or bear false witness. Now if those who have no faith can
do this for the sake of themselves and their reputation, why
is it not possible for those who have faith to do this for the
sake of God?

But, as we have said, there is much more involved in
the Lord's fulfilling the Law than just keeping the Commandments. We read:

Think not that I am come to destroy . . . but to fulfill. For verily I say unto you, Till heaven and earth pass, one jot or one tittle shall in no wise pass from the law, till all be fulfilled. (Matthew 5:17,18)

And it is easier for heaven and earth to pass, than one tittle of the law to fail. (Luke 16:17)

A jot, or *yoth*, was the smallest of Hebrew letters, and a tittle was the little horn on the Hebrew letter.

Compare this with what the Lord said: "And beginning at Moses and all the prophets, he expounded unto them in all the scriptures the things concerning himself." (Luke 24:27.)

Taking the above quotations together, it can be seen that every jot and tittle of Moses and the Prophets treats of the Lord, and there was not a jot or tittle that He did not fulfill. But it may be asked, How can this be?

The Bible or Word of God

There are many now who would agree that we must not be literalists, that we must seek the spirit of the Word of God or Bible, and not remain in the mere letter, as was said by Paul:

Who also hath made us able ministers of the new testament; not of the letter, but of the spirit; for the letter killeth, but the spirit giveth life. (II Corinthians 3:6)

We should serve in newness of spirit, and not in the oldness of the letter. (Romans 7:6)

Circumcision is that of the heart, in the spirit, and not in the letter. (Romans 2:29)

But if we regard the spirit and have no regard for the letter, what have we? Those who seek only for the spirit often speak of "the Spirit of the Gospels," but as to what that spirit is they are very vague. It is sometimes called "the Fatherhood of God and the brotherhood of man," but as to what is the Fatherhood of God and the brotherhood of man they have vague and different ideas in which there is no agreement.

Some regard the Ten Blessings as expressing the spirit of the Gospels, but with no clear idea of what is meant by "the poor in spirit" or "the meek." The idea obtained from them is often a sentimental idea of Christ, such as mere love, apart from any judgment—any definite stand; this is quite contrary to the teaching of the Gospels, where we read of the Lord making severe judgments: casting out the thieves from the temple and denouncing the self-righteous Pharisees. Some look for a spiritual meaning in all parts of the Bible, but to them the meaning is vague and uncertain.

The Word, spiritually seen, is a Divine Man. Its spirit is its soul and its letter is its body.

The letter without the spirit is a corpse. The spirit without the letter is a ghost or disembodied spirit having no form, an indefinite something on which no two persons agree.

Those who regard only a spirit and those who regard only the letter are at the extremes. What is the golden mean? It is to see that the body of the Word of God is its letter and the spirit is its soul, and that both are from God.

The Old Testament, in every last detail, does not appear to treat of our Lord, nor can it easily be seen how the Lord could fulfill every least thing of the Books of the Old Testament during His life on earth.

When the Lord lived on earth with His twelve Apostles, they saw and were deeply impressed by His person as they knew it. Yet what they knew of Him was relatively little. They saw His acts and listened to His teaching, but His inner life, His struggles and combats, were hidden from them except on rare occasions, as in Gethsemane and at Calvary.

The Lord could not reveal His inner thoughts to the Apostles, for these men were too simple to understand, and, besides, they had not the character to understand, for even James and John, who were two of the three leading Apostles, had the audacity to ask to sit, one on His right hand and the other on His left hand in His Kingdom. As the Apostles were not prepared to enter into the inmost truths of faith, Jesus said to them: "I have yet many things to say unto you, but ye cannot bear them now. Howbeit when he, the Spirit of truth, is come, he will guide you into all truth." (John 16:12,13.)

Still, all the inner and hidden life of the Lord is contained in the Law and the Prophets, if they are opened up as they were by the Lord, in a brief and general way, to the two disciples as He walked with them to Emmaus. Concerning this we read: "Then he said unto them, O fools, and slow of heart to believe all that the prophets have spoken: Ought not Christ to have suffered these things, and to enter into his glory? And beginning at Moses and all the prophets, He expounded unto them in all the Scriptures the things concerning Himself." (Luke 24:25–27.)

1

Noah and the Dove

In a work consisting of twelve large volumes, *The Arcana Coelestia,* by Emanuel Swedenborg, Genesis and Exodus are explained with respect to their spiritual meaning. We cannot attempt even to summarize the contents of this work in a volume such as this, but we shall give an idea of certain chapters from this work. We have already spoken of Adam and Eve, of the tree of life and the tree of the knowledge of good and evil, and of the serpent.

We shall now treat of an episode in the story of Noah.

Adam stands for the first or Most Ancient Church on earth; Noah, for the second or Ancient Church. Frequently in the Word of the Lord, a church is spoken of as if it were a person, usually as a woman. The church is called the wife of the Lord, as in the book of Revelation, where the New Jerusalem is called the wife of the Lamb.

In the Prophets, Judah is spoken of as an unfaithful wife. Such a form of speech has come down to the present day, in relation to nations: we speak of Uncle Sam, John Bull, and Marianne. In the first eleven chapters of Genesis, the persons mentioned are not literally persons, nor are the events literal events. For example, the flood was not a literal flood of water, but a flood of evil and falsity. "The flood" has a similar meaning when the Lord said that the floods came and carried away the house built on sand.

The human race has had its infancy, childhood, and adult life. Whereas the stories in the Word, in their historical sense, treat of the churches which have been in the past, these stories also have an application to every real church, and to every man and woman who is regenerated, for the history of the individual man corresponds to the history of the human race. In the supreme sense, they treat of the life of our Lord.

The flood, as has been recognized from the earliest Christian period, stands for temptations. Spiritual temptations come to a man or to a church when there is the beginning of a strong love for the Lord, for His Word, and for one's neighbor. When a man has acquired such loves and begins to come into doubts and obscurities, even to the point where he begins to feel that his faith and spiritual life are failing, he comes into temptations; he suffers from the fear of losing his spiritual life—at times even to despair. The greater has been his love to the Lord and His Word, the greater his suffering at the thought of losing such a life of love and faith. Yet he finds difficulty in shaking off his doubts; many objections against faith come to his mind and torment him. Waters signify truth, but every word also has an opposite meaning. A destructive flood of water signifies false ideas and reasonings.

Noah Opens a Window and Sends Forth First a Raven, Then a Dove

After a man has undergone the distress of temptations, doubts, and obscurities, false ideas tend still to disturb him; for, even though he has overcome the temptation, time is necessary entirely to remove the false reasonings.

A window is to a house or to the Ark as is the eye to the body, and the eye signifies an inner sight of the mind. Noah's opening the window and sending forth a raven signifies that false ideas and reasonings still disturbed. A man in this state has a certain inner light, like the light of early dawn, that he has acquired as the result of overcoming temptations; but still the shades of night have not been dissipated. As he progresses, he comes to a new, holy faith in what is good and true. This new faith is represented by the dove which Noah sent forth.

The Dove

As is known from the Gospels, a dove represents the Spirit—the Spirit of God or the Holy Spirit. The words "Holy Spirit" do not occur in the Old Testament, but instead "the Spirit of Jehovah" (translated, "the Spirit of the Lord") occurs frequently, also "the Spirit of God" and "the Spirit of the Lord." In three places in the Old Testament—once in the Psalms and twice in Isaiah—the phrase "the spirit of holiness" occurs (mistranslated in the King James Bible as "the Holy Spirit").

The reason why the Holy Spirit is not spoken of in the Old Testament is given in the Gospel of John: "But this spake he of the Spirit, which they that believe on him should receive; for the Holy Spirit (Ghost) was not yet, because that Jesus was not yet glorified." (John 7:39.)

In the King James Bible, it says "The Holy Ghost was not yet given." By adding the word "given," which does not occur in the Greek, the meaning is entirely changed. There are some other places where the translators changed or added words in their translation of the Bible to make it agree with their theology, altering the Greek text—an example of which is found in the King James Bible in Matthew 24:3, where the words "the consummation of the age" (Greek *aion*) are mistranslated "the end of the world."

That a dove signifies the spirit is evident in Matthew, where it is said: "He saw the Spirit of God descending like a dove." (3:16.)

In a cross reference in the reference Bible, we are referred to Isaiah 11:1,2, where we read: "And there shall come forth a rod out of the stem of Jesse; . . . and the spirit of Jehovah shall rest upon him."

In Mark it is merely said: "He saw the Spirit like a dove descending upon him." (1:10.) And in Luke 3:22, it is said: "The Holy Ghost descended in a bodily shape like a dove."

In John 1:32, John the Baptist is quoted as saying: "I saw the Spirit descending from heaven like a dove, and it abode upon him." In the above the dove is said to be "The spirit of God" and "the spirit," whereas in the prophecy of Isaiah it is said to be "the Spirit of Jehovah."

How do we reconcile these passages? The word translated "spirit" in its root meanings in the Hebrew and Greek is air, wind, or breath. Air stands for or signifies the breath of God, that is, His Spirit.

We read in the second chapter of Genesis, verse seven: "And Jehovah God formed man of the dust of the ground, and breathed into his nostrils the breath of life; and man became a living soul." By "the breath of life" is here meant not man's animal life, but his spiritual life, which causes man to be a spiritually living soul—the life that is arrived at by following the "narrow . . . way, which leadeth unto life" (Matthew 7:14), that life which the Lord spoke of when He said: "I am come that they might have life, and that they might have it more abundantly." (John 10:10.)

It is this life which the Lord meant when it is said that "He breathed on them, and saith unto them, Receive ye the Holy Spirit." (John 20:22.)

It is obvious that the breath of Jehovah God is the spirit of Jehovah God, and the breath of the Lord Jesus Christ is His spirit which goes forth and is received by man. How the church could have come to the idea that the Holy Spirit was a person from the beginning is indeed strange, for there is no support for such an idea in the Word, and it is an unreasonable idea. In John the Holy Spirit is called "the Spirit of truth." (16:13.) It is the Spirit of truth of our

Lord, which proceeds from the Lord and is received in the mind of man.

Before the Lord came on earth, this spirit of truth, or the spirit of Jehovah God, inspired men. (The literal meaning of "inspire" is to breathe into.) When mankind had so turned away that they could no longer receive the spirit of Jehovah God, the Lord had to come down by birth into the world—and to come on a lower plane, where He was "the way, the truth and the life," in order that from Himself He could again breathe upon or inspire into men the breath of a new life.

In the world, Jehovah God took to Himself a Human nature by birth from a virgin, as we read: "The Holy Spirit shall come upon thee, and the power of the Highest shall overshadow thee." (Luke 1:35.) The Holy Spirit is the Divine Truth and the power of the Highest is the Divine Good of love, both proceeding from Jehovah God.

At the Lord's baptism, there was a new infinite influx of the Divine Truth from Jehovah God, which was the soul of our Lord Jesus, into His Human, called the Son.

By the inflowing of the Divine Itself, the Infinite Divine, into the Human, the human was gradually made a Divine Human, and all the Infinite power of Jehovah God was transferred into this Divine Human, as the Lord said after His resurrection: "All power is given unto Me in heaven and in earth." (Matthew 28:18.)

The Divine and the Human called the Father and the Son were then entirely one, one in essence and one in person, as the soul and body are one person.

This making Divine the Human is called in the Gospels glorification. That it was a gradual process is taught in the Gospel of John:

> Therefore, when he was gone out, Jesus said, Now is the Son of man glorified, and God is glorified in Him. If God be glorified in Him, God shall also glorify Him in Himself. (John 13:31,32)

Father, glorify thy name, . . . I have both glorified
it and will glorify it again. (John 12:28.)

That the Lord was not fully glorified, or made Divine,
and thus one with the Father in essence and person until
after the resurrection, is taught as follows: "These things
understood not His disciples at the first; but when Jesus
was glorified, then remembered they that these things were
written of Him." (John 12:16.)

And shortly before the crucifixion, He said: "The hour
is come, that the Son of man should be glorified." (John
12:23.)

It was after our Lord was fully glorified and had risen
from the dead that His Holy Spirit, signified by the breathing upon the disciples, could go forth from Him.

Because this long process of glorification commenced
with the Lord's childhood, in the beginning of the Gospels
it speaks of the Holy Spirit; yet, as was shown above, the
Holy Spirit in its fullness did not exist until the Lord rose
again in the fullness of His glorified Divine Human. At the
Lord's Baptism the "Spirit of God," spoken of in Matthew,
which came upon Jesus, was the influx of the Divine Truth
into Him from His Divine soul called the Father; and not
the Divine Truth which proceeded from Him and was received by others. It is, indeed, called the Holy Spirit in
Luke, because the work of glorification was already progressing. But that it was not the Holy Spirit itself which
proceeds from Him is evident from the words spoken later:
"The Holy Spirit was not yet, because that Jesus was not
yet glorified." (John 7:39.)

The dove in the story of Noah stands for or signifies
the goods and truths of faith which man is in when inspired
by the Spirit of God.

Noah is said to have first sent forth the dove to see if
the waters were abated from off the face of the ground.
When the truths of faith are first inspired into man, false
ideas still disturb his mind, for he is not yet in clear light

as to what is true and what is false, and therefore the truths
of faith are like truth of the Word, which the Lord called
seed, but which in the first state cannot take root on account
of false ideas that still cling to man.

On account of the flood of waters that still remained,
the dove found no rest for the sole of her foot and returned
to Noah. This signifies that, on account of the false ideas
that still clung to him, the spirit was not free but returned
to Noah and the confinement of the ark—that is, to the
church signified by Noah, and the like happens to every man
who is in a similar state. One in such obscurity supposes
that the good he does and the truths he thinks are from
himself, and he takes them to himself as Noah took the dove
to himself.

John the Baptist said: "A man can receive nothing,
except it be given him from heaven." (John 3:27.) Whereas
a man may, as it were, know this because he has read it
in the Word, or heard it in the church, still he feels so
strongly that the good he does and the truth he thinks are
his own, that for a long time he does not realize that they
are from God out of heaven.

"He [Noah] put forth his hand, and took her, and pulled
her in unto him into the ark." (Genesis 8:9.) The hand and
also the arm signify power, for the power of the body is by
means of the arms and hands; wherefore frequent mention
is made in the Word of the hand and arm of Jehovah to signify His power or omnipotence, as in the Psalms, "Jehovah
upholdeth him with His hand." (37:24.) "Thou art the God
that doest wonders: Thou hast declared Thy strength among
the people. Thou hast with Thine arm redeemed Thy people."
(Psalm 77:14,15.) "Sing unto Jehovah . . . His right hand,
and His holy arm, hath gotten Him the victory." (Psalm
98:1.) "The heavens are the work of Thy hands." (Psalm
102:25.) In an unfavorable sense, a hand represents a man's
vanity in trusting in his own power, as in Isaiah: "They
worship the work of their own hands." (2:8.)

Noah's putting forth his hand and taking the dove signifies man's thinking that he can take to himself the truths of faith by his own power. Most leaders of the church say that all power is from the Lord, and that also all of faith is from the Lord; yet in their hearts they feel they have acquired the truths of faith by their own power.

After seven days, that is, in a holy state, the dove was sent forth again, and returned with an olive leaf plucked off. An olive tree signifies the love of God and one's neighbor; and for this reason the Lord dwelt on the Mount of Olives. Fruit, as is well known, signifies deeds, particularly deeds of love to God and one's neighbor. Leaves signify the truths of faith. As faith without deeds is not saving, therefore the Lord cursed the tree which had leaves but no fruit.

An olive leaf in the mouth of the dove signifies some little truth of faith, a truth of life, inspired by the Spirit of God.

Seven more days had to pass, that is, a following holy state, before the dove was again sent forth. This time the dove was free and did not have to return, for the flood was no longer covering the land. After living imprisoned in the ark, the free state of the dove—and afterward of Noah when he left the ark—recalls to our mind the words of the Lord: "And ye shall know the truth, and the truth shall make you free. . . . Whosoever committeth sin is the servant of sin. . . . If the Son therefore shall make you free, ye shall be free indeed." (John 8:32, 34, 36.)

There is no one who thinks he is more free than one who trusts solely in himself and his own ability to find the truth aided by no one. Yet such a one is the slave of his own vanity and conceit and can never find the truth, no matter how hard he searches. On the other hand, one who trusts in the Lord and in His Word is free, for it is the very nature of God to make man free to find the truth, and to live it freely and joyfully.

2

The Tower of Babel

All churches and civilizations have had their infancy, childhood, and adult age, followed by a decline. When a church comes to its spiritual fall, although it may long continue for many centuries as an external organization, a new church is raised up. At the end of the Most Ancient Church, represented by Adam and his descendants, the church was first cast out of Paradise and then came to an end in an overflowing of evil and false things, represented by a flood, and a new church called Noah and his sons was established. Later a church was established with Abraham and his descendants which, when it fell into hypocrisy, was judged by the Lord, at His Coming into the world, and the Christian Church was established. The fall and judgment of the Christian Church by the Lord, at His Second Coming, are prophesied in the Gospels and the book of Revelation. Following this a New Church is instituted, called, in the book of Revelation, the New Jerusalem or, to use the Greek of the Gospels, *Nova Hierosolyma.*

The fall of the Noachic Church is represented by what is said about the tower of Babel.

We read: "The whole land was of one lip, and their words were one." (Gen. 11:1.)

Lips and words signify the doctrine or teachings of the Church, for it is by the lips and by words that the teachings are communicated from man to man. To have one lip, and the words being one, signifies that there was one teaching or doctrine. The church called Noah, which included his descendants, was widespread, and there were many nations around the land of Canaan which belonged to this church. In these nations there was a variety of worship and teachings, yet this variety was a harmonious variety, a harmony which made them one and united them into one church.

As long as there is a spirit of spiritual or real charity, different organizations of the church in different lands make it one, for all have good will and therefore understand each other.

Take two men who are humble and are of good will but who differ as to their doctrinal position. In speaking together, if one points out the error that the other is in, the one who has his position criticized carefully considers the criticism to see whether there is any truth in it; and if, after prayer to God, he finds that there is, he modifies his point of view. He may then point out errors in the other's point of view. Thus, although the emphasis may remain different, an ever-increasing harmony of thought develops between them. If, however, there is no humility and no good will, antagonism on account of doctrinal difference increases. The same is true of churches. If all churches were in good will and were willing to humble themselves before the Word of God and give up all their cherished ideas which do not agree with the Word of God, there would be internal unity. This, however, does not mean that there should be an ecumenical coming together of churches at the sacrifice or compromising of the truth. For example, if those who believe in the Divine nature of the Word of God —and therefore believe that the Lord Jesus Christ is their Lord and their God—compromise and join with those who believe that the Bible is a human production and deny the Virgin birth and the Divinity of the Lord, they still have nothing spiritually in common. When a compromise is made as to the very essence of faith, those having no faith in the Word of God prevail and all living faith perishes.

The prevailing idea is that charity involves abstaining from a forceful exposure of false ideas. But this is not a Christian idea, for the Lord condemned the false ideas of those with whom He dwelt on earth in the sharpest of language; yet He did this out of pure love, saying, "O Jerusalem, Jerusalem, which killest the prophets, and stonest them that are sent unto thee; how often would I have gathered thy children together, as a hen doth gather her brood under her wings, and ye would not!" (Luke 13:34.)

Union of church organizations may have as its purpose increase of power and influence, protection from a common enemy, improvement of one's image before others, or reduction in the cost of running a church. Such union has nothing to do with good will or charity, although it may put on such an appearance, just as thieves are friendly to each other in order to protect themselves or for the sake of uniting to carry out their ends.

It is said of those who built the tower of Babel that they journeyed from the east. The east, or sunrise, signifies love to the Lord and charity. To go from the east means that they departed from love and charity.

> They said, Go to, let us build us a city and a tower, . . . and let us make us a name. (Genesis 11:4)

A city signifies doctrine or teaching, and a tower in the unfavorable sense signifies the loftiness that comes from loving one's self in the first place. " . . . and its head in heaven" signifies even having dominion over the things of heaven, or the divine things of the church. ". . . and let us make a name" signifies that they desired to have a reputation for power.

It is the nature of a man who has not been born again to long for power and influence, to long to be able to command and domineer over others. In churches the leaders who have such ambitions invent teachings which add to their power and authority. Examples of this in the Christian Church are claims involving the power to admit or not to admit into heaven; also, the idea that one has been called by the Lord to the ministry, when frequently the call was an imaginary response to a personal ambition. Every doctrinal position taken by a church or congregation for the sake of influence or popularity, every political attitude which does not humbly submit to the Word of the Lord, no matter what the consequences, but strives for the prosperity of this world or the increase of membership or wealth, becomes a city and tower of Babel.

When such an attitude prevails, to prevent profanation the Lord is said to go down, confound their lip that they hear not the lip of their fellow. (Genesis 11:7.) This signifies that the inner truth in the Word of God is taken from them and they are left "in the letter"—which is not understood and about which they begin to quarrel and dispute, so that there is no agreement and they are deprived of their power.

3

The Patriarchs

From the beginning of the Christian Church up until the present, it has been recognized by some that the Patriarchs were types or representatives of the Messiah who was to come.

It has been recognized by some that Israel represents the Lord, on account of the verse in the Gospels which reads: "He took the young child and his mother by night, and departed into Egypt, . . . that it might be fulfilled which was spoken of the Lord by the prophet, saying, Out of Egypt have I called my son." (Matthew 2:14,15.) The passage here referred to reads: "When Israel was a child, then I loved him, and called my son out of Egypt." (Hosea 11:1.)

That Abraham was also a type of the Messiah who was to come and thus represented the Lord is evident from the fact that it is repeatedly said in Genesis concerning Abraham: "In thee shall all families of the earth be blessed." (12:3, 18:18.) Now no one is blessed in Abraham or in the name of Abraham; but all are blessed in the Lord, the Messiah, whom Abraham represented or prefigured. This is also confirmed by the verse in Galatians 3:7 which reads: "Know ye therefore that they which are of faith, the same are the children of Abraham"; and by these words of John the Baptist in the Gospels: "Think not to say within yourselves, We have Abraham to our father; for I say unto you, that God is able of these stones to raise up children unto Abraham." (Matthew 3:9.)

The literal-minded in the above passages will think of the man Abraham, but those who think more deeply can see that Abraham represents the Lord, whose children we may become. To Isaac it is also said, "In thy seed shall all the nations of the land he blessed" (Genesis 26:4), and to Jacob it is said: "Blessed be he that blesseth thee." (Genesis 27:29.)

4

The Call of Abram

In the commencement of the twelfth chapter of Genesis we read: "And Jehovah said unto Abram, Get thee out of thy country, and from . . . thy father's house, unto a land I will cause thee to see." (12:1.)

Abram here represents the Lord in His early childhood. He also represents the presence of the Lord with man. Man's life, if he is born again or regenerated, is an image of the Lord's life.

The Lord commenced to glorify Himself, that is, perfect or make Divine His Human nature, from earliest childhood; as He said to Mary and Joseph when He was twelve years old, "Wist ye not that I must be about My Father's business?" (Luke 2:49.)

Man on the other hand is not regenerated and born again until he reaches adulthood. Then, being born again involves the Lord's coming to man, His birth in man.

This new birth is signified by the statement that Jehovah called to Abram to leave his land and go to the land of Canaan. It is generally known that the land of Canaan signifies heaven, wherefore in spiritual songs the expression "heavenly Canaan" occurs. But heaven is not just some place where we go after death; as the Lord said, "The Kingdom of God is within you." (Luke 17:21.)

The words to Abram have a signification very similar to that of the words of the Lord to His disciples: "He that loveth father or mother more than me is not worthy of me;

and he that loveth son or daughter more than me is not worthy of me. And he that taketh not his cross, and followeth after me, is not worthy of me." (Matthew 10:37, 38.)

What is this leaving we are asked to do? It is a leaving of our loves that are centered in the outer world and a turning to the "Kingdom of God which is within you," a Kingdom where an inmost love to the Lord and a spiritual charity, which looks to the eternal welfare of one's neighbor, reign. It is not a going away from the world and its occupations and recreations, but a lifting of our spirit and ruling love and joy above the world, so that the Kingdom of God, the Kingdom of Heaven within, is more real and of immensely greater significance than the external world.

Such an elevation is not possible except after our moral, civil, and social life has been brought into order. Consider the story of the young man who came to the Lord and asked Him what he should do to inherit eternal life. The Lord said first: "Thou knowest the commandments. Do not commit adultery, Do not kill, Do not steal, Do not bear false witness, Defraud not, Honor thy father and mother." When the young man said he had kept all these commandments, it is said, "Jesus beholding him loved him." (Mark 10:21.) Having been prepared, he could now come to a new state if he was willing, but to come to this state he had to sell all that he had, take up his cross, and follow the Lord. That is, he was to take his heart away from the things of this world as the center of his life, to do as the Lord commanded. "Seek ye first the kingdom of God, and His justice; and all these things shall be added unto you." (Matthew 6:33.)

Much of Genesis treats of going in and out of the land of Canaan. Abram enters the land of Canaan, and then goes to Egypt. He then returns to the land of Canaan, and later goes to Philistia, from which he again returns to Canaan. Isaac goes to Philistia and returns to Canaan. Jacob goes to Padan-aram in Syria and returns, and later goes to Egypt; and finally the children of Israel return to Canaan.

As we have said, Canaan stands for the Kingdom of

God, or Kingdom of Heaven, and in relation to man, the
Kingdom of God within man; whereas the other lands
around Canaan stand for the lower faculties of the mind.

Man's spiritual life consists of ascending and descending, and this repeatedly. Man must ascend to the things of
the spirit, and out of the vision which he comes to when in
the elevation of the things of the spirit, he must again descend and reorder the things of his outer mind and life.
On the basis of such a reordering of his outer or external
mind and life, he can again ascend into a fuller vision of
the spirit, and this repeatedly; thus man is perfected as to
the things of the spirit and as to his life in the world. This
whole process is explained, with thousands of particulars,
in the explication of Genesis and Exodus in the *Arcana
Coelestia* by Emanuel Swedenborg. As we have said, in this
book we can treat only of a very few of the things involved,
but we hope this will be sufficient to give the reader some
little idea.

As we have said, Abram's first being called and going
to the land of Canaan signifies a feeling of love to the Lord
in the inner things of the spirit, which we call celestial love,
out of which love there is a new vision of the Lord and His
Kingdom. With the Lord in His childhood, it was a new
love and vision of Jehovah, from whom He was conceived
and who was His soul within Him. Many things occur in
this exalted state of mind that are described in the twelfth
chapter of Genesis but which we shall not treat of here.

Abram Goes to Egypt

After being in this elevated state for some time, the
Lord—and man in His image—must descend into Egypt.

In the *Arcana Coelestia* "Egypt" is said to signify the
"scientific." In the Writings of Swedenborg words are sometimes used with a different meaning than in ordinary English, for words had to express new ideas. In Latin, in which

the Writings of Swedenborg were written, as in French, Dutch, German, and other languages, there are two words for "to know," and hence two words for "knowledges." In Latin, there is the word *scire*, "to know," and *"scientifica,* "knowledges," from which come the English words "science" and "scientific"; also there is the Latin word *cognoscere,* "to know," and *cognitiones,* "knowledges," from which come the English words "cognitions" and "cognize," which are related to the English word "know."

Man has two memories, an inner or internal memory, and an outer or external memory. The internal memory is his book of life according to which he is judged after death, which contains all things of his spirit and whereon are, as if written, all things of his life, including those that, as to his conscious or external memory, he has forgotten. That there is a memory of which man is unconscious in ordinary states of life is now generally known. In the inner memory, wherein are all things of man's very spirit, are the knowledges which in the Writings of Swedenborg are called "cognitions"; in the outer conscious memory are the knowledges that in Swedenborg's Writings are called "scientifics." In some translations of the Writings of Swedenborg they are called "memory-knowledges."

"Egypt" stands for the knowledge of things in the external or outer memory. To go into Egypt is to be instructed in those knowledges that we call "scientifics." These knowledges especially include all the knowledges man has of the letter of the Word.

If man has been elevated into an inmost love to God, and if in the Kingdom of Heaven within him he has undergone new experiences, and he then again reads and reflects on the Word and the knowledges he acquires from the Word, he sees the truths of the Word in a new light; he sees many things he could not see before, and he is thus instructed anew.

Sarai Called Abram's Sister

As Abram and Sarai were coming to Egypt, Abram asked Sarai to say that she was his sister instead of his wife, for, because she was beautiful, he feared that the Egyptians would kill him and take Sarai.

This story of a man asking his wife to say she was his sister is thrice repeated in Genesis: here in Egypt; later (in the twentieth chapter) in Gerar in Philistia; and (in the twenty-sixth chapter), this time also in Gerar, where it is Isaac who asks Rebecca to say that she is his sister. Is it not evident that this thrice-repeated story has a remarkable significance?

In the twelfth chapter, Abram, in relation to man, stands for the inmost love of the Lord, which we call celestial love, and Sarah is the celestial wisdom, or truth that makes one with this love. The heart can sometimes perceive truths of wisdom that the understanding by itself can never grasp; a great love opens the eyes to see things that a cold viewing can never see. A truth can be clearly seen by one who has love into the Lord, although it cannot be demonstrated to one who demands a cold, scientific demonstration of its validity.

When man is in an elevated state, he sees such truths; but when he descends into the plane of his external memory, his "scientifics" and natural reason, the truths in his outer memory are in a region separated from the Kingdom of Heaven, in a part of his mind not yet purified and one that may easily abuse the truths that are from love, or make one with love.

Abram's asking Sarai to say that she was his sister signifies that the truths were to be regarded as intellectual truths and not as truths inspired purely by love.

When a man comes down from a spiritual elevation in which he was inspired by love, he must come to have an intellectual view of the truth—a seeing of truth in light. He must have a clear, objective grasp of truth, apart from his love; for if he does not have such a sight of truth, the emotions in his outer or external mind may do violence to the love that he had when in a state of celestial inspiration.

The danger then exists that the external knowledges in his outer memory may grasp with delight the truths that have descended from the Kingdom of Heaven within, and the man may come to desire and care for the knowledges, and not for the love of the Lord that inspired them.

Not until man has gone through the fire of temptations and his natural or outer mind has been purified can he have the inmost love to the Lord, present in his outer thought and memory, without the danger of mixing the pure thoughts of his inner man with the impure emotions of his outer man and thus of profaning them.

Pharaoh seeing Sarai to be beautiful signifies delight in the knowledges of truth, which captivate the external mind. There are those who love to have knowledges of truth just for the sake of knowing them, without any other use. Every man in the beginning of spiritual life has a curiosity about spiritual knowledges which as yet has not as its end the inner Kingdom of God. Such curiosity or such mere desire to know is represented by Pharaoh and the Egyptians.

All truths have as their end or use the purification of the mind as a preparation for conjunction with God and for the sake of knowing how to serve God and our neighbor. If we become fascinated with acquiring more and more knowledges of truth, apart from their use of conjoining ourselves more closely with God and our neighbor, we come into the danger of being only in dry, outer shells of truth.

It is said that Jehovah smote Pharaoh with plagues. This signifies that dry knowledges of truth, which had not been made of use in increasing our love to the Lord and toward our neighbor, were destroyed.

In certain states we must love the knowledge of truth

without any feeling for the end or objective of truth, namely,
that it may serve the love of God and our neighbor; for in
the first delight of merely knowing, a man learns to think
intelligently. But if he stops here, his thinking dries up
and he becomes what is called "merely a brain." Such a one
is useless in the Kingdom of Heaven.

A man in this state must leave the useless dry knowledges
for the sake of the Kingdom of Heaven and return to
the internal things of the spirit. This is signified by Abram's
returning to the land of Canaan.

Although there is a danger of bogging down in mere
knowledges, still the going down into Egypt that is the acquiring of knowledge is of essential importance for any
advance. A child has to learn letters, words, and sentences
before he can read and write, and his curiosity stimulates
his efforts. It is only after he has acquired a facility in these
things that he can understand the ideas in what he reads
and writes and can express his thoughts and feelings in
writing. It is the same in every science and art; a man commences with the love of the subject to which he wishes to
devote himself and with the desire to develop or express
something new, something of value to mankind, but he has
first to concentrate on acquiring knowledge of the subject
and perfecting his technique. Many, however, become so absorbed in the knowledge or technique that they lose sight
of the original end they had in view. It is the same in matters
of religion. A man, if he is to contribute anything of spiritual value to others, must acquire a knowledge of the Word
of God and of theology; but if he becomes so absorbed in
the knowledges that he loses sight of the end in view, namely,
that such knowledge may serve God and his neighbor, he becomes lost.

It was similar with the Lord. He perfected Himself in the
knowledges of the Word, even commencing in His childhood
—as is evident from His talking to the doctors in the temple
when twelve years of age. But when He entered into His
ministry, His love was solely for things useful for the sal-

vation of the human race. His instruction in the letter of the
Word was represented by His being brought into Egypt.

The Lord at birth had a human inherited from Mary;
as to this human He had to learn like any other child, and
to grow in wisdom; but little by little, as He perfected His
Human, by means of the Divine that was in Him, He expelled all the infirmities or weaknesses from His maternal
heredity. In this way He glorified His Human, that is, made
it Divine; until when He rose from the dead, His Human
was purely Divine, entirely one with His Divine soul called
the Father, one in Essence and one in Person.

5

Lot

In the thirteenth chapter of Genesis there is described the contention between the herdmen of Abram and the herdmen of Lot. Lot and his herdmen signify the pleasures of the external or lower mind, just as Pharaoh and the Egyptians signify the knowledges of the lower or outer mind. The leaving of Egypt signifies the leaving of knowledges that do not serve a genuine love of the Lord and of one's neighbor and are therefore dry and useless for man's spiritual life.

Leaving Lot signifies leaving pleasures that do not serve or minister to man's spiritual life. There are pleasures that serve the things of the spirit and pleasures that draw man away from the Kingdom of God. These two may appear similar or even the same, viewed from without, but they are opposite when seen from within. For example, consider the enjoyment of eating food. With those who make good food a primary thing of life and have their life to a degree centered in the enjoyment of the table, the pleasure of eating draws the mind away from the things of the spirit.

If, however, man's love is centered in the Lord, in the things of His Kingdom, and in love toward his neighbor, to enjoy eating together a well-prepared meal adds to the feeling of friendship and can serve love toward his neighbor.

Also in the arts, one who is concentrated on the sound of music or the color of paintings and centers his life on the sensual delights of such things is drawn away from the things of the spirit. But if one sees the arts as an expression of worship, or as an expression of the nobility of the human spirit, then the arts serve the things of the spirit. There is an ancient saying that the arts are the handmaidens of religion.

Until three or four hundred years ago, the great works of art were mostly religious art. This applies to Egypt, Greece, and the Orient, as well as to the Christian art of Europe. Art was made not to glorify man, but for the glory of God, and often, as in the instance of the great cathedrals, the names of the artists are not known.

Genuine nonreligious art gave expression to love toward one's neighbor. It gave expression to noble human ideals; it communicated a human feeling. The ugly was used to bring out the beautiful by contrast, or to arouse sympathy for those who suffered or had been misled. In modern times the prevailing saying is "Art for art's sake."

No great art has ever been inspired by this slogan, nor will it ever be. An art which does not communicate something of value, an idea or feeling of what the Divine or human is, is not art.

Many in the so-called artistic world are primarily interested in appearing cultured, in gaining a reputation, and in appearing up-to-date, and have very little real love of art, with the result that they seek out the latest novelty—the superficially striking—no matter how little it communicates of a normal noble feeling for what is Divine or human. A sick, ugly, and degenerate generation looks to a sick, ugly, and degenerate art, calling anything healthy and normal sentimental or naïve. Nowadays, indeed, most objective art, particularly religious art, is excessively sweet and sentimental and is of no more value than the nonobjective art.

The same law which applies to the love of art applies also to the love of nature. Nature was created to manifest the love and wisdom of God, as is said in the Psalms: "The heavens declare the glory of God; and the firmament sheweth his handywork." (Psalm 19:1.)

There is not the least good thing in creation that does not show forth or represent something of the Divine Love and Wisdom with its beauty and harmony. The sky, the mountains, every animal and plant, all are examples.

In ancient times, when men lived more in the order of life that God designed for man, and life was less artificial, there was a feeling and knowledge of what each thing of creation represented, and the Word is written throughout in accordance with such representations.

Nowadays there is only some little feeling remaining of this relation of the things of the body and the world to those of the spirit. Many people have a feeling that spring stands for a resurrection of the life of the spirit; that morning, with the rising of the sun, represents a coming of the Lord to man; that mountains signify that which is high and, thus, things that are elevated above the things of the world. Wherefore we read, "I will lift up mine eyes unto the mountains (not "hills," as in the King James translation), from whence cometh my help. My help cometh from Jehovah, which made heaven and earth." (Psalm 121:1, 2.) But as to the particular things that each animal signifies, with maybe the exception of the lamb and a few others, this knowledge has been lost.

The sophisticated and sensual man strongly resents the idea that every word in the Word of the Lord has a spiritual significance and that everything in creation corresponds to a spiritual idea or to some Divine or human affection, for such an idea threatens the center of his life, which resides in his conceit, in relation to his scientific ideas, and in his sensual delight in pleasures as such. He does not want to lift up his eyes to the mountains; he does not look to the Lord for help, for he trusts in himself and delights in his scientific or philosophic ideas and sensual pleasures. He will therefore combat against the above idea with all his might and with every argument at his disposal; for he does not wish to leave the life he is in, although he is aware at times of its emptiness. He cannot realize that all good pleasures can serve love to God and one's neighbor, and that when such pleasures serve these higher ends, man is far happier than he was before. The Lord Himself did not reject good pleasures, for He said: "The Son of man came eating and drinking." (Matthew 11:19.) But the Lord left all pleasures which did not serve His Divine purpose, nor did He care for pleasures merely for their own sake. He would not have mentioned that He came "eating and drinking" unless this had a spiritual significance, representing His spiritual eating and drinking. He said: "My meat is to do the will of him that sent me." (John 4:34.)

6

Wars in the Word of the Lord

The fourteenth chapter of Genesis describes wars, which were waged first by Chedorlaomer and three other kings with him against five other kings, and then the war of Abraham against Chedorlaomer.

The Word of the Lord in its spirit or internal meaning cannot possibly describe wars between nations. For what have wars between nations to do with the Divine Love and Wisdom, which the Lord's Word reveals? All wars in the Word signify spiritual combats, that is, combats against the evil and the false, or against the power of hell. A man must carry on this combat in himself to become a spiritual conqueror and gain the crown of life. The Lord, when in the world, carried on such spiritual warfare in an infinitely greater way than others, overcoming the power of evil or hell and thus saving those in the human race who were willing to follow Him in fighting against the evil and false things in themselves and in the world.

That the Lord is a spiritual conqueror is evident from the book of Revelation, where we read:

And I saw, and behold a white horse and he that sat on him had a bow, and a crown . . . and he went forth conquering, and to conquer. (Revelation 6:2)

And he was clothed with a vesture dipped in blood: and his name is called The Word of God. And the armies . . . in heaven followed him upon white horses. . . . And out of his mouth goeth a sharp sword, that . . . should smite the nations: . . . And he hath on his vesture and on his thigh a name written, KING OF KINGS, AND LORD OF LORDS. (Revelation 19:13–16)

It is to those who follow the Lord and conquer with Him that the Lord makes the promise, "To him that overcometh will I grant to sit with Me in My throne even as I . . . overcame, and am set down with My Father in His throne." (Revelation 3:21.)

Why is it that so much of the Old Testament describes wars between nations? Why do internal things which are those of the spirit have to be described in a letter in which cruelties and at times unjust and apparently trivial or even indecent things are recounted?

In the *Arcana Coelestia* the following reasons are given: The Word had to be written so that all, even children and the most simple, can have some idea; and on account of the fallen state of the human race, the Word of the Lord in its letter had to be written in accommodation to the world as it is. This is represented in the thirty-second chapter of Exodus by the story of Moses breaking the tables of stone on which the Ten Commandments were written. The first "tables were the work of God, and the writing was the writing of God." But after Moses, on seeing the people worshipping the golden calf, broke the tables of stone on which were written the Ten Commandments, he was told to "hew . . . two tables of stone like unto the first," and Jehovah said: "I will write upon these tables the words that were in the first tables." (Exodus 32:16; 34:1.)

A golden calf stands for natural good works, that is, all good works which are done not from a real love of God or one's neighbor but for the sake of being seen of men; also all worship, or sacrifice, made in a spirit of vanity—thus, all things which are done for the sake of reward either here or in heaven. Because the Children of Israel, and the human race in general, had come to worship such appearances of good, an external good for the sake of one's own glory with no real internal of love to God and one's neighbor, the Word of God had to be written in accommodation to such a state of the human race and of the Israelitish church.

The tables of stone signify the literal sense of the Word and also the externals of the church and of worship.

If the Israelitish church had not been such that they would worship the golden calf, the Word of God would have been written differently and they would have had a different kind of worship. They would not have made the chief thing of their worship the sacrifice of animals. The Word would not have described cruelties, wars between nations, or immoral deeds. Jehovah would not have been said to be angry or jealous, or to have commanded wars and cruelties. But the letter would have been pure and beautiful, obviously in harmony with its internal sense or spirit. The written Word of God, free from all such cruelties, is represented by the tables which were the work of God, which were broken. But the tables which Moses hewed signify the literal sense of the Word, such as it is in the Word as we have it. Yet it is said that "the writing was the writing of God," and was the same writing as on the tables made by God, which were broken. This signifies that the internal of the Word is the same now as it would have been if the Israelites had not been in the state represented by the worship of the golden calf.

The following illustration will make this clear. It is frequently said that Jehovah God is angry; whereas Jehovah God is infinite Divine Love and Mercy, far above anything resembling anger. Yet on account of the fallen state of the human race, God has to appear angry for the sake of the reformation of man. This may be compared to a wise father out of love telling his children that he is very angry on account of something bad that they have done. It is obvious in this case that the word "anger" stands for the father's love of his children and his hope of their improvement, and is the outward expression of such love. We return now to the wars in the fourteenth chapter of Genesis. In their internal sense the combats described are against evil and false things and are those the Lord waged, when in the world, for the sake of man's salvation. They represent also the spiritual warfare of those who follow the Lord.

In the beginning, five kings, after serving Chedorlaomer for twelve years, rebelled. Chedorlaomer and three other kings with him then smote the five kings and other nations.

The four kings, including Chedorlaomer, signify apparently good and true things. There are two kinds of things which are apparently good and true. There are apparently good and true things done by hypocrites who do good deeds and speak what is true solely for the sake of their personal reputation and often use this as a means of hiding their sinister ends. Then there are apparently good and true things that children and simple people do who act with good intentions but often unwisely, with the result that what they do does more harm than good in the long run.

Anything good or true is an apparent good or truth if it stems from a certain pride in which the heart does not acknowledge that a man can do nothing good and can be in nothing of truth as to his spirit unless it is given him from heaven, or if the Lord's words are not believed: "As the branch cannot bear fruit of itself, except it abide in the vine; no more can ye, except ye abide in me." (John 15:4.)

The appearance that we can do good and think truth by following our own ideas is so strong that it is with great difficulty, and only after many spiritual experiences, that we can come actually to realize fully that we cannot do any good or think anything true from our heart that is not given us from the Lord out of heaven.

When a man is progressing toward the Kingdom of Heaven, he must do all in his power to think the truth and to do what is right; and if he does this from conscience and duty, such things are accepted as being good and true. They are not, however, the good and the true itself until he has advanced to the state in which he perceives from the heart that all the good he does and all the true he thinks is from

the Lord and not from himself. In the meantime he must act
with all his might to do what is right, with the feeling that
he is doing this from himself, until he can come to the perception that nothing is good and true that has not been
given him by the Lord.

In every new state, man is in a state of peace, in which
his hereditary evils are not active. A little child is in no
spiritual struggles. In the first stage of marriage things are
usually peaceful and one's innate selfishness does not manifest itself. When a person first comes to a church, if he does
it with all his heart he has a period of delight and peace, and
this is also true of the state when man is reborn as a spiritual
child. As we have stated, Abram when he first enters the
Land of Canaan represents the Lord's early childhood. He
also represents the spiritual childhood when man is first
reborn. The rebirth of man internally seen is the birth of
the Lord in man's inner mind or in his heart.

The twelve years wherein the five kings served Chedorlaomer stand for the early states in which man is in peace,
for then his innate inclination or hereditary evil things do
not rise up and disturb the peaceful new state that the man
has come into.

The time comes, however, when the selfish things in man
rebel against the good and true things he has been given,
and he must fight. In this state, because he has not yet come
to the living feeling or perception that all that is good and
all that is true is the Lord's with him, he fights from the
apparent good and true things he is in against the obviously
evil, selfish, and false things that rise up in the mind. A
man in this state fights against the things of hatred, revenge, cunning, and deceit which rise up to tempt him, although the true and good things from which he fights are
not yet the genuine good and the truth itself, but apparent
good and truth. In this battle Lot is carried away. Lot
represents the outer mind or the sensual part of the mind,
that part of the mind which is formed by those things
which enter directly from the bodily senses.

Lot in the best sense signifies the sensual truth which "consists in seeing all earthly and worldly things as being created . . . for a purpose, and in all things whatsoever a certain image of God's kingdom." (*Arcana Coelestia*, Number 1434.)

When Lot's herdmen are quarreling with Abram's herdmen and Abram and Lot have to separate, as we have said, Lot then stands for pleasures which do not agree with a genuine love to the Lord and toward one's neighbor. Here when Lot is carried off by Chedorlaomer and the kings with him, he stands for the external or outer mind; this was done under the appearance that man, in his warfare against the evil and the false, had overcome by his own power or ability. Abram's going to the rescue of Lot and overcoming Chedorlaomer and the kings who were with him signify that the inner or internal mind perceives that it is solely from the power of the Lord that man has won in his spiritual warfare; and that from this inner perception he rescues the lower mind, represented by Lot, from the appearance that it has power to overcome evil and do good of itself. After this warfare a blessing is given by the Lord: Melchizedek blesses Abram—that is, man comes into the joy of the things of the Lord's Kingdom.

Man must fight against evil and falsity as if of himself, but he must acknowledge that it is the presence of the Lord with him which alone brings the victory. Man's warfare against the power of evil and false things is relatively very little compared to the Lord's combats against evils and falsities and the hells that inspired them. The Lord executed a great judgment not only on the church into which He was born, but also a judgment on the church in the spiritual world. He said: "Now is the judgment of this world: now shall the prince of this world be cast out. And I, if I be lifted up from the earth, will draw all men unto me." (John 12:31, 32.) "For judgment I am come into this world." (John 9:39.) "I beheld Satan as lightning fall from heaven." (Luke 10:18.)

Note that it was after the judgment, that is, the overcoming of the power of hell represented by Satan, that the
Lord was lifted up, that is, was glorified, or became Divine
—entirely one with the Father, one in Essence and one in
Person.

In the Gospels little is said about the judgment and of
the casting down of the hells which had penetrated into
heaven; but in the Old Testament all the descriptions of
warfare signify the Lord's combats with the hells and His
victory over them, by which He re-established order and
made it possible for men to be saved. If He had not come
and overcome, the hells would have prevailed and there
would have been no possible salvation for mankind.

In all the chapters we are considering there are innumerable particulars or details described in the *Arcana Coelestia* which we can hardly touch upon here. In fact, there
is an infinity of wisdom, signified by the words: "And there
are also many other things which Jesus did, the which, if
they should be written every one, I suppose that even the
world itself could not contain the books that should be
written." (John 21:25.)

Every word in the book of Genesis and every word in
the *Arcana Coelestia* by Emanuel Swedenborg opens to
Infinity, and can be seen in deeper meanings and with
increased inspiration and wonderment both in heaven and
earth to all eternity.

We read in the *Arcana Coelestia*: "These are some of
the things set forth in this chapter, but those set forth
here are but few. . . . If anyone could know how many
arcana each particular verse contains he would be amazed,
for the number of arcana is past telling." (Numbers 166
and 167.) Not only Genesis itself, but the explications of it
in the *Arcana Coelestia,* contain an infinity of truth not set
forth obviously—that is, they do not appear in the unopened
letter.

The letter of the Word contains all Divine Truth in the
same way that the things of creation contain all the laws

of nature. But little of the inner laws and structure of nature is obvious to the five bodily senses. It has taken many generations of scientists to come to the understanding of nature that we have arrived at. To have an idea of the hidden things of creation, instruments, like the magnifying glass, the microscope, and many others, had to be invented. To penetrate to the internal of the Word of the Lord, there must come into existence doctrines whereby its internals can be seen, as a microscope enables us to see those things not visible to the unaided eye.

How many learned, sophisticated theologians there are who do not believe in the Bible as purely the Word of God, of which one jot or tittle cannot pass till all is fulfilled! They try to find God in their science or in their subjective experiences alone, and they doubt that God has fully revealed Himself in His written Word, not realizing that the Word contains Infinite Truth which, except for His Hands and Face, are still veiled by the letter.

7

The Terror of Great Darkness

In the fifteenth chapter of Genesis Abram complains that he is childless and that Eliezer, the steward of his house, is his heir, and he is then promised a son.

In relation to the Lord, this signifies that the Lord saw that, after its combats with temptation, the church He came to form was a church only in external love, faith, and worship, and that it did not look primarily to the things of the Kingdom of God within but rather to the most external things of faith, charity, and life in the world. Such a looking to outward or external things of worship, faith, and works has characterized the fall of churches throughout history, including that of the Christian Church. The promise of a son is the promise that a church would arise that would center its love in the things of love, faith, and worship in the Kingdom of Heaven in the hearts of men.

Abram's complaint that he had no heir signifies the perception that man's outer or external mind directs itself to the outer world and does not look upward with all its strength to the formation of a Kingdom of Heaven in the inmost part of the heart, where the Lord can find a dwelling place.

Abram then asked how he was to know that his seed would inherit the land of Canaan, that is, the Kingdom of God that is within man. This signifies a doubt, on the part of the Lord, on seeing the character of the human race, as to whether such a pure, internal church could be formed in the human race; and on the part of man, a doubt whether such a pure, internal church could be formed in himself.

Then there was given a terrible vision of great darkness, with a furnace of smoke and a burning torch, signifying the false things and the selfish things, the hatreds, revenge-fulness, deceits, and hypocrisy that the human race, the church, and the man of the church were coming into.

But before this, Abram was commanded to take a heifer, a she-goat, and a ram and a turtledove and a young pigeon, and to divide each animal, with one part on one side and the other half on the other over against each other, but not to divide the birds.

The animals signify the things pertaining to love to God and one's neighbor, or what we call celestial things, whereas the birds stand for the things of faith or spiritual things.

All things of genuine love are from the Lord to man, and then return from man to the Lord. Thus there is a parallelism between the things of love on the part of man and on the part of the Lord, but there is not a similar parallelism and correspondence in relation to the truths of faith as first taken up from the Word and the church from without by reading or hearing the Word or the teachings of the church.

The reason is that the truths of faith as taken up from without, that is, by the reading of the Word of the Lord, or from instruction by the church, are in obscurity, and many doubtful or even false ideas are mixed with the truth. Man is uncertain of his opinions as to what is true, and he observes that there are many opinions in the church as to what is true, with little agreement, and this adds to his obscurity; for passages in the Word are interpreted one way by this man and another way by that one.

The truths in the Word of the Lord are pure, Divine truths; but as taken up by man, from reading of the Word, they are not pure truths but are opinions, because at first they are not seen in a clear light of heaven. Nevertheless these truths are of such a nature that by them, if the man is sincere, a conscience can be formed by influx from the Lord.

A man who has lived according to a conscience formed by his opinion of truth as taken up from without can come subsequently into a state in which he is given a "perception, internal dictate, and conscience" from the Lord from within; that is, he can receive pure truths, as distinguished from the opinions he was in before. Such truths of faith, with one who has love to the Lord and toward his neighbor, are from the Lord and are represented by the ram which was divided. In the *Arcana Coelestia* it is said of the ram that "it is faith in which is charity, or faith . . . begotten by charity." (Number 1824.)

There are few in the world, and there are few even in what is called the Swedenborgian Church, who believe that such pure truths, that are from within from the Lord by a perception and internal dictate, can be given to man when he is reading and meditating on the Word of the Lord; for they know only those things taken up from without, by reading, that form their uncertain opinions.

The Lord underwent the grievous temptation of seeing the terrible evils and falsities that were taking possession of the human race: evils that were signified by the sun going down, the thick darkness, the furnace of smoke, and the torch of fire. He underwent the most grievous suffering— a suffering far more grievous than any man could endure. After such suffering He was granted consolation.

The Lord suffered far more than any man ever did or could because He had an infinite love for the human race, and His suffering was in accordance with the ardor of His love. The more one loves, the greater his suffering when he sees the evil that overtakes the one who is loved; wherefore, when the Lord saw the evils and falsities that threatened the damnation of the human race, His suffering was unbelievably severe. The consolation was the promise from the Divine within Him that an internal church would be raised up, signified by the words "Unto thy seed will I give this land" (Genesis 24:7), that is, the heavenly Canaan, or an internal church.

The consolation of the Lord after temptations is spoken of in the Gospels, where we read, after the temptation in the wilderness: "Then the devil leaveth him, and behold, angels came and ministered unto him" (Matthew 4:11), and after the temptation in Gethsemane, where He was in agony, we read: "And there appeared an angel unto him . . . strengthening him." (Luke 22:43.)

The Lord's consolation was that He was given to foresee that an internal church would arise in accordance with His desire.

Ishmael

In the sixteenth chapter of Genesis the conception and birth of Ishmael are treated of, along with, later, the flight of Hagar from her mistress Sarai. Sarai was barren, and she gave Hagar, her handmaid, to Abram in order that she might have a son. Such an act is not according to a true order, but it was done according to the custom of the times. The wonderful thing is that the Lord used such things in His Word to represent wonderful things in the glorification of His Human and the regeneration of man.

Abram signifies the internal man as to the good of love to the Lord; and Sarai, the internal man or mind as to the true of faith: these make man's heaven, whence there is an influx of spiritual life into man's external mind, whereby he acts in the world. Sarai being barren signifies that as yet there was no influx of truth from the Kingdom of God within man that could give birth to a truly rational understanding of the Word.

Hagar, the Egyptian, signifies a love of the knowledges of the Word as taken into the mind by the bodily senses, that is, by reading and hearing. By an influx of the Lord's love or life into our love for the things of the literal sense of the Word a new thing is born in the mind. This new thing is signified by Abram coming to Hagar and Ishmael's birth. This new thing signified by Ishmael is called in the *Arcana Coelestia* "the exterior rational." An interior rational is represented by Isaac, born later to Abraham and Sarah.

In the *Arcana Coelestia* the "rational" has a distinct meaning different from the meaning in ordinary English. In ancient Greece it was said that man was a rational animal. Man differs from animals in that he is born with the ability to become rational. The rational faculty distinguishes a man from a mere animal. It enables him to view things contrary to their appearance to the bodily senses. The rational faculty enables a man to see relations, especially the relation of cause and effect, and therefore confers on him the ability to adapt means to an end.

Every man of normal intelligence has a kind of scientific rational. For example, one can see that the sun is the center of the solar system and that the earth turns on its axis although this is contrary to the evidence of the bodily eye. All scientific discoveries are based on what might be called a "scientific rational"; yet such things are not the rational proper, for they are all on the plane of the material world, whereas the rational proper that makes a man to be a man, truly above the plane of the animal, is due to his ability to rise into the plane of the spirit. He who has in him the Kingdom of God and from this Kingdom looks down on the kingdom of the world, both within himself and outside himself, is rational; he has a spiritual life above the mind that he has in common with animals. One who has come to this plane sees the relation between the things of the spirit and the knowledges of the body and the world. He sets for himself goals different from and often contrary to those of one who follows his natural inclinations or desires. He is therefore truly a man and not just an animal who can speak and contrive things in relation to the natural world. He also can see the difference between the spirit or internal sense of the Word of the Lord and its literal sense, as well as the relation between these two.

As long as man reads or hears only the things of the literal sense of the Word and obeys them but does not rise above these to the Kingdom of God that the Lord said was within him, man is not properly rational, although he may be on his way to becoming rational.

As we have said, Hagar represents the affection for or love of the things of the sense of the letter of the Word as seen from without, with obedience to it. Into this affection there is an influx from God out of man's internal mind or from the Kingdom of God within, raising him up and giving him a conscious view of things above the plane of the literal sense of the Word. Thus the first or external rational mind is formed, represented by Ishmael; later the second or internal rational, represented by Isaac, can be formed in man.

Concerning these two rationals the following is said in the *Arcana Coelestia*:

> The first rational can be conceived only from the influx of the internal man into the affection of the knowledges of the external man; and can be born only from the affection of knowledges of the external man. . . . But the second or Divine rational is not thus conceived and born; but through the conjunction of the truth of the internal man [Sarah] with the good of the same [Abraham] and of the influx . . . of the good into [this] truth. (Number 2093)

Nowadays men are so occupied with the things of this world that very few even in the "New Church" (Swedenborgian) ever come to the first rational, represented by Ishmael, and scarcely anyone reaches the second rational, represented by Isaac, that rational which descends as to both the good things of love and the true things of faith from the Lord out of the Kingdom of Heaven within man, on the basis of man's living according to the truths of the Word taken up from without, by direct reading. There are relatively many who read or hear the Word of God, and the teachings of the church, but who do not deeply reflect or meditate on the meaning or spirit of what they read or hear.

Such have a knowledge of the Word, but do not yet have what is meant in the *Arcana Coelestia* by the first or Ishmael rational. Some even have a very extensive knowledge of the Word, and are able to reason about it most acutely and still lack the Ishmael rational, whereas others with less knowledge and a less-sharp reasoning faculty, but who delight in meditating on the Word, may have the spiritual rational represented by Ishmael.

When the first rational, "Ishmael," is born in man, man sees the truths of faith in a new way; he feels them as his own and desires to be independent in relation to the truths he has acquired. He does not realize that he will lose the truths he has gained if there is not a continual influx of truths conjoined to the good of love from the Lord out of the Kingdom of Heaven within.

The fact that the rational at this stage of man's development lightly esteems the Divine Truths in the inner mind, which is above the rational, is signified by Hagar despising her mistress, the internal man, which is above. Wherefore when the inmost mind disciplines and subjugates the rational, the rational becomes indignant and tries to flee from the power of the true that is above it so as to lead its own independent life, apart from the truths of the Holy Spirit. In the story of Genesis this is represented by Hagar, now carrying Ishmael, fleeing from Sarah. Man in this state has a conscience, and he hears a voice warning him that his rational must return and submit itself to the influx of truth from the Lord coming from the inner man within him. This is represented by the angel speaking to Hagar and telling her to return and humble herself before Sarai.

In recent times in what is called "existentialism," many have centered their attention on man as the important thing and have turned away from materialism and the concentration on the material world. But in trying to find the nature of the subjective man, they have wandered into all kinds of obscure and often fanciful ideas as to what man really is. In the Word of the Lord the whole nature of man is revealed, yet it remains hidden until the veils of the letter of the Word are removed.

Man's soul and mind are a complex thing—more complex than the body; in fact, there is nothing in the body that does not correspond to something in the soul and mind. The soul and mind have their ears, eyes, nostrils, touch, heart, and every other part that the body has, and man is in the image and likeness of God. Wherefore in the Word of God it speaks of the eyes, arms, hands, and other like implements of God—not that God has material or spatial eyes, ears, arms, or hands.

Man is also the result of development and growth. If he develops, he is born again, a long and wonderful process; the Lord comes to man, and man is conjoined with the Lord.

We read in John: "But as many as received him, to them gave he power to become the sons of God." (John 1:12.) When a man has been born again from the Lord, he becomes a son of God and is a new man, entirely different from what he was before; it makes no sense to investigate the question of what man is unless we make the distinction between what man is when he has become a son of God and what he was before.

The very brief outline we are giving here contains but a hundredth part of what is stated openly in the *Arcana Coelestia*, and is as but a cup of water compared to the ocean of what is hidden in the description of the spiritual growth and development of man—a description of an inner life whereof most men know nothing and, alas, are desirous of knowing nothing, for they are too busy with the business and pleasures of the world to care.

9

Abraham Goes to Gerar

In the twentieth chapter of Genesis, as in the twelfth chapter, a famine is spoken of—that is, a lack of knowledge. Abram in the twelfth chapter goes to Egypt; that is, in the highest sense, the Lord, and in a lesser sense the man who is being regenerated, is instructed in the obvious teachings of the Word, the outer knowledges, or the things of the letter of the Word.

In the twentieth chapter there is again represented a lack of knowledge, but this time a lack of inner knowledge concerning the doctrinal things of charity and faith that are hidden in the inner recesses of the Word.

Abraham goes to Abimelech, king of Gerar in Philistia. Abimelech represents or stands for the doctrine of faith which looks to rational things or is the result of viewing things rationally. Sarah as a sister represents the rational truth, and Sarah as a wife represents the truth that belongs to the Kingdom of Heaven, the truth that is above the rational and is married to the Divine good of love.

Abimelech's regarding Sarah as a sister signifies the desire to consult the rational in regard to the truth of doctrine. Genuine doctrine or teaching comes from a perception that an idea drawn from the Word of the Lord is true, that it is a truth seen in the light of heaven. When a man sees such a truth, he sees it by inspiration. For such an idea to take form, it must descend into the rational mind, where a man grasps it as his own idea. If a man then from a certain pride begins to reason about it too much, the truth is often brought into doubt, becomes null and empty, and may even be rejected. A man must realize that his perception of truth is given him from above, that the ability to perceive a truth in the Word grows out of his love to the Lord and is not merely a product of his rational faculty. Such a perception of truth is of Divine origin or essence—the truth is a thing which God has given him to see.

Because of his pride a man likes to put his trust in his rational ability to find and know what is true. Yet if he has a certain humility, he somewhat fears to trust solely in his rational ability, and he hears the voice of the Lord saying: "Behold thou wilt die because of the woman whom thou hast taken, for she is married to a husband" (verse 3). That is, if he were just to trust in his rational faculty, the Doctrine would become null and void.

Genuine Doctrine or teaching is indeed rational, and is in the rational faculty of man; but if the rational faculty is not an inspired rational, the truth is not accepted as genuine truth, for truth in the rational mind is not a product of the rational mind, but is inspired by God out of heaven into the rational.

The Lord, when in His Human nature on earth, in a Divine way was far above men, yet he went through this experience and struggle. And man, if he is to progress, must go through a corresponding struggle in an image of the Lord's life while on earth.

Also, the genuine and living Church, as a greater or greatest man, goes through a similar struggle and thus comes to a genuine doctrine or understanding of the Word of the Lord. In the *Doctrine of the Sacred Scripture*, by Emanuel Swedenborg, it is said:

> The Church is from the Word and is according to the understanding of it with man. . . . There are those who believe that they are of the Church because they have the Word, read it or hear it from a preacher and

know something of its sense of the letter, yet how this or that in the Word is to be understood, they do not know, and some of them little care. . . . The Word is the Word according to the understanding of it in man. . . . If it is not understood the Word is indeed called the Word, but it is not the Word with man. . . . The Word is spirit and life according to the understanding of it, for its letter if not understood is dead. . . . As a Church exists by means of faith and love, and according to them, it follows that a church is the church through the understanding of the Word . . . ; a noble church if in genuine truths, an ignoble church if not in genuine truths, and a destroyed church if in falsified truths. (Numbers 76 and 77)

There is always the danger that a man or the church may make false doctrine and think he or it has received such doctrine by inspiration of God, when yet it is false, and it is asked how it can be known whether the doctrine or teaching of the church or of the individual man is true or false. If a man has real humility and approaches the Lord with an earnest prayer for enlightenment, he can be given to see clearly whether the doctrine or teaching is true or not. As long as vanity or pride rules in a man, he will say that we have to trust in our rational ability to decide what is true; and as man's unaided ability is limited, he regards all truth as being merely a matter of human opinion.

The question as to how one could know whether a doctrine was true or not was put to the Lord by the Jews; to this question the Lord replied: "My doctrine is not mine but His that sent Me. If any man will do His will, he shall know of the doctrine, whether it be of God, or whether I speak of Myself. He that speaketh of himself seeketh his own glory; but he that seeketh His glory that sent him, the same is true." (John 7:16–18.)

The Lord in saying: "My doctrine is not mine but His that sent Me" means that His Doctrine was not from the

human He took on in the world through Mary, but from
the Divine Itself which was in him—His very soul from
His conception, which is called the Father. It was not the
human He took from Mary whose glory the Lord sought,
but the glory of the Divine Itself that was in Him; this
was the origin of His Doctrine, and He taught that if any
man did the will of God, he could know whether the Doctrine was of God or not. If a man does not do the will of
God, he can never know if a doctrine is false or true; but
the Lord taught that if man did the will of God, then he
could know. Knowing is immensely more than merely having
an opinion.

The Lord promised that if a man did the will of the
Father, he would know of the Doctrine whether it be of
God; but to do the will of God involves much. It involves
keeping the Lord's Commandments, of which we have
treated above.

The Lord said that He was sent, but He was sent in
such a way that He was not separated from the Father
within Him. As to the human nature He took on, there was
a kind of separation from His soul, which gives the appearance of two natures, before He completely glorified
the Human and rose again as completely one with the
Father, one in Essence and one in Person.

In an infinite sense, in relation to the Lord, it is said:
"He that speaketh of himself seeketh his own glory; but
he that seeketh his glory that sent him, the same is true."
In a limited or finite sense this has an application to man.
The Lord said to His disciples, "I send you forth" (Matthew
10:16), and the disciples did not seek their glory but the
glory of Him that sent them. The Lord was the very truth
Itself. The disciples were not the truth, but they were in
the true way, the truth which the Lord gave them. A man
now, if he advances to the state described in the inner sense
of the twentieth chapter of Genesis, can also be sent by the
Lord and can testify that the Doctrine is not his but is the
Lord's who sent him.

This idea opens the possibility of men becoming religious fanatics, of their coming into the fantasy that they are sent by God when they are merely talking fantasies of all kinds, and there is therefore a certain natural fear of such ideas, for "false Christs and false prophets," of whom the Lord said that they would deceive many, are far more common than true prophets.

A prophet, as spoken of in the Old Testament, was one through whom the Word was given; but when the Lord spoke of false prophets who would arise, He referred to those who make false doctrine, whereas the true prophet is one who teaches true doctrine.

The Lord referred to those teaching false doctrine when He said: "This people draweth nigh unto me with their mouth, and honoreth me with their lips; but their heart is far from me. But in vain they do worship me, teaching for doctrines the commandments of men." (Isaiah 29:13, Matthew 15: 8,9.)

The sophisticated will never accept the idea that doctrine is given to men by God, but, like the Jewish leaders of old, they are averse to anyone speaking with authority, as it is said: "The people were astonished at his doctrine: for he taught them as one having authority, and not as the scribes." (Matthew 7:28, 29.)

Because there are many fanatics who claim an authority for their teaching that is false, and this causes intelligent persons to be very careful and hesitant in accepting any of those who claim unique inspiration, this is no reason for denying the possibility that a man can be inspired in his understanding of the Word of the Lord. Certainly, if a man is not inspired, he will have no true understanding.

The great majority will either, like the sophisticated, desire to have only the opinions or doctrines of men; or they will, like the literalists, stick to the letter and never come to any understanding of the spirit of the Word. The mere literalist, although protected from the fantasies of crazy interpretations of the Word, still remains in the deadness of the letter alone. Those who believe in the interpretation inspired by the Lord's spirit are in danger of accepting "false Christs and false prophets"; still, if they have a living faith, they will trust in the words of the Lord quoted above: "If any man will do His will, he shall know of the doctrine, whether it be of God."

It is often thought that the attitude opposite to sophistication is naïveté, or credulousness. A wise man is neither sophisticated nor naïve or credulous when a new idea or doctrine arises. He believes that God can manifest Divine Truth to man, but he very carefully examines it with prayer to see whether it be of God or of man. He tries to remove all prejudices from his habits of thought, to see with an open mind whether the idea be true or not. Not loving mere novelty, he is not hasty to accept any idea that comes along, for he has no ambition to be among the avant-garde; nor will he hastily reject new ideas, knowing that it often takes much reflection and meditation to see whether a thing is true or not. He must question habits of thought which he has acquired. He waits with the prayer that he may be enlightened and see clearly whether it is true or false. He knows that Divine truth must appear to him as rational; but he also knows that the rational mind cannot clearly see truth unless it is enlightened by God, and that if the rational mind does not look to the Lord for enlightenment, it turns away to things which are irrational in the sight of heaven no matter how rational they may appear to a materialist or to one prejudiced by the rut his mind has slipped into. No man is truly rational who is not regenerated or born again, for before regeneration man is in the obscure light of the things of the world, whereas a man who is being regenerated sees in the light that comes from the Lord, who, as it is written, is "the true Light, which lighteth every man that cometh into the world." (John 1:9.) But many "loved darkness rather than light, because their deeds were evil." (John 3:19.)

Note that it is the teaching of the Lord that it is not

the ability to reason cleverly that enables a man to distinguish between spiritual truth and falsity, but whether one does the will of God (John 7:16–18) or whether one's "deeds are evil." This the sophisticated will never accept.

A man who accepts the teaching of the Lord, if he is in doubt as to whether a thing is true, will question his attitude toward God as to whether it is right or wrong, knowing that if his heart is purified he can be given the light to see, as is said in the Ten Blessings, "Blessed are the pure in heart: for they shall see God." (Matthew 5:8.)

We have treated of certain things of the twentieth chapter in relation to the spiritual development of man, but we shall now quote from the *Arcana Coelestia* a number in its application to the Lord.

In the internal sense of the Word the Lord's whole life is described, such as it was to be in the world, even as to the perceptions and thoughts, for these were foreseen and provided because from the Divine. . . . As regards the Lord's life itself, it was a continual progression of the Human to the Divine, even to absolute union, . . . for in order that he might combat with the hells and overcome them, He must needs do it from the Human; for there is no combat with the hells from the Divine. It therefore pleased Him to put on the human like another man, to be an infant like another, to grow up into sciences and cognitions [that is into outer and inner knowledges] which things were represented by Abraham's sojourning in Egypt (Chapter 12) and now in Gerar; thus it pleased Him to cultivate the rational as another man, and in this way to disperse its shade, and bring it into light, and this from His own power. That the Lord's progression from the Human to the Divine was of this nature, can be denied by no one if he only considers that He was a little child and learned to talk like one, and so on. But there was this difference: that the Divine Itself was in Him, seeing that He was conceived of Jehovah. (Number 2523)

10

Abraham's Temptation to Sacrifice Isaac

In the *Arcana Coelestia*, the word "celestial" signifies the inmost love to the Lord, a state in which a man, as to his whole heart, soul, mind, and strength, is directed to the Lord, and all things of his life are qualified by this love. The word "spiritual" signifies all the truth man perceives from having such a love. From the marriage of this love and truth, the internal rational represented by Isaac is born—a new faculty of the mind, a rational mind that only those who are being regenerated or born again have. This faculty is the inmost of the human; what is above it is the Divine Good and truth. With the Lord, the Divine love and wisdom itself was what is called in the Word "the Father"; the Human, when glorified and made one with the Divine, is called "the Son."

We shall now consider the following verses:

And it came to pass after these things, that God did tempt Abraham. . . . And he said, Take . . . thy son, thine only son Isaac, whom thou lovest, and get thee into the land of Moriah; and offer him there for a burnt offering upon one of the mountains which I will tell thee of. . . .

And Abraham took the wood of the burnt offering, and laid it upon Isaac his son; and he took the fire in his hand, and a knife; and they went both of them together.

And Isaac spake unto Abraham his father, and said, My father: and he said, Here am I, my son. And he said, Behold the fire and the wood: but where is the lamb for a burnt offering?

And Abraham said, My son, God will provide himself a lamb for a burnt offering. . . . And Abraham built an altar there, and laid the wood in order, and bound Isaac his son, and laid him on the altar upon the wood. . . . And the angel of the Lord called unto him out of heaven, and said, Abraham, Abraham: and he said, Here am I. And he said, Lay not thine hand upon the lad, neither do thou any thing unto him: for now I know that thou fearest God, seeing thou hast not withheld thy son, thine only son from me.

And Abraham lifted up his eyes, and looked, and behold . . . a ram caught in a thicket by his horns: and Abraham went and took the ram, and offered him up for a burnt offering in the stead of his son. (Genesis 22:1,2,6–13)

Each word in the above has a significance, but to explain each word, and why each word has the significance it has, as explained in the *Arcana Coelestia* by Swedenborg, would go beyond the purpose of this book. We shall here confine ourselves to giving a general idea of the subject.

If we accept the idea that the whole of the Old Testament involves a prophecy of the Lord's life, it is evident that the chapter we are considering stands for or represents the Lord's most grievous temptations, even to the passion of the cross.

In the first verse of the chapter, we read: "God did tempt Abraham." It is self-evident that God, who is Divine Love and Wisdom Itself, could never tempt anyone, and still less tempt a man to slay his son. Nothing but the evil and the false can tempt man: hell, called the Devil, is the tempter; yet all things are under the rule of the Divine Providence. God permits evil for certain reasons, including man's free choice, but He turns evil to some good purpose. Because children and simple people cannot distinguish between a thing which is of the Lord's will or good pleasure and what the Lord permits, and yet it is important to believe that all things are under the Lord's government, the letter of the Word speaks of God's tempting, and of His becoming angry and punishing; but in the internal sense or spirit of the Word, by such expressions nothing is signified but God's love and mercy.

By Abraham is signified the Internal Divine essence in the Lord, called the Father; Isaac stands for or represents the inmost of the Lord's Human. The inmost of the human is the inner rational mind that, when inspired by the Holy Spirit, perceives Divine Truths. Before treating of the Lord, we shall say something about this story as it applies to man. If a man is born again, he comes to a perception of Divine Truths; nevertheless there are falsities and fallacies that adjoin themselves to his rational mind. Man's mind is to be sanctified. He has to, as it were, let his rational mind, represented by Isaac, die that it may be united to his soul, wherein the Lord is present. Man must be willing to give up his rational, and after temptations even to despair, he is given a new rational mind, which is a mind inspired by the Lord. The altar to which man brings his rational thinking and feeling is the Divine Human of our Lord. The fire on the altar is the Divine Love. The wood is the merit of our Lord. The knife is the Divine Truth, whereby that which is not genuine dies. All that is merely human, growing out of pride and the conceit of man's own intelligence, must be put away. This takes place imperfectly with man, but with the Lord it took place fully and with Infinite perfection, so that He became God even as to His Human. He put off all the weaknesses of His heredity from Mary, a putting off finally completed on the cross when He said, "It is finished," or "It is fulfilled."

Abraham was commanded to go to the land of Moriah, that is, to Jerusalem, where our Lord endured the most grievous temptations. That the mount which Abraham and Isaac went to was the site whereon Jerusalem later arose is clear from II Chronicles, where we read: "Then Solomon began to build the house of the Lord at Jerusalem in mount Moriah." (3:1.)

"Isaac spake unto Abraham his father, and said, My father, and he said, Here am I, my son." These words signify the conference of the Divine Truth with the Divine Good in the Lord, or, as expressed in the New Testament, of the Son with the Father.

Love can work only through wisdom or truth. Love without wisdom can do nothing. A man who truly loves his neighbor seeks for wisdom and truth so that his love may go forth and serve others. Love without the truth of wisdom is blind and does more harm than good. The harm that a foolish love may do is well known. The Lord's love, which was the Father, loved the Divine Rational or the Son, by which He was to save the human race. As the Lord said several times in John, "The Father loveth me."

To have an idea about the temptation treated of in this chapter, consider how you would feel if you were told that you had to give up your rationality completely because it leads you into human errors. A man would feel in this case that if he did this, he would become a useless and worthless creature. If he were told that, by giving up his own rational, he could come into a new and sanctified rational, he would scarcely believe it. There is in such case a great temptation to let one's rational abilities die, as it were, in order to have them sanctified and raised up to a new life.

The Lord saw that it was by His Divine Rational or the Divine Human that He was to save the human race; but when He received the command to have His rational as it were die, and finally the whole of His Human destroyed on the cross, so that His Human could be sanctified on the altar and rise again, He prayed that "this cup might pass from" Him and, in His agony, He "sweat as it were drops of blood."

This great suffering which the Lord underwent was not for Himself, for He did not love Himself. His only love was the love of the salvation of the human race. He suffered because, in the obscurity He was in, He did not see how, if He gave up His Human to death, the human race could be saved.

This is also involved in the words of Isaac to his father, "Behold the fire and the wood: but where is the lamb [or kid] for a burnt offering?" (verse 7). That is, there was the warmth of love and the merit represented by the fire and wood, but where were those in the human race who could be sanctified, that is, formed into an internal or spiritual Church? A man who has a great love for the salvation of the human race and sees how far removed the race is from an inner spiritual life also at times comes into states of corresponding despair.

Compare the words: "And the angel of the Lord called unto him out of heaven, and said, Abraham, Abraham: . . . Lay not thine hand upon the lad, neither do thou any thing unto him: for now I know that thou fearest God" (22:11,12) with the words: "And being in an agony he prayed more earnestly: and his sweat was as it were great drops of blood falling down to the ground." "And there appeared an angel unto him from heaven, strengthening him." (Luke 22:43,44.)

An angel signifies Divine consolation, for the angel did not speak from himself but from God.

"And Abraham lifted up his eyes, and looked, and behold . . . a ram caught in a thicket by his horns; and Abraham went and took the ram, and offered him up for a burnt offering in the stead of his son." (Genesis 22:13.) A ram here signifies the spiritual men in the human race that the Lord came to sanctify and save. The ram being caught by his horns in a thicket signifies that they were entangled in external knowledges, so that they could not find their way. The ram's horns signify power; here, that they lacked power, because the horns were caught in a thicket. The Lord was "the way, the truth and the life." The Lord said, "The truth shall make you free." It was this freeing of those who were spiritual which was signified by Abraham taking the ram from the thicket.

The question may arise as to how it was possible for Abraham to believe that God would command him to sacrifice his son, when the sacrificing of sons is an abomination. In explanation of this, we read in the *Arcana Coelestia* by Emanuel Swedenborg, as follows:

To slay his son. That this signifies until whatever was from the merely human was dead, is evident from the internal sense of these words; for they signify the Lord's most grievous and inmost temptations, the last of which was that of the cross, in which it is evident that what was merely human also died. This could not be represented by Abraham's son or Isaac, because to sacrifice sons was an abomination; but it was represented so far as it could be, namely even to the attempt, but not to the act. Hence it is evident that by these words, "Abraham took the knife to slay his son," is signified until all that was merely human was dead.

That it was known from the most ancient time that the Lord was to come into the world, and was to suffer death, is evident from the fact that the custom prevailed among the Gentiles of sacrificing their sons, believing that they were thus purified, and propitiated to God; in which abominable custom they could not have placed their most important religious observance, unless they had learned from the ancients that the Son of God was to come, who would, as they believed, be made a sacrifice. To this abomination even the sons of Israel were inclined, and Abraham also; for no one is tempted except by that to which he is inclined. That the sons of Jacob were so inclined is evident in the Prophets; but lest they should rush into that abomination, it was permitted to institute burnt-offerings and sacrifices. (Number 2818)

In the chapter we have been considering, there are two persons, Abraham and Isaac. It is common in the Word of the Lord for various persons to represent or stand for different things in the mind of man. Thus, though Abraham and Isaac were two persons, they represent two things in the one person of our Lord; for the Father was in the Lord as our soul is in our mind and body. In the Gospels, it is sometimes clearly taught that the Father and Son are one Person; as when the Lord said that "I and my Father are one," for which saying, "the Jews took up stones again to stone Him." (John 10:30,31.)

Again, "He that hath seen Me hath seen the Father. . . . Believest thou not that I am in the Father and the Father in Me?" (John 14:9,10.)

In other places, according to the sense of the letter, there is an appearance that the Father and Son are two Persons. And in this chapter that we have been considering, the Divine and the human of the Lord are represented by two Persons. On account of the appearance of two—called the Father and the Son—the Christian Church fell into the error of thinking that God was two Persons and, with the Holy Spirit, three Divine Persons. Yet it is impossible to think of God as being three Divine Persons without thinking of three Gods, no matter how much one says with the mouth that there is one God.

11

Jacob and Esau

From the Divine good or the Divine love of the rational represented by Isaac and Rebecca, a new natural mind and life are born, represented by Jacob and Esau.

This is an entirely new natural mind; that is, it is a new natural mind in relation to all things of life in the world. When this is born, man leads a totally different kind of life, a life which in all things looks to the Kingdom of God as its end.

This change may not be evident to others; it may not be clearly evident to the man himself. A man continues his work and his social relations, and even appears to enjoy his pleasures, as he did before. But in the sight of God and of heaven he has become a new man, for his ruling love is no longer directed to the things of the world, but to the things of the Kingdom of Heaven.

Jacob represents the natural or outer mind as to the truths of faith and Esau, this mind as to the goods of love. A conflict arises in the mind as to which is prior or superior, the truths of faith or the goods of love and charity. This conflict is represented first by the twins struggling in the womb, and then by Jacob stealing Esau's birthright and later his blessing.

The first thing of the church appears to be the truths of faith, for one who does not know and accept the truths of faith does not really belong to the church. But truth, by it-self, has no life. In order for a man to accept the truths of faith from the heart, he must have a heart, that is, he must have some love, will, or desire that motivates him to accept the truth. If a man does not have some love, will, or desire for the truth, the truths of faith he may have been taught and may have in his memory are dead and lifeless —mere knowledges in the outer memory that we call dead scientifics. It is therefore obvious that the good of love is the first-born or Esau.

Here we shall not consider the whole subject of Esau and Jacob, but shall confine ourselves to a consideration of certain things in relation to the blessing of Esau and Jacob.

The following is a summary account of the twenty-seventh chapter of Genesis:

Isaac, being old and blind, calls his elder son, Esau, to him to hunt for food and bring it to him, with the promise that he would then bless him. Rebecca, hearing what Isaac said, calls Jacob, and after calling Jacob sends him to get kids of the goats from the flock, and after making a savory dish, putting the garments of Esau on Jacob, and covering his neck and hands with the skins of the goats, sends him in to Isaac to receive a blessing.

Isaac, upon smelling the garments of Esau and feeling the skins—for Esau was a hairy man—says that the voice is the voice of Jacob but the hands are the hands of Esau; yet he blesses Jacob in place of Esau.

When Esau returns, having brought the dainties he had prepared, he finds that Jacob has stolen his blessing. Isaac had promised Jacob that he would be master of his brethren, and that his mother's sons would bow down to him.

Isaac then blesses Esau and in the blessing promises that the time would come that he, Esau, should have the dominion and break the yoke of his brother Jacob from off his neck.

One might well ask how such a story could occur in the Word of the Lord and what the use of such a story might be. If the Word did not have an inner sense, there would be no possible answers to these questions. As we have said, Isaac stands for or represents the rational mind open to heaven; Isaac, for the love or good in such a mind, and Rebecca, for the truth in such a mind.

If he is being regenerated, or born again, a man comes to see the truths of the Kingdom of Heaven in the Word. He sees the true things of doctrine in the light of heaven and he loves them. Thus his inner man or inner mind comes into the order of heaven. In this state a man realizes that his outer mind—the mind having to do with the world, and his wife, family, and social relations—must be brought into a new order, so that it may come to agree with, or correspond to, the new inner life that he has acquired.

Man's natural life in this world is the foundation of his spiritual life: "The Kingdom of God within you."

Many give all their attention and efforts to improving their external life and neglect the Kingdom of God; others give all their attention and efforts to the Kingdom of God and neglect the things of life of this world. The one is like a foundation without a house; the other is like what the Lord called a house built on sand. Both the former and the latter attitudes, as seen in the light of heaven, lead to useless lives.

The story we are considering describes the condition of one whose inner mind has been ordered but whose outer or natural mind is still in disorder; for the love of himself and the love of the things of this world are very powerful in his outer mind and life, and he does not see how he is to bring the outer mind and the things of his daily life in the world into an order corresponding to his inner mind. This obscurity as to how he is to live in the world is represented by the blindness of Isaac.

Isaac desires to bless Esau—to "bless" signifying to give to the lower mind the good and true things of life. Esau represents goods, that is, good will in the natural mind.

The true order of life is for love, or what is good, which is in man's Kingdom of Heaven, to flow into man's outer or external will, and thus to lead him in the way of life. Ani-

mals, which are born into the order of their life, know by
instinct the way of their life, and this without instruction.
If man were born into the order of his life, he would instinctively know the order of human life, and this spontaneously.

But man nowadays has not a human instinct corresponding to the instinct of animals. Man, unlike animals, having
free choice, has over countless generations destroyed this
instinctive order of life in himself. Man from his hereditary
nature tends to be selfish, and to look primarily to the things
of the world; he has lost the human instinct to stand spiritually erect and to look upward to the things of heaven. Man
must therefore be instructed, trained, and disciplined if
he is to become truly a man. He must learn the truths of
faith and the laws of spiritual and natural life from others;
he must first be disciplined by others and later discipline
himself by living according to what he knows to be true.

A wise man is one who from good will immediately perceives the truths of life and, thus, how he should speak and
act. He does not think, "I must say or do this because this
is something I have been taught," but out of his love and experience he knows what is right and wrong and does what
is right.

Isaac's wishing to bless Esau signifies a longing of the
inner mind to bring the lower mind into such a spontaneous
order of life in which man finds spontaneously the truths
of natural life out of his love to the Lord and his neighbor.
These truths are represented by the things that Esau
hunted for food for his father.

The inner love represented by Isaac longs immediately
for the end that man may come immediately to the things
of wisdom. This is represented by Isaac calling Esau; but
the inner truth of enlightenment represented by Rebecca
sees that such an immediate coming to a spontaneous wisdom is not possible. Man must go through a long period of
instruction and discipline according to truths of faith to
come to this end. This is represented by Rebecca, who sig-

nifies the truth of the inner rational as she sends Jacob to receive the blessing of Isaac. Jacob here represents the teachings of doctrine according to which man is to live and discipline his outer life. Man must live and discipline his life for a long time before he acquires a second nature from which he can spontaneously speak and act wisely in all things.

Very few at this day arrive at such a state, but the Lord, whose life is described in the inmost sense of the Word, went through the states described here until He made all degrees of His mind purely Divine and even rose, unlike others, with a body made Divine.

We have said that the hunting of Esau represents the spontaneous truths of life which arise in man from his love of the Lord and his neighbor. These are from the Lord immediately and have flowed into him from the Lord.

The flock from which Jacob took the she-goats signifies the goods of love a man receives not immediately by influx from the Lord, but by inheritance from his parents. These affections are strengthened by education. Although these loves are mixed with many impure, selfish, and worldly loves, they are yet of great importance, and without them man could never be saved. Man, with the heredity he has, would not at the commencement of reformation have the strength to acquire a knowledge of the Word and to struggle to make something important of his life if at the commencement he did not have ambitions, motivated by the love of glory, of praise, and of success as seen in the light of the world. Later on, indeed, these loves must be discarded in order that man may come to pure loves and the perception of genuine truths out of pure loves.

The flock from which Jacob took the she-goats signifies the desires man inherits from his parents to learn truths so that he may know many things and appear intelligent, and so that he may not only excel others in knowing but may also gain a reputation for leading an honorable life.

A man who disciplines himself in order to gain such a reputation imagines that he has become intelligent and that he leads an honorable life from the pure inspiration of God, although in fact his motives are not at all pure. This is represented in our story by Jacob saying, "I am Esau thy firstborn; I have done according as thou badest me." (Genesis 27:19.)

Isaac's saying, "The voice is Jacob's voice" (Gen. 27:22), signifies that, seen interiorly, he acted according to the truths which he knew, but not out of a pure love inspired from God. "But the hands are the hands of Esau" signifies that, as to the speech of his mouth and the acts of his body, he appeared to be acting from a pure love to God and his neighbor.

When Esau returned to his father, and his father knew what had taken place, it is said that "Isaac shuddered with exceeding great shuddering." This signifies the great perturbation of mind a man comes into when he realizes that the honorable life he has been leading is not the result of pure motives inspired by God but is motivated by things mixed with earthly ambitions, or maybe by a desire to be rewarded in heaven—not purely by a love of God and his neighbor.

After the blessings it is said that: "Esau hated Jacob, . . . and Esau said in his heart, . . . I will slay my brother Jacob." (Gen. 27:41.)

In the internal sense, this signifies that the good represented by Esau was averse to the life which is from self and not from inspiration from God, averse to the ambitions and other worldly loves; and hence he desired to remove such loves. The meaning of the words here is similar to the meaning of the words of the Lord: "He that loveth his life shall lose it, and he that hateth his life in this world shall keep it unto life eternal." (John 12:25.)

The good of love represented by Esau can by no means hate or desire to kill, but it desires that the old life may die in order that man may receive new life from the Lord. In the letter it appears entirely different, the appearance being that Esau acted out of hatred. In the letter of the Word such appearances frequently occur, as when it says that Jehovah is angry, is jealous, curses, and condemns, whereas being Infinite Mercy and Love, Jehovah is infinitely above such merely human emotions.

In the thirty-second and thirty-third chapters of Genesis are described Jacob's great fear when he came to meet his brother Esau and how he humbled himself before him; how Esau ran to meet him, embraced him, fell upon his neck, and kissed him. When a man who has loved the truths of faith out of a merely human desire to know and the desire to lead a life according to them in order to excel others in reputation comes to humble himself before a life which is out of a love into the Lord, that is, out of a pure spiritual life, then his love to the Lord embraces the truths of faith that he has learned by study and application from motives mixed with ambitions and purifies them.

Jacob, therefore, after he humbled himself before Esau and after Esau embraced him, signifies the pure truths of faith which are conjoined with love toward the Lord and love toward one's neighbor.

As we have said, man's regeneration is an image of the glorification of the Lord. The Lord had a Divine heredity from the Divine Itself, called the Father, and a heredity having all human weaknesses from Mary. As to His Human, the Lord had to be instructed, to learn and to struggle like mankind in general, although with far greater wisdom, as is indicated by His speaking with the doctors in the temple when He was twelve years old, at which time the doctors were astonished at His understanding.

The Lord read and meditated on the Word; He learned the Law represented by Jacob in the chapter we are considering. By living the Law of Moses, He finally came to the spontaneous life according to the inner good of life represented by Esau; but as with other men, this came only after a life of obedience to the Word of God as taken up by study and reflection. The Law so taken up at first necessarily appeared as if it were in the first place represented by Isaac regarding Jacob as his firstborn. It was on account of the Lord's maternal heredity that this was necessary. The Lord in His temptations, in which He overcame, finally put off all the hereditary weakness inherited from Mary, so that He was no longer her son, as He said: "Who is my mother? and who are my brethren? And He stretched forth his hand toward His disciples and said, Behold My mother and My brethren! For whosoever shall do the will of My Father who is in heaven, the same is My brother, and sister, and mother." (Matthew 12:48–50.)

The whole of the Lord's life, as interiorly represented in the chapters we are considering, treats of how the Lord completely expelled the maternal heredity and glorified His Human until He was completely one with the Father —one in Essence and one in Person.

But before a man who has loved the truths of faith can come to humiliate himself before the good of love to the Lord and his neighbor, he has to pass through severe temptations, represented in this chapter by Jacob serving twice seven years for his wives, and his fleeing from Laban, his father-in-law.

12

Joseph

Abraham, Isaac and Jacob represented the Lord, but in the Christian Church particularly, Joseph has been recognized as a type of the Messiah who was to come. For example, we read concerning Joseph in the *Catholic Encyclopedia*:

A character so beautiful made Joseph a most worthy type of Christ, the model of all perfection, and it is easy to point out some of the traits of resemblance between Jacob's beloved son and the dearly beloved Son of God. Like Jesus, Joseph was hated and cast out by his brethren, and yet wrought out their salvation through the suffering they had brought upon him. Like Jesus, Joseph obtained his exaltation only after passing through the deepest and most undeserved humiliation, and in the kingdom over which he ruled, he invited his brethren to join there to whom theretofore they had looked upon as a stranger, in order that they might also enjoy the blessings which he had stored up for them. Like the Savior of the world, Joseph had but words of forgiveness and blessing for all, who recognizing their misery, had recourse to his supreme power. It was to Joseph of old, as to Jesus that all had to appeal for relief, offering homage of the deepest respect, and yielding ready obedience in all things. Finally, to the Patriarch Joseph, as to Jesus, it was given to inaugurate a new order of things for the greater power and glory of the monarch to whom he owed his exaltation. While thus recognizing the typical meaning of Joseph's career, one should not lose sight that one is in the presence of a distinctly historical character.

Also in the Protestant Churches it has not been uncommon to speak of the "Heavenly Joseph," meaning the Lord. Although the above statement from the *Catholic Encyclopedia* in general is true, it does not tell us anything new about the Lord, nor does it help us much to lead a new life. It does not reveal anything new about what Bishop Sheen calls the "inner thoughts" of the Lord, which is the primary purpose of Revelation. In the twelve-volume work *Arcana Coelestia* we referred to before, Emanuel Swedenborg has done just this. In this work it is shown that the whole of the Old Testament has an internal sense which treats in its inmost sense of the life of the Lord, of His internal life, of His thoughts, His affections, and His temptations. Deeply hidden there are wonderful things which the Lord referred to when He said to His apostles: "I have yet many things to say unto you, but ye cannot bear them now. Howbeit when he, the Spirit of Truth, is come, he will guide you into all truth." (John 16:12, 13.)

From the Lord, Swedenborg has opened up the Books of Genesis and Exodus in such a way as to reveal the inner life of the Lord and the inner life of the man who is on the way to heaven. We shall now give some examples of this, in the simplest language possible, rather than in the more exact theological language, which would not at first reading be so readily understood. To see the particulars in their exact series would require a careful study of the *Arcana Coelestia*. The whole of the Word is written in a Divine series. More and more of the wonders of the Word can be seen if one's mind is opened to heaven; but even the knowledge of the wisest of men is only as a cup of water compared to the ocean relative to all the wonders of the Lord's life and the regeneration of man that are involved in the Word of the Lord. As it is written in the closing verse of the Gospel of John: "And there are also many other things which Jesus did, the which if they should be written every one, I suppose that even the world itself could not contain the books that should be written." (21:25.) In this verse by "the world" is meant the church.

Not only do these stories in their inner sense reveal the Lord's thoughts and the manner in which He glorified His Human, but, because the life of the man who is regenerated is an image and likeness of the Lord's life, this is also described. And because the church commences as an infant and develops like a man, the whole progress of the church is described.

Joseph and Potiphar and His Wife

We shall now consider the thirty-ninth chapter of Genesis:

And Joseph was brought down into Egypt; and Potiphar . . . bought him. (v. 1)

And Joseph was a prosperous man . . . in the house of his lord the Egyptian. (v. 2)

And it came to pass after these things that his lord's wife . . . said, Lie with me. (v. 7)

And he refused and said unto his lord's wife, . . . How . . . shall I do this great evil, and sin against God? (v. 8, 9)

And it came to pass . . . and no men of the house were in the house. And she caught him by his garment, saying, Lie with me; and he left his garment in her hand, and fled and got him out. (v. 11, 12)

And Joseph's master took him and put him in the prison. (v. 20)

To understand the spiritual significance of the above

verses, we must have some understanding of the spiritual significance of marriage and its opposite. The Lord, in the Word of the Lord, is in many passages called the Husband and the Church His Bride and Wife. When the Church is unfaithful, it is called a harlot and is said "to go a whoring after their gods" as in Exodus 34:15, and there are many similar verses.

In all things of creation there is a conjunction of two into one. Even in the mineral kingdom, hydrogen and oxygen combine to make water; sodium and chlorine, to make salt. All such things represent things of the spirit. In man, the will and the understanding are conjoined to make the mind of man. As love is of the will and truth is of the understanding, it is a conjunction of these two which makes a true man. The will without being married to the understanding, and the understanding without being married to the will, can produce nothing. Every good intention must have its own truth or knowledge to accomplish anything; and every truth of faith is of no importance unless it has behind it a will to act, that is, to do good. A man without a will has no motivation even to acquire truth or faith. Without a will, a man cannot even lift his hand or open his eyes.

This is represented in the relation of husband and wife, or of man and woman. With hypocrites, the will and the understanding are indeed divided. Hypocrites understand how to appear to act well; but their will or intention, being centered in their own advantage at the expense of others, is evil.

The outstanding inner characteristic of a man who is truly a man is the love of becoming wise and of being actively engaged in acquiring the things of wisdom. This love forms man's inner mind or soul, and from this he acquires in a lower degree or plane of the mind an understanding of truth; thus, the inner or higher mind of a man is love, that is, the love of acquiring wisdom, and the outer or lower mind is the understanding of truth which he has acquired.

The ruling characteristic of a woman is different. A

woman who is truly feminine is affected or moved by truth; she loves the truth, and thus her love has an exquisite sensitivity to the things of wisdom and is receptive of wisdom. Her longing is not so much an eager desire to acquire knowledge, to struggle intellectually, but rather a delight in being affected by or moved by the truth when she hears it. This delight in the things of wisdom forms her inner mind or soul. From this, her inner sanctum of truth, she is filled with the love of clothing the truths developed in the Church, of applying them to life. Wherefore Eve was called the mother of all living; thus the internal of woman is truth and her external is love, the love of giving form to truth, and from this she loves her husband, if he is truly a man.

The above is all involved spiritually in the story of the creation of Eve from the rib of Adam, but we shall not stop here to unfold this story in detail.

When a man and woman are spoken of in the Word of God, in the higher sense, the man or husband stands for and represents love and the woman or wife, truth. But when the lower or more external meaning is involved, then the man stands for the understanding of truth and the woman or wife, for the love of what is good. In the Hebrew language, there are two words for "man," *adam* and *ish*. When *adam* is used, it refers to the inner mind of man, which is the love of being actively engaged in the things of wisdom; when *ish* is used, it is the lower mind of man that is referred to, namely, the understanding of truth. And the reverse applies to woman. When the higher meaning is involved, a woman or wife stands for or signifies truth; when the lower or more external meaning is involved, a woman or wife stands for the good of love.

In the chapter we are considering, the man under whom Joseph served was called his lord, not his master. A lord leads, a master instructs. Jesus Christ was called sometimes "Lord," and sometimes "Master" or "Rabboni." When He is called "Lord," it refers to His leading by the good of His love; when He is called "Master," it refers to His instructing in the truths of faith. Even in English, we call one who instructs another a "master."

In the story of Joseph and Potiphar, Joseph stands for the inner mind or soul in which the Holy Spirit of our Lord is received: Potiphar, for the outer or lower mind.

Man is born with animal-like traits, both good and evil. Some men by nature are faithful, friendly, good-natured, and generous, as are some animals. Others are born more pugnacious, unfriendly, and ill-natured, like other animals. Potiphar, in the chapter we are considering, stands for a kind of instinctive good which man has in common with animals; and his wife, for the thoughts or the truths which agree with such an outer good.

In childhood and youth, man's natural affections rule. He does not as yet have principles of truth which rule over or govern his life. Yet the Lord works in his outer or natural good affections out of His presence in the inner mind, secretly leading him. As long as this state lasts, man is blessed as the Lord blessed Potiphar and his house on account of Joseph.

The natural affections or loves, meant by Potiphar, are such things as the love of one's friends, love of one's family, even love of one's church, and, if one is brought up in a religious family, love of the Lord. These loves are at first spontaneous with man, and some of them are instinctive with animals. But with a man who is truly a man, there is an inner presence of the Lord in man's natural affections that makes him different. This presence of the Lord is represented by Joseph; but in this state, Joseph is a servant, for man does not, in this state, submit himself to the Divine Good and Divine Truth which are above his natural loves and affections.

The Lord, when on earth, had such natural loves on account of His maternal heredity. These loves later had to be entirely changed as to their quality. While the Lord was still a boy twelve years of age, this struggle had already commenced, as is indicated by His reply to Mary in the temple in Jerusalem. Mary said to Him, "Son, why hast thou thus dealt with us? Behold, thy father and I have sought thee sorrowing. And he said unto them, How is it that ye sought me? Wist ye not that I must be about my Father's business? And they understood not the saying which he spake unto them. And he came down with them and came to Nazareth and was subject unto them." (Luke 2:48–51.)

Compare this with the following:

> Then cometh Jesus from Galilee to Jordan unto John, to be baptized of him. But John forbad him, saying, I have need to be baptized of thee, and comest thou to me? And Jesus answering said unto him, Suffer it to be so now: for thus it becometh us to fulfill all righteousness. Then he suffered him. (Matthew 3:13–15)

These submissions of the Lord have a similar signification to Joseph, being, as it were, a servant to Potiphar his lord. But as the Lord said, "Suffer it to be so now." This indicates that it was only temporary. The time came when the Lord's relation to Mary was completely changed. When certain persons came to the Lord and said that His mother and brethren desired to speak with Him, He replied, "Who is My mother and who are My brethren? And He stretched forth His hand toward His disciples and said, Behold My mother and My brethren. For whosoever shall do the will of My Father which is in heaven, the same is My brother, and sister, and mother." (Matthew 12:47–50.)

Thus the Lord put off any special relation to Mary and His brethren. He rose above all merely human relationships and viewed all things from the Divine and from His love for the universal salvation of the human race.

The same applied to His love of His home town, His country, and the church in which He was brought up. He had to rise above all merely human affections and view all from an infinite Divine Love; and this involved temptations, for a man cannot remove merely natural affections without temptations, nor could the Lord.

In this struggle, Potiphar stands for such natural affections and his wife for the apparent truths which were married to these loves. These apparent truths, represented by Potiphar's wife, appear even to be confirmed by things of the letter of Scripture. The garment of Joseph, which Potiphar's wife took from him, represents such confirmations, and these confirmations persuaded the natural affections, represented by Potiphar, to put Joseph in prison.

We shall illustrate this by things that take place with a man who is becoming regenerated or a spiritual man by placing the love of the Kingdom of Heaven above the things of this world. Such a man comes into a new relation to his children. He no longer loves his children because they are his, but he loves them for the sake of the Kingdom of Heaven. His desire is no longer primarily directed toward his children's becoming successful citizens of this world, but toward their becoming good citizens in the Kingdom of Heaven, and only secondarily good citizens of this world. If, on becoming adult, they do not direct themselves toward the Kingdom of Heaven, this results in a kind of separation. Not that he does not long for their spiritual welfare, but he does not keep them attached to himself.

In this connection, consider the parable of the Prodigal Son. A father who was guided merely by his natural affections would have gone in search of his son, or at least would have sent messengers to look for him and bring him back. But such an act would have been contrary to the real welfare of his son. There could be no real conjunction until the son repented and of his own free choice came back and submitted himself to his father.

A man who acts from merely natural affections will help all kinds of people, especially the poor and miserable, and will quote Scripture in support of such actions. But such a man often does more harm than good; for he is easily persuaded to help the evil, who misuse his help, especially if they are friends, and his help often results in making others lazy and irresponsible.

If one does not take a superficial heartiness as an expression of genuine love, he is regarded as too critical. If one does not manifest a love for his alma mater by contributing to it generously, for the reason that he sees that the alma mater is not serving spiritual or eternal goals, one is criticized. If one takes a stand against being excessively mild toward those who have broken the laws, on the grounds that the welfare of society as a whole must be served, and that severe punishment is necessary for the protection of society and is most salutary for those who commit offenses, he is regarded as hardhearted.

Many speak of the Lord as if He were mild and gentle, and they think a good Christian should always be mild and gentle. The Lord was indeed quite mild to the humble and repentant; but to the hypocrites, to the self-righteous, and to the proud He was exceedingly sharp.

Consider His words to the woman taken in adultery: "Neither do I condemn thee: go, and sin no more." (John 8:11.) The whole spirit of the Gospels implies that the Lord's words were said in such a way as to make such an impression on the woman that she would not consider disobeying them.

A syndicated sermon in the daily press speaks of the Lord as He went away, as turning to the woman and quietly saying,"Go and sin no more." What a perversion!

The Lord said: "I have given you an example, that ye should do as I have done." (John 13:15.) If a man follows the example of the Lord and condemns most harshly the counterfeit, the self-righteous, and the false; pride parading as humility; vanity in the guise of piety; ambition posing as charity and service; sophistication palmed off as erudition, especially in those in high places, will he not be condemned? Will he not be accused of lacking "Christian charity"? Such false accusations are especially signified by the accusation Potiphar's wife brought against Joseph.

To condemn hypocrisy is a work of real charity, for if

there is no exposure of the hypocritical, the false, the pretended, there can be no cure, no health; it will be like new skin covering a hidden abscess.

The Lord said, "As ye would that men should do to you, do ye also to them likewise." (Luke 6:31.) These words of the Lord can be badly misunderstood. Most men like to be flattered, to be praised and patted on the back, whether it is meant sincerely or not; they desire that their faults remain hidden or be ignored; they do not desire their just reward. In turn, they flatter and praise others, they manifest an appearance of friendship, mildness, and gentleness, in order to be liked or spoken well of by others. Thus they think they do unto others as they wish others to do unto them. But this is a mockery of the Lord's words.

The Lord addresses the earnest, the sincere—those who wish to change their lives. Such are glad when their faults are shown to them. They do not resent a reprimand but value it if it is just and constructive; they appreciate the value of being disciplined. They therefore appreciate any words or actions of others in relation to themselves which are useful, whether pleasant or unpleasant. It is only to such that the words of the Lord quoted above apply.

Those who think of the Lord as only gentle and mild, who regard the so-called social gospel as the all of religion, make much of the Ten Blessings; but not many desire the tenth blessing: "Blessed are ye, when men shall revile you and persecute you, and shall say all manner of evil against you falsely, for my sake. Rejoice and be exceeding glad; for so persecuted they the prophets which were before you." (Matthew 5:11, 12.)

How many Christians take seriously the words of the Lord: "Woe unto you, when all men shall speak well of you! for so did their fathers to the false prophets." (Luke 6:26.)

One who speaks the truth without fear or favor knows that many will not like him. Yet do not most men, even those called Christians, including their ministers, wish to be liked above everything else?

This of course does not refer to one who speaks his mind on all occasions whether it is appropriate or not. Some want or like to speak the unvarnished truth just for the sake of shocking people or of getting attention; they have no love of truth for the sake of truth. Some speak from a persecution or martyr complex; they may be ambitious to gain a martyr's crown. Such are stupid.

The world's rejection of those who stand for the truth —truth that manifests the state of the world—is represented by Joseph's being placed in prison. In the supreme sense this rejection applies to the Lord, who was crucified. In a relative sense it applies to those who follow the Lord.

The Lord said:

Ye shall be hated of all men for my name's sake. (Mattthew 10:22)

If ye were of the world, the world would love his own; but because ye are not of the world, but I have chosen you out of the world, therefore the world hateth you. (John 15:19)

In contrast, many think that the fact that they are loved by all men is a sign that they are good Christians. Why else is it considered a reproach to be called a Jeremiah?

It is often said that everyone has his good and his bad side, with the implication that we should treat all more or less alike; and this is regarded as charity. In contradistinction to this, if it is pointed out that everyone has a ruling love, inspired by either heaven or hell, and that no one can serve two masters, God and mammon, this is regarded as indicative of a lack of spirit of charity or brotherly love. Such illustrations could be multiplied, for in everything of human life there is either an approach from an apparent good, with apparently reasonable arguments in favor of it, or a genuine approach, having in it the warmth and light of heaven. With all who see only in the light of this world, the former will be praised as being good and wise; whereas the latter will be condemned as lacking charity and normal human sympathy and despising wholesome normal feelings. In recent times this false idea of charity has often characterized governments.

The most important thing for a man's natural as well as his spiritual development is for him to become responsible, to assume obligations, to become truly independent—in a word, to become a man or woman, and not remain a child. Does not indiscriminate government assistance destroy these qualities, taking away man's initiative and independence, making many lazy and irresponsible, and often making the undeserving worse than they otherwise would be? Yet any protest against the misuse of public assistance is regarded as uncharitable. By this we do not mean to imply that there should not be public assistance to those who are worthy and cannot help themselves or that there should not be wise public assistance to the handicapped to enable them to become more responsible and to help themselves, but the removal of difficulties at the expense of the development of character is wrong.

A wise judge who orders such severe punishments as are in order to protect society and put fear into evildoers is criticized by some as not having Christian charity. Such things are false charges, such as are signified by the accusation Potiphar's wife brought against Joseph. That is, those who have a sentimental idea of charity accuse the spirit of the Word, signified by Joseph, of lacking love toward a neighbor, and they quote Scripture to support their acccusations. Thus, by the literal truths of the Word, misunderstood and misapplied, the outer loves and affections are turned against the inner good and truth, represented by Joseph. When the wife of Potiphar took Joseph's garment and used it to witness against him—that is, took away the appearance of truth with which man is clothed—it is said, "There was none of the men of the house there within." There was no one to help or witness for him. This brings to mind the prophecy of Isaiah concerning the Lord:

And he saw that there was no man, and wondered that there was no intercessor; therefore his arm brought salvation. . . . (Isaiah 59:16)

And of the people there was none with me. . . . And I looked and there was none to help; and I wondered that there was none to uphold. (Isaiah 63:3,5)

Also, at the temptation in Gethsemane, the disciples slept and the Lord said unto Peter, "What, could ye not watch with me one hour?" (Matthew 26:40.)

The Lord's temptations were much more profound than we can comprehend; still, the above illustrations may give a little idea of what they were like.

They all had to do with putting off the merely human love and affections He inherited from Mary and putting on in their place Divine Love and Wisdom, whereby He saved the human race. This putting off of all that was merely human from Mary and putting on the Divine, that is, making His Human Divine, is what is meant by the Lord's saying: "Now is the Son of man glorified, and God is glorified in him" (John 13:31 and other similar passages.)

The Lord, having put off all merely natural human affection for the Jewish Church in which He was brought up, by exposing the evils and hypocrisy of the Jewish Church so offended the Church that He was persecuted and finally crucified in like manner as Joseph was accused by Potiphar's wife and put into the prison house by Potiphar.

13

Joseph, His Brethren and the Egyptians

We shall now consider the following verses of Chapters 37, 44, and 47 of Genesis.

(From Chapter 37:) And Joseph dreamed a dream, and he told it his brethren, and they hated him yet the more. And he said unto them, Hear, I pray you, this dream. . . . For, behold, we were binding sheaves in the field, and lo, my sheaf arose, and also stood upright; and behold, your sheaves stood round about, and made obeisance to my sheaf. And his brethren said to him, Shalt thou indeed reign over us? or shalt thou indeed have dominion over us? And they hated him yet the more for his dream, and for his words. (verses 5–8)

(From Chapter 44:) And he [the servant of Joseph] overtook them and he spake unto them [the brethren of Joseph] . . . . Wherefore have ye rewarded evil for good? Is not this it [the silver cup] in which my lord drinketh, and whereby indeed he divineth? ye have done evil in so doing. . . . And they said unto him, . . . God forbid that thy servants should do according to this thing: [that is, that they should steal Joseph's cup] . . . . With whomsoever of thy servants it be found, both let him die, and we also will be my lord's bondmen. . . .

And Judah and his brethren came to Joseph's house; for he was yet there: and they fell before him on the ground. . . .

[And Judah said] Now therefore, I pray thee, let

thy servant abide instead of the lad a bondman to my
lord. (Genesis 44:6,4,5,7,9,14,33)

(From Chapter 47:) . . . all the Egyptians came
unto Joseph, and said, . . . there is not ought left in the
sight of my lord, but our bodies, and our lands: Wherefore shall we die before thine eyes, both we and our
land? buy us and our land for bread, and we and our
land will be servants unto Pharaoh: and give us seed,
that we may live, and not die. (verses 15,18,19)

Joseph's Dreams

The Lord in His parables at times compared the Church
to a field and the truths of the Word, by which man is spiritually fed, to the seed. The sons of Jacob with their sheaves
represent the teachings or doctrine of those who instruct
the Church. Joseph's sheaf stands for or represents the
teaching that the Lord Jesus Christ is the God of heaven
and earth, and that His Human is Divine, and that we are
to be conjoined with Him in love by the keeping of His commandments. The brethren of Joseph in the thirty-seventh
chapter stand for those in the Church who live by faith
alone and teach salvation by faith but do not have a
genuine love to God and their neighbor and do not live
according to the Lord's commandments; such do not believe that the Lord's Human is Divine. To believe in the
Divine Human is to believe that God is a Divine Man. a
Man of Infinite Love and Wisdom, who came to earth and
made His Human Divine. We can know the Lord from the
description of His life on earth, as recounted in the Gospels,
but He is now in the Kingdom of Heaven.

When asked when the Kingdom of God should come, the
Lord said: "Neither shall they say, Lo here! or, lo there!
for, behold, the kingdom of God is within you." (Luke
17:21.)

The Lord is in His Kingdom not only outside of man, but

He is in the Kingdom of Heaven within man. Here He can appear to man in His Divine Human, and here man can internally adore Him. If a man comes to a full state of regeneration, a state now very rare, he sees the Lord as Divine Love, Wisdom, and Mercy, working in man for his salvation.

In the *Arcana Coelestia* of Swedenborg, we read: "Man is sensible of that which flows in by an external way, [that is, through man's senses] but not, until he is regenerated, of that which flows in by an internal way" [that is, through the soul]. (Number 4977.)

A man who has a kind of faith but does not lead a worthy life, or one who is conceited, proud, or vain, may be willing to worship an invisible God, an unknown creator of the universe, an intellectual abstraction; but to bow down and worship and submit his life to the visible Lord in His Divine Human in the Kingdom of Heaven within runs counter to his pride and vanity. This asks for an entire change in his life; and this but few come to and many reject, feeling an aversion for the truth which teaches this. It is this that is signified by the hatred which Joseph's brethren felt for him and by their rejection of him.

Although in one sense Joseph and his brethren stand for different classes of persons, in a deeper sense Joseph and his brethren stand for different things in every man in the Church, for Joseph stands for the presence of the Lord in the inmost of man's mind; and his brethren, for lower faculties of the mind which at first are unwilling to submit themselves to the rule of the Lord in the inmost of the mind. Even the Lord, when on earth, had in His natural mind a knowledge of the Church which He had acquired from the Jewish Church, conjoined with affections which had in them hereditary weakness inherited from Mary. This lower mind resisted total submission to the Divine Love Itself, called the Father, until He had overcome these weaknesses in the temptations which He underwent and until He had totally submitted Himself to the Divine Itself in His soul.

The final submission of Joseph's brethren to Joseph had to take place by a free choice, or willingly. Joseph's brethren came and fell down before Joseph, and Judah offered himself as his slave of his own free choice. Yet it was Joseph who brought this about, by controlling the circumstances which led up to this. In the same way the Lord in the inmost of the mind of man leads man, by a way that is unknown to him, to submit his life to the Lord as a servant, and yet man does this of his own free choice.

The circumstances were that Joseph sent his servant to accuse his brethren of theft, particularly the theft of his silver cup, which was in the bag of Benjamin. The story of Joseph revolves around the fact that Joseph could not be united to his brethren without Benjamin as an intermediate. As we read: "Judah spake unto him [his father], saying, The man did solemnly protest unto us, saying, Ye shall not see my face, except your brother be with you." (Genesis 43:3.)

To understand the story, we must have an idea of what Joseph stands for, what Israel stands for, what Benjamin stands for, and what the ten brethren stand for. Joseph, as we have said, stands for the presence of the Lord as the Divine Truth in the love of God which is in the inmost of the mind; his ten brethren stand for the truths of the Church in the external or outer mind; and Benjamin stands for the intermediate or conjoining truth by which the internal flows into the external. If we compare the inmost to the head and the external to the body, the intermediate may be compared to the neck.

Israel stands for the good of life, or a good life according to the truth which man knows by his reading and meditating on and obeying the Word of God. When Benjamin is with his father, he stands for the new truths which a man out of such a life sees in the Word of God. There are truths which a man cannot see before he comes into such a life. There are many truths in the Word which can be seen only as the result of the experience of living a spiritually good life of love to God and one's neighbor. Such truths are meant by Benjamin, when with his father. These truths, that is, Benjamin, can be elevated to the Lord in the Divine Truth in the inmost of the mind, that is, to Joseph. Joseph stands for and represents the Lord as the Divine Truth in the highest degree of the mind. It is by means of the new truths developed out of a spiritual life of love to the Lord and one's neighbor that the mind is opened to its inmost where the Lord has His dwelling place in man. Man can finally come to a state wherein the Lord as the Divine Truth, that is, Joseph, can manifest Himself to the natural or lower mind of man in which are teachings that man has gathered together from his study of the Word.

It is only by living the truths we know from a study of the Word, and thereby coming to a life of love to the Lord and our neighbor, and from such a life seeing new truths in the Word, represented by Benjamin, that the Divine Truth in the inmost of man's mind, represented by Joseph, can manifest itself to our outer mind, represented by Joseph's ten brethren.

As long as we have not come to a life of love and faith, and out of such a life have perceived new truths we did not know before (Benjamin), the Lord as the Divine Truth in the inmost (Joseph) will appear as a stranger, as a severe ruler, not manifesting His love, as was the case of Joseph in relation to his brethren when Benjamin was not with them. An analogy of such new truths, represented by Benjamin, is as follows: It is realized that out of a lifetime of experience in his profession a man comes to knowledge that can never be acquired by mere book learning. An elderly man comes to what is sometimes called the wisdom of life as the result of a lifetime of many experiences. But it is not realized by many that such wisdom does not become the real wisdom of life unless it totally submits itself to the presence of the Holy Spirit of our Lord in the Kingdom of Heaven with man, that is, to Joseph, and that such a submission is an acknowledgment from the heart that, of ourselves, we have no wisdom, but that all wisdom flows into us from God.

Benjamin, when Joseph had manifested himself to him, stands for truths flowing from the presence of the Lord in the inmost of the mind into the truths of the Church in the outer or external mind, represented by the ten sons, through the intermediate truths spoken of above. But before this can take place, Joseph accuses his brethren of stealing his silver cup. In the Bible story, wine stands for or represents spiritual or inner truths. The silver cup stands for the vessels of the mind into which these truths inflow. To steal the silver cup is to think that the faculty of receiving Divine Truth from the Lord is man's own faculty, and not to see it as something bestowed on man, as something loaned, as a talent which man may indeed feel as if it were his own but which he must acknowledge as being continuously from the Lord with him. Everyone, to begin with, steals the good and the true things of the Word and the Church, because he feels they are his own, and therefore such stealing is forgiven man if he later comes to acknowledge that all that is good and true is from the Lord and must be ascribed to the Lord because it is Divine, and thus is the Lord's and not man's own and is given to man only as a talent to be used. Truths are living truths only as long as man's mind is open to receive the Spirit of our Lord. The moment we do not acknowledge that truths are with us continually from the Lord and are the Lord's, they become mere knowledges in the memory, lifeless shells which have lost their kernel. Many have had the experience of hearing truths which have stirred their souls; but when later recalled from the memory, the same truths seem dry and lifeless, the reason being that they have come to a state in which they are no longer open to the Lord. Such a dry, dead attitude, in which one can find no nourishment for the soul, is represented by the famine that caused Jacob and his sons and the Egyptians to come to Joseph for food.

Joseph's brethren stand for or represent the truths or falsities of faith in man's natural or outer mind. When they submit themselves to Joseph, they represent truths. When they hate Joseph, they represent false teachings. The Egyp-

tians stand for or represent the knowledges of the Word
that a man has in his outer memory. When he reads the
Word of the Lord out of the conceit of his own intelligence
or out of pride, man misinterprets whatever he reads in the
letter of the Word of the Lord and opposes the genuine spiritual meaning of the Word; he regards himself and those
who agree with him as being a chosen people. This perver-
sity is represented by the Pharaoh who knew not Joseph
and the Egyptians who were persecuting the children of
Israel. When the Lord rules in the Kingdom of Heaven within man, then all the knowledges he has from reading the
Word submit themselves to the Lord and become true knowledges in the memory. In order to represent the instruction
of the Lord in the knowledges of the Word, Joseph, like
our Lord, was carried down into Egypt.

A man may know many things from the Word of the
Lord, yet they may not be living in him—-they may not feed
his spirit, and he thus feels that he is starving.

The Egyptians, after their silver and cattle were gone,
came to Joseph and offered themselves and their ground unto
Joseph for food. That they offered themselves signifies that
they gave up their own will, the receptacle of the good of
love, so that they might receive a new will, namely, the
Lord's, in them. That they gave up their ground signifies
that they gave up their own understanding so that they
might receive a new understanding from the Lord. That
they were given food by Joseph signifies that they then received love and wisdom from the Lord. When a man comes
into such a state of mind, all knowledges he has from the
Word become vessels for receiving spiritual life from the
Lord.

Many read the Word from their own intelligence and
look for things in the Word which confirm their preconceived ideas. Such never come to a true understanding of the
Word. It is only those who read the Word in order that their
loves and thinking may be changed by the Lord who can
come to a real understanding of the Word.

The Egyptians then said: "We shall live, and our ground, servants unto Pharaoh." In explanation of these words, we read in the *Arcana Coelestia*, by Emanuel Swedenborg, as follows:

> That this signifies total submission . . . "we and our ground" [are] . . . the receptacles of good and truth . . . "servants [signifies] to be without freedom from man's own [or self], thus total submission. By receptacles are meant the very forms of men; for men are nothing else than forms receptive of life from the Lord, and these forms are such by inheritance and by actual life that they refuse to admit spiritual life which is from the Lord. But when these receptacles have been so far renounced that they no longer have any freedom from the man's own, there is total submission. A man who is being regenerated is at last so far reduced by repeated alternations of desolation and sustenance that he no longer wills to be his own, but the Lord's; and when he has become the Lord's he comes into a state of such a nature that when he is left to self he grieves and is seized with anxiety; and when he is delivered from this state of self he returns into his happiness and bliss. In such a state are all the angels. In order that He may make a man blessed and happy, the Lord wills a total submission, that is, that he be not partly his own and partly the Lord's, for then there are two lords, which no man can serve at the same time. (Matthew 6:24)
>
> Total submission is also meant by the Lord's words in Matthew: "He that loveth father and mother more than Me is not worthy of Me: and he that loveth son and daughter more than Me is not worthy of Me." (10:37) ; where by "father and mother" are signified in general those things which are man's own from inheritance, and by "son and daughter" those things which are his own from actual life.
>
> Man's own is also signified by "soul" in John: "He

that loveth his soul shall lose it; but he that hateth his soul in this world shall keep it unto life eternal. If anyone will minister to Me, let him follow Me; and where I am, there shall also My servant be." (John 12:25, 26)...

That submission must be total is very evident from the first commandment of the church: "Thou shalt love the Lord thy God from all thy heart, and from all thy soul, and from all thy mind, and from all thy forces; this is the first commandment." (Mark 12:30) Thus because love to the Lord does not come from man, but from the Lord Himself, therefore all the heart, all the soul, all the mind, and all the forces, which are recipients, must be the Lord's, consequently submission must be total. Such is the submission which is here signified by the words "we shall live, and our ground, servants unto Pharaoh," for by Pharaoh is represented the natural in general which is under the auspices of the internal celestial, in the supreme sense under the auspices of the Lord, who in this sense is "Joseph." (Number 6138)

We have considered the above quotation in relation to the regeneration of man; but as man's regeneration is an image of the Lord's glorification, inmostly these verses treat of the glorification of our Lord. But as this is so profound a subject, we shall not enter into it now. We shall only say a few words as to the difference between the Lord's glorification of His Human, by which He made it Divine, and the regeneration of man's human, by which it is made spiritual.

Man is not life, not a spark of the Divine, but a vessel which receives the Lord's life. This may be crudely illustrated by the filament of an electric light bulb which receives electric current and becomes a light as long as the current is received; the moment the current is cut off, the light goes out. If a man does not receive love and wisdom from the Lord every moment, his life of love and the light of his intelligence immediately ceases. "A man can receive nothing, except it be given him from heaven." (John 3:27.) And the Lord said: "He that abideth in me, and I in him, the same bringeth forth much fruit; for without me ye can do nothing." (John 15:5.)

Whereas man is a vessel that receives the Lord's life, and has no life from himself, the Lord communicates His life to man in such a way that man feels it as his own and can act as if of himself. If this were not so, man would not be man, nor could he feel the joy of cooperating with the Lord, in his love to God and his neighbor. Yet though man feels love and wisdom as his own, he should acknowledge that he has nothing of the life of genuine love and wisdom if it is not given from the Lord out of heaven.

That the Lord is life itself, and that man is the recipient of life, the Lord taught in many passages in the Gospel of John, as follows:

> For as the Father hath life in himself: so hath he given unto the Son to have life in himself. (5:26)
> In him was life; and the life was the light of men. (1:4)
> Whoso eateth my flesh, and drinketh my blood, hath eternal life. (6:54)
> I am come that they might have life. (10:10)
> And I give unto them eternal life. (10:28)
> I am the resurrection, and the life. (11:25)
> I am the way, the truth, and the life. (14:6)

The Lord totally submitted Himself to the Father, and thus became life itself, entirely one with the Father—one in Essence and one in Person. Man submits himself to the Lord and receives his life, and is thereby conjoined to the Lord. But he is not totally united to the Lord, nor does he become one with the Lord, for he can never have life in himself as his own, as the Lord had, but he has life as if of himself from the Lord.

In the *Arcana Coelestia* we read the explication of the words: "And Jehovah was with Joseph."

> By "Jehovah was with him" is signified that the Divine was therein; for the Divine was in His Human, because He was conceived of Jehovah. In the case of the angels, the Divine is not in them, but is present with them, because they are only forms recipient of the Divine from the Lord. (Number 4971)

There are two opposite extreme opinions with man. One is that man has in him a spark of the Divine as his own, which would make him a little god; the opposite opinion is that man cannot receive the Divine of the Lord in his soul or mind, which makes of man an animal.

The Lord said: "But seek ye first the kingdom of God, and his righteousness; and all these things shall be added unto you." (Matthew 6:33.)

The Kingdom of God which man is to seek is the "Kingdom of God which is within you," in which is the Lord. For if the Kingdom of God is not within you, it is impossible to be in the Kingdom of God round about you.

Many desire to go to heaven, but their main goal in life is not seeking the Kingdom of God within them.

There are many who strive for the improvement of the world, but an apparent improvement of the world is only a palliative cure and short-lived if the Kingdom of God is not established in men's hearts.

If man does not seek the Kingdom of Heaven within, with all his heart, soul, mind, and strength, and if he does not there totally submit himself to the Lord, little is accomplished. How few there are who see that the primary work of man is to form his mind as a dwelling place of God in His Kingdom! This does not mean that man must not do his work in the world sincerely, faithfully, and justly, for this is part of the work of forming the Kingdom of God within; but man's work in this world should be regarded as that of a servant for a more noble end, for the sake of the Kingdom of God within and without.

14

The Ten Commandments, or Decalogue

We are told that the Ten Commandments were written by the finger of God on Mount Sinai, when Jehovah descended upon the mount in fire. The tables of stone were placed in the Holy of Holies in the ark. And by the ark were done great miracles, such as the drying up of Jordan, so that the Children of Israel could pass over. The truths in the Ten Commandments were commonly known: that they were to worship God and hallow His name; that they were to keep holy days sacred; that they were to honor father and mother; that they were not to kill, steal, commit adultery, or bear false witness. These commandments were known to nearly all peoples, for without some of these laws, human society is impossible.

The reason why the Ten Commandments were given with such great miracles was to make it plain that these laws are not only civil and moral laws, but also Divine Laws, and that to sin against them is not only to sin against one's neighbor and society, but to sin against God.

The keeping of these laws in their literal sense is not only the basis of society and the state, but also the basis of the Kingdom of God. The Lord, when in the world, taught that it is not sufficient to keep these laws only in their letter, but that it is necessary to keep them also in their spirit:

Ye have heard that it was said by them of old time, Thou shalt not kill; and whosoever shall kill shall be in danger of the judgment: But I say unto you, That

whosoever is angry with his brother without a cause
shall be in danger of the judgment. (Matthew 5:21,22)

Ye have heard that it was said by them of old time,
Thou shalt not commit adultery: But I say unto you,
That whosoever looketh on a woman to lust after her
hath committed adultery with her already in his heart.
(Matthew 5:27,28)

There is, however, much more involved in the Ten Commandments than the Lord here expressed. The Lord said:
"I have yet many things to say unto you, but ye cannot bear
them now." (John 16:12.)

There are many things in the Word of the Lord that
could not be revealed to the Apostles, including the inner
meaning of the Ten Commandments.

We read in the *Arcana Coelestia*, by Emanuel Swedenborg:

> "And God spake all these words, saying." That this
> signifies truths Divine for those in the heavens and for
> those on earth. . . . From this also truth Divine is called
> "the Word," and "the Word" is the Lord, according to
> John 1:1, for the reason that when the Lord was in
> the world He was the Divine truth itself, and after-
> ward when He was glorified He became the Divine
> good, and thenceforth all Divine truth proceeds from
> Him. This Divine truth is light to the angels, which light
> is also that which illuminates our internal sight, which
> is that of the understanding. . . . It has for its objects
> in the spiritual understanding the truths which are
> called the truths of faith; but in the natural under-
> standing it has for its objects truths of the civil state
> which relate to what is just, and also truths of the
> moral state which relate to what is reputable. (Num-
> ber 8861)

"I am Jehovah (the Lord) thy God"

(Exodus 20:2)

Who is Jehovah, our God? On the answer to this question depends the nature of our worship of God. What God do we worship?

As we have said, the entire Old Testament is a prophecy of the coming of the Lord, but there are some verses which are more obvious prophecies of His coming than others, and are commonly recognized as such; many of these are quoted in the New Testament. The obvious prophecies clearly teach that it was Jehovah (the Lord) who was to come into the world. For example, the last two verses of the Old Testament read:

Behold, I will send you Elijah the prophet before the coming of the great and dreadful day of Jehovah [the Lord]: And he shall turn the heart of the fathers to the children, and the heart of the children to their fathers, lest I come and smite the earth with a curse. (Malachi 4:5,6)

(In place of "Jehovah," "the LORD" is used in the King James translation of the Bible.)

In reference to this, Jesus said:

For all the prophets and the law prophesied until John. And if ye will receive it, this is Elias, which was for to come. He that hath ears to hear, let him hear. (Matthew 11:13–15)

But the angel said unto him [Zacharias]. . . . And many of the children of Israel shall he [John the Baptist] turn to the Lord their God. And he shall go before him in the spirit and power of Elias, to turn the hearts of the fathers to the children, . . . to make ready a people prepared for the Lord. (Luke 1:16–17)

Jehovah [the Lord] is called the only Saviour and Redeemer, as in Isaiah:

"I, even I, am Jehovah, and beside me there is no savior." (43:11)

Who hath declared this from ancient time? . . . Have not I, Jehovah? . . . a just God and a Savior; there is none beside me. Look unto me, and be ye saved . . . for I am God, and there is none else. (45:21,22)

I, Jehovah, am thy Savior and thy Redeemer. (49:26)

Yet I am Jehovah [the Lord] thy God . . . and thou shalt know no god but me; for there is no savior beside me. (Hosea 13:4)

Thou, Jehovah, art our father, our redeemer; thy name is from everlasting. (Isaiah 63:16)

He [Jehovah] bowed the heavens also, and came down. (II Samuel 22:10; Psalm 18:9)

The voice of him that crieth in the wilderness, Prepare ye the way of Jehovah. . . . Behold, the Lord Jehovah will come with a strong hand. . . . He shall feed his flock like a shepherd. (Isaiah 40:3,10,11)

From the above, it is clear that it was Jehovah who came into the world as our Lord Jesus Christ, our Savior and Redeemer. When it says in the opening words of the Ten Commandments, as addressed to Christians, "I am Jehovah thy God," we must think of our Lord Jesus Christ, who is God and man, now present in His Divine Human, for the Gospel says:

No man hath seen God at any time; the only begotten Son . . . he hath manifested Him. (John 1:18)

Jesus saith unto him, I am the way, the truth and the life: no man cometh unto the Father, but by me. If ye had known me, ye should have known my Father also: and from henceforth ye know him, and have seen him. Philip saith unto him, Lord, shew us the Father,

. . . Jesus saith unto him, Have I been so long time with you, and yet hast thou not known me, Philip? He that hath seen me hath seen the Father; and how sayest thou then, Shew us the Father? Believest thou not that I am in the Father and the Father in me? . . . Believe me that I am in the Father and the Father in me. (John 14:6–11)

Jehovah was then evidently in the Lord, as our soul is in our human—the invisible God in the visible God—and we can approach God only in His Divine Human. This is the great truth concerning which the Lord said: "I thank thee, O Father . . . because thou hast hid these things from the wise and prudent, and hast revealed them unto babes" (Matthew 11:25), for the sophisticated, those who are proud of their learning, have a profound aversion to this truth. Such are unwilling to bow down to our Lord, who came into the world and made His Human to be God, having, as He said, "All power . . . in heaven and in earth." (Matthew 28:18.)

The Ten Commandments involve all things of man's life. If one keeps the Ten Commandments for the sake of God and for the sake of the Kingdom of God, and not merely for the sake of himself and his reputation in the world, he comes to love the Lord with all his heart, soul, mind, and strength. The Lord then comes to reign universally in the Kingdom of God which is within him, and also in man's earth or land, which is the human in which man lives in the world.

"Which have brought thee out of the land of Egypt." This signifies that man is made free from the power of the world and the flesh, free from the power of evil inflowing from hell.

"Thou shalt have no other gods before me"

(Exodus 20:3)

This signifies that a man must not attempt to think truths from any source other than the Lord, for the Lord is the only source of truth, for, as He says, "I am the way, the truth, and the life." (John 14:6.)

If a man raises his mind to heaven, truths flow into his mind from the Lord. In ancient times, men made many gods and worshipped them. Modern man does not make gods in the same way, yet any idea which he makes out of the conceit of his own intelligence or the evil desires of his heart is a thing that he worships and is, therefore, to him a god. Jesus said: "There shall arise false Christs, and false prophets." (Matthew 24:24.)

False Christs and false prophets signify false doctrines which come out of the conceit of one's own intelligence. When a man is unwilling, on account of his conceit, to submit himself to the rule of our Lord—when he does not trust in the Word of the Lord, but in himself—he immediately begins to worship other gods, that is, the concoctions of his own imagination. These are the modern man's graven images, likenesses or counterfeits of things in heaven above —that is, false theological things; in the earth beneath— false philosophical and psychological things; and in the water under the earth—false sensuous and scientific things. These are the gods which so many modern men worship in place of our Lord and Savior.

In recent years it has become customary to speak of creating an image of a man or organization in order that such an image may be adored or admired, and much effort is put into the creating of such an image. In a word, it is not the man himself that is adored, but the image that is made of him. To adore an image of a man is far worse than to adore images of wood or stone, as is done by simple primitive peoples.

"Thou shalt not take the name of Jehovah thy God in vain"

(Exodus 20:7)

A name stands for a man and all that is known about him, and thus for a man's quality. In ordinary language we speak of a man's good name, or of a man with a bad name, signifying the quality of a man or his reputation. We read in the book of Revelation: "His name [the Lamb's] shall be in their foreheads." (22:4.) That is, they will have a new quality from the Lord. The Lord is made known to us in the Word and in genuine doctrine from the Word. Wherefore, to take the name of Jehovah in vain means not only to use the names of God disrespectfully, but also to make light of the Word of God and, especially, to immerse the things of religion in worldly and political matters in such a way as to advance one's self-interest. Especially do those take the Lord's name in vain who live an outwardly Christian or holy life and inwardly have no living faith, and also those who make much of faith but lead an evil life. With such, either the will looks toward heaven but the understanding looks toward hell, or the understanding looks toward heaven and the will toward hell. Such, therefore, have a divided mind. It is such who are meant by the "lukewarm, and neither cold nor hot," of whom it is said, "I will spue thee out of my mouth." (Revelation 3:16.) Of such it is especially said: "For Jehovah will not hold him guiltless that taketh his name in vain." (Exodus 20:7.)

"Remember the sabbath day, to keep it holy"
(Exodus 20:8)

Six days shalt thou labor, and do all thy work: But
the seventh day is the sabbath of Jehovah thy God; in
it thou shalt not do any work . . . For in six days Jehovah made heaven and earth, the sea and all that in
them is, and rested the seventh day; wherefore Jehovah
blessed the sabbath day, and hallowed it. (Exodus 20:
8–11)

If we believe that there is a Divine end or purpose in
creation, that end and purpose must be the conjunction of
God and man. Material creation must then be regarded as
one of the means to this end. The things of creation have
no living significance unless they are in the mind of man;
a created world in which there is no consciousness is useless
and meaningless. The things of heaven and the things of the
world can be in man's mind. The Lord said: "The Kingdom
of God is within you." (Luke 17:21.) Certainly the things
of the world are also within. A man without the five bodily
senses could know nothing; sensation is the ultimate means
of forming the mind. But how the mind, with its understanding, its thoughts, its loves, and its desires, is formed
on the basis of sensation is a miracle which no one can
comprehend. The lower or external mind is opened first;
then the Kingdom of God can be formed within it. The
lower mind is the earth or kingdom of the world within
you. The inner mind is heaven or the Kingdom of Heaven
within you. These kingdoms are the ends of creation and
are spiritually meant by: "For in six days Jehovah made
heaven and earth." (Exodus 20:11.)

It is the Lord who creates the Kingdom of Heaven and
earth in the mind of man, but at first it appears as if a
man created his own mind by study and application. Man

has to struggle as if of himself to bring his mind into order; he has to combat the disorder of his mind. It is this that is signified by "Six days shalt thou labor, and do all thy work." (Exodus 20:9.) Finally, a man totally submits himself to the Lord and comes into a state of peace and rest. Looking back then, he can recognize that the Lord has created all things within him. Wherefore, when a man has come to a state of peace or rest, he sees that it is the Lord who can now rest from the combat. This is what is meant by "Remember the sabbath day, to keep it holy." (Exodus 20:8.) Man then lives a life of love to God and his neighbor, free from labor and combat. He does his work, spiritual and natural, freely from the inspiration of the Lord; his mind is at rest. To remember the sabbath day is to keep perpetually in the thought the belief that it is the Lord who has brought him to this state of peace and rest.

The Lord also, when in the world, went through combats and labors, until He fully united the Divine to the Human and the Human to the Divine and thus came to a Divine peace or rest. From Him comes all peace of soul and rest of mind. Wherefore He said: "The Son of man is Lord even of the sabbath day." (Matthew 12:8.) And again: "Peace I leave with you, my peace I give unto you; not as the world giveth, give I unto you. Let not your heart be troubled, neither let it be afraid." (John 14:27.)

"Honor thy father and thy mother"

(Exodus 20:12)

The Lord said, "And call no man your father upon the earth: for one is your Father, which is in heaven." (Matthew 23:9.)

Wherefore, spiritually seen, God is our Father. That our heavenly Father is the Lord Jesus Christ is taught in Isaiah, where we read: "For unto us a child is born, unto us a son is given: and the government shall be upon his shoulder: and his name shall be called . . . The mighty God, The everlasting Father." (9:6.)

It is known in the Church that the genuine Church is the bride and wife of the Lord and is our spiritual mother, from whom we are born again.

To honor includes to love, for honor without love means little, as does also love without honoring. Separate loving and honoring, and neither is of value.

We have said that the genuine Church is our spiritual mother, that is, the Church which is truly the Kingdom of God, or the Church insofar as the good of love and the truth of faith reign. So-called churches often have things ruling in them which do not originate in love from the Lord, or love to the Lord and one's neighbor; things such as ambitions, pride, envy, the love of power, and jealousy often enter into churches and acquire the upper seats there because the Kingdom of God is not in them. Wherefore, insofar as such things are in the so-called church, it is not a spiritual mother. The church is our spiritual mother insofar as it is in the spirit of the Word of the Lord and is formed by this spirit.

"Thou shalt not kill"

(Exodus 20:13)

To kill, spiritually seen, is to take away spiritual life from another. Anything we may say which weakens a man's faith, which takes away innocence; anything we do which makes others lose faith in God, in His Word and in His Kingdom, or in His Providence or Mercy is spiritual murder. As we have already pointed out, the Lord taught that hatred involves killing, for all hatred does harm to the soul.

To kill also involves killing the faith in the Lord within oneself. Anyone who comes to deny that the Lord Jesus

Christ is God, having all power in heaven and earth, kills
the Lord in himself; that is, he kills the Lord's power to
work in him, so that the Lord, as far as he is concerned,
is no longer living. This is the meaning of the words, "And
all that dwell upon the earth shall worship him [the beast],
whose names are not written in the book of life of the Lamb
slain from the foundation of the world." (Revelation 13:8.)
That is, they refer to those who have not acknowledged the
Lord in His Divine Human from the beginning of the
Church.

"Thou shalt not commit adultery"
(Exodus 20:14)

In relation to the story of Joseph we have already treated
adultery, but we shall add the following:

The Lord when in the world said that "whosoever looketh
on a woman to lust after her hath committed adultery with
her already in his heart." (Matthew 5:28.)

Not only is the adultery of the heart most widespread
in so-called Christian lands, but actual adultery is becoming
shockingly widespread, and with very many people there
is no conscience in relation to this. Every act has a spiritual
cause. The prevalence of natural adultery has its source in
spiritual adultery. Spiritual marriage is the marriage of
love and wisdom or of good and truth. Spiritual adultery
is the adulteration of love by false ideas and the falsification
of truth by evil loves, especially the adulteration or falsification of the Word of the Lord.

Every vain, proud, and sophisticated man adulterates
the Word when he reads it, for he interprets it to favor his
own self-interest. He "goes a whoring after other gods,"
that is, he interprets it in such a way as to favor his love
of himself and makes his opinions false gods which he worships. He makes his church a chosen people, haughtily stand-

ing far above all others, forgetting the words of the Lord,
"That servant, which knew his lord's will, and prepared
not himself, neither did according to his will, shall be beaten
with many stripes." (Luke 12:47.) It is therefore the vain
and proud leaders of the church who receive the greatest
condemnation. A wise man knows that of himself he can do
nothing good and looks to the Lord continually to teach, en-
lighten, and lead him lest he be lost. The vanity of the heart
is the cause of both spiritual and natural adultery.

Where there is little faith in the Deity of the Lord and
the Divinity of His Word; where adultery is prevalent;
where the name of God is abused; where false statements
are made with no conscience about causing harm; and where
dishonesty is commonplace, a country is not Christian, and
churches in such countries in which but few of the members
are profoundly distressed at such happenings are Christian
in name only. Between such churches the ecumenical spirit
is of no significance.

"Thou shalt not steal"

(Exodus 20:15)

We have already treated of stealing, but shall add the
following: To steal, regarded spiritually, is to take away a
man's spiritual faith and knowledges. It also involves claiming anything which is one's neighbor's for oneself, as, for
example, claiming ideas which one has got from someone
else as one's own original ideas, especially claiming inspirations which one has been given from God out of heaven as
one's own. We read: "A man can receive nothing, except
it be given him from heaven." (John 3:27.)

All that is good and true comes to man from the Lord
out of heaven. If a man does not ascribe such things to the
Lord from whom they came, he steals from the Lord. The
Word of the Lord was given from heaven, but if the light

by which the Word is read and the understanding obtained
is not also given from heaven, the things of the Word remain
in man's mind as a dead letter.

Anyone who says that the truths which man has are
only human opinions steals from the Lord, for human opinions cannot be ascribed to God, but are necessarily claimed
as man's own.

Man is faced with this great problem. To begin with,
nearly everything of spiritual truth is obscure. Man is sure
of very little in regard to the truths of faith. Many of his
ideas are false. Man may imagine that he has been inspired
by a new idea, and yet the idea may be false. Now, to
ascribe a false idea to the Lord as being an inspiration out
of heaven is a serious matter. It is only slowly that a man
comes into a clear spiritual light in which he can see clearly
what is from heaven and what are his own human and
fantastic ideas.

It may be better for a man to believe that his ideas are
merely human and his own than out of vanity to ascribe
ideas that are of his own concoction to God and therefore
to regard them as Divine. A man should, however, progress
until he comes to acknowledge that all the truth which he
thinks and all the good which he does are the Lord's.

We read in the *Arcana Coelestia* of Swedenborg: "A
man . . . cannot be admitted into heaven until he acknowledges at heart that nothing of good or truth is from himself,
but all from the Lord, and that whatever is from himself
is nothing but evil." (Number 5758.) Furthermore, we read:
" 'To steal' denotes to claim for self that which is the Lord's,
namely, good and truth; and as in the beginning of regeneration all do this, and as this is the first state of innocence,
the expression is milder than it sounds in the letter." (Number 4002.)

Spiritual theft is committed by the heads of churches,
or ministers and priests, who claim special powers and inspiration on account of their position or ordination. An
office in the Church does bring enlightenment if a man is

humble, if he submits himself to the Lord and thus acquires
wisdom. But to claim wisdom and inspiration on account
of the office comes from pride and leads to folly; for wisdom
comes from being born again from the Lord and not on
account of being exalted by the Church.

"Thou shalt not bear false witness against thy neighbor"

(Exodus 20:16)

In the spiritual sense, to bear false witness is to call
the good evil, or truth falsity. As an example of calling what
is good evil, consider the following: There are many who
think that it is charitable to treat those who commit crimes
or even those who harm others by slander with great lenien-
cy. Such persons place the imagined welfare of undeserving individuals above the welfare of society. Thus they call
the good of those who act with reasonable severity evil.

It is very common for persons to bear witness against
the truth. When a new truth is being born into the world,
many will declare it to be false and bring many things to
witness against it, even from the Word of God, which they
misunderstand.

When a new idea appears which is obviously of significance, a man should examine it with an open mind and pray
for enlightenment. Many, instead of this, view a new idea
from prejudices of many kinds, from habits of thought
practiced from childhood, from the rut of professional opinion, or from fear of the reaction of others. This fault is the
worst of all with those who are in a profession, such as
ministers or medical doctors. Many, from the pride of their
profession, are unwilling even to consider open-mindedly
anything which comes from others without a high standing
in their branch of the profession, and are still more prejudiced against it if it comes from one outside the profession.

The supreme example of this was the trial of our Lord: "The chief priests, and elders, and all the council, sought false witness against Jesus, to put him to death; But found none. . . . At the last came two false witnesses, And said, This fellow said, I am able to destroy the temple of God, and to build it in three days. . . . Jesus saith unto him [the high priest] . . . Hereafter shall ye see the Son of man sitting on the right hand of power, and coming in the clouds of heaven. Then the high priest rent his clothes, saying, He hath spoken blasphemy. . . . What think ye? They answered and said, He is guilty of death." (Matthew 26:59–65.)

Here we note that those who bore witness took the words which the Lord had said and, applying them in a merely literal way, contrary to their real meaning, used them to bear false witness against the Lord. We may in our hearts condemn those who did this; but every man who is proud in his profession and in the conceit of his intelligence acts in the same way toward a truth and at times persecutes those who bring forth a truth, if he sees it as a threat to his professional standing. It is only those with a "broken heart and contrite spirit" who are willing to accept a truth which will manifest their ignorance and the disorders of their own lives. We should therefore take the commandment not to bear false witness as a great warning.

"Thou shalt not covet thy neighbor's house, thou shalt not covet thy neighbor's wife, nor his manservant, nor his maidservant, nor his ox, nor his ass, nor any thing that is thy neighbor's"

(Exodus 20:17)

The preceding commandments treat of things which are not to be done with the body. This commandment treats of the things of the spirit, of desires that are to be shunned. Coveting comes from the love of self and the love of the world as opposed to the love of God and one's neighbor. If a man does not shun these evils of his will, he can never come to a genuine love of God and his neighbor. The evils mentioned in the former commandments are acts; yet not only must evil acts be shunned, but also the desires of the will from which they proceed. If a man is to be saved, he must examine himself and repent not only as to his acts, but also as to his desires from which the acts proceed. If a man would know his ruling loves, let him reflect as to what he concentrates on. What does he think about in his free time; what gives him the greatest delight? Are they things of love to God and the neighbor, or are they things of his ambitions, his pleasures, and his selfish desires?

It is said in the *Arcana Coelestia* by Swedenborg:

Man is not allowed to divide his mind [namely, his will and understanding] . . . that is, to understand and speak truth, and to will and do evil; for then the one faculty would look upward or toward heaven, and the other downward or toward hell, and thus the man would hang between the two. But let him know that the will carries him away, and the understanding favors. . . .

Nothing is more necessary to man than to know whether heaven be in him, or hell. . . . In order that he may know this, it is necessary that he should know what good is, and what evil, for good makes heaven, and evil makes hell; the doctrine of charity teaches about both. (Numbers 7180 and 7181)

If a man will look to the Lord, he can be granted to see how heaven or hell rules in him. He can then shun the things of hell and receive the things of heaven, not by his own power, but by the power of the Lord in him. But if man does not do this, as if from himself, the Lord cannot do it for him, for this would be to destroy man's freedom and thus his manhood.

The last words of the commandment tell us we are not to

covet "his ox or his ass or any thing that is thy neighbor's."

A commandment which was written by "the finger of God" must be an important and eternal truth. Nowadays few have an ox or an ass or covet one. From this it can be seen that there must be more involved in the Word than appears in the letter. An ox, in the spiritual sense, represents natural good, that is, external good things which man does for his neighbor. Such things serve the internal things of the spirit. They serve the inner things of the spirit of charity which look to man's eternal welfare. The primary use of the ox was to plow the ground. By being useful to our neighbor, we prepare the ground of the mind for more internal usefulness for the things of the spirit.

An ass stands for knowledges in the external or outer memory; such knowledges serve the thinking of the spirit of man: they prepare man's mind for inspirations of the spirit. Those who do not do their duty are often envious of those who do, as illustrated by the five foolish virgins, who coveted the oil in the vessels of the five wise virgins. (Matthew 25:8.)

We have presented a few things, but the Ten Commandments, which are in the holy of holies of the Church, contain infinitely more things than have ever entered into the mind of man.

15

The Writings of Emanuel Swedenborg

The explanations of the stories from Genesis and Exodus are based on the *Arcana Coelestia* of Emanuel Swedenborg. As was said before, this is a large work of twelve good-sized volumes, unfolding the inner meaning of Genesis and Exodus. The interested reader is referred to this work. But the reader may be warned that to enter into this work is not so easy. In the first place, there is the language. Every study involves new words, or words used with special meanings. A man commencing a serious study of a science or philosophy has to acquire a vocabulary. In the case of the writings of Swedenborg, this is not nearly so difficult as in many other studies, but it does require effort. I know Zulus and Basutos in Africa with little education who, from practice, can more easily read the writings of Swedenborg than they can read a newspaper or a novel.

The greatest difficulty in reading the writings of Swedenborg is that they treat of things that are not well known. Most people have reflected and meditated little on what takes place in the mind and how the mind develops and grows spiritually, how the Kingdom of Heaven "within you" is formed, and what pertains to that kingdom. It is therefore only gradually, as the mind ponders these things, that the understanding of them develops. But what is more important, a man can really understand only that which he has experienced. It is therefore only insofar as man has struggled with spiritual concerns and experienced them in his life that he comes into real light on the matter; and this comes little by little. Many have had the experience of sections of the Writings of Swedenborg, when first read, seeming difficult and tedious, but when read later, after the reader has undergone new spiritual experiences, they are felt to be alive and inspiring. Another difficulty is that, with a long work, at the first reading it is difficult to follow the line of development that runs throughout and gives it significance, a significance that at first cannot be realized.

Also, there are many things stated that are brief and are not illustrated whose significance can be grasped only by meditation. For example, there are innumerable things which represent good and truth. The truth of faith, as we have already shown and shall show in the following chapter, is represented by light, water, wine, blood, rock, and innumerable other things—whereas the good of love is represented by fire or heat, by bread, flesh, ground, and innumerable other things.

The great difference between these natural objects, which appear to have little in common, is obvious. We have few words to express the things of the Kingdom of Heaven within, all of which have to do with the good of love and the truth of faith. Indeed, there are as many kinds of truth and good as there are objects in nature; and these all have totally different characteristics, differing as much as light and rock, or as flame and ground. These differences can often be comprehended only by reflecting and meditating on the characteristics of the object mentioned, its function and usefulness, and then coming to see the nature of the good or truth to which the natural object corresponds. As this is frequently not illustrated in the Writings of Swedenborg but only the general idea presented, it takes much meditation to come to a living idea.

The best-known work of Swedenborg is the book entitled *Heaven and Hell*. A large part of this work describes things seen in heaven and hell, such as the houses of angels and spirits, their clothing, their gardens, and all things of their surroundings, and the relation of the angels to these.

Everything in heaven corresponds to and exists according to the state of mind of the angels. The Kingdom of Heaven around them is an image of the Kingdom of God within them. And in hell, the hell around them is nothing but an image of the hell within them.

If one has the Kingdom of Heaven within, little by little one can come to see how this kingdom is represented in the things seen by the angels outside of themselves. If, however, the Kingdom of Heaven is not in man, and if man has no idea of the nature of that kingdom, when he reads a book like *Heaven and Hell*, in the outward description or letter of the book he sees nothing of the essential living things within. Wherefore to understand such a work requires not only meditation, but also a spiritual development involving many inner experiences, and this comes only slowly.

16

The Samaritan Woman at the Well

We have considered various chapters of the Old Testament; we shall now give an explication of a chapter of the New Testament. We read:

> Jesus therefore, being wearied with his journey, sat thus on the well; and it was about the sixth hour. There cometh a woman of Samaria to draw water; Jesus saith unto her, Give me to drink. . . . Jesus . . . said unto her, If thou knewest the gift of God, and who it is that saith to thee, Give me to drink; thou wouldest have asked of him, and he would have given thee living water. . . . Whosoever drinketh of this water shall thirst again: But whosoever drinketh of the water that I shall give him shall never thirst; but the water that I shall give him shall be in him a well of water springing up into everlasting life. (John 4:6,10,13,14)

The Lord in this passage was speaking to the woman of Samaria. The Samaritans were despised by the Jews and were not considered true worshippers of Jehovah. The Samaritans represent and stand for the Gentiles, and for the simple. Here the woman of Samaria represents those who have a simple understanding of the Word—those who are not learned but who love the literal sense of the Word and are open to instruction from the Lord. The Jews in the unfavorable sense represent the learned who have formed false ideas of religion according to their conceit and love

of themselves and despise those who have a simple love of
the literal sense of the Word. The well was Jacob's well.
Jacob's well represents, or stands for, the literal or natural
sense of the Word, and the waters thence, the external or
literal understanding of the Word. The Lord, sitting on the
well, represents the spiritual or internal sense of the Word,
which seen spiritually is the Lord Himself, who is the Word,
the Logos described in the first chapter of John; sitting
on the well represents the fact that the spiritual sense of
the Word rests on its literal sense.

In *Doctrine of the Sacred Scripture,* by Emanuel Swedenborg, it is said: "The Doctrine of the church is to be
drawn from the sense of the letter of the Word, and is to
be confirmed thereby." (Number 50.)

The internal sense of the Word, which is the genuine
Doctrine of the church, is drawn from the Word as water
is drawn from a well.

It is taught in the *Arcana Coelestia* that when man is
reading the Word, the angels are in the internal sense, and
from them the spiritual and even the celestial sense can be
communicated to man. As we read: "The literal sense is
such that the interior sense can be communicated to man,
and also the internal and supreme sense, for man communicates with the three heavens." (Number 4279:2.)

Again: "When man suffers himself to be enlightened
by the Word . . . the internal way is opened, thus there
is effected influx and communication through heaven from
the Lord." (Number 3708.)

This passage speaks of influx and communication
through heaven from the Lord. Many in the churches acknowledge the influx of the Lord through heaven, which is
imperceptible; but few really believe in the communication
of ideas from God out of heaven—perceptible and compre-
hensible ideas, which may be given to man while he reads
and meditates on the Word.

The reason for this can be seen if the truth in the following quotation from the *Arcana Coelestia* is considered.

> Those who are being reformed and are becoming
> spiritual [in their first state] suppose they do good
> and think truth from themselves ... nor do they know
> otherwise; and when told that all good and truth are
> from the Lord, they do not indeed reject it, but do not
> acknowledge it at heart, because they do not feel it,
> nor interiorly perceive that anything flows in from any
> other source than themselves. (Number 2678)

That is, they feel they can understand the Word by their
own intelligence without enlightenment from the Lord.

As the angels, all of whom were once men on earth,
are in the internal sense from the Lord and not from themselves, the internal sense which is communicated is from
the Lord, out of heaven. In the above quotations there is
an apparent paradox. One statement is that the doctrine
is drawn from the sense of the letter of the Word; the
other, that it is communicated through heaven from the
Lord. The first statement treats of the apparent physical
influx, through the bodily senses of seeing and hearing. A
man must read and study the Word, apart from which he
can know nothing of spiritual truth. The other passage
treats of the spiritual influx; for if there is not an influx
and reception of the Holy Spirit, that is, of truths communicated from the Lord out of heaven, man is only in the
outer forms of truth, but not in the truths themselves.

When the Lord said: "Whosoever drinketh of the water
that I shall give him shall never thirst, but the water that
I shall give him shall be in him a well of water springing
up into everlasting life" (John 4:14), the woman replied:
"Sir, give me this water, that I thirst not, neither come
hither to draw." The woman here was thinking merely naturally about drawing water from a well. In the same way
it is our tendency to think merely naturally about drawing
truth from the Word; and when the Lord promises living

truth from Himself from within, we may think we can
avoid the labor of drawing truth from the Word, as if of
ourselves, by study and meditation.

What is the merely natural idea of drawing doctrine
from the Word that is represented by the answer of the
woman?

There are those who think they can acquire internal
truth by study of the Word and the doctrine, by comparison
of passages, and by a knowledge of correspondences or
types, or who place all the emphasis on this. Others put all
the emphasis on the presence of the Lord and inspiration
from the Lord, with little study, meditation, and labor, as
if of oneself. Both these attitudes when separated and regarded by themselves are merely natural and do not lead
to an opening of the Word. It is only by a conjunction of
these two, which, internally seen, is a conjunction or marriage of the Divine and the Human, that man can be admitted into the internal of the Word. Wherefore the Lord's
reply to the woman was, "Go call thy husband." To which
the woman replied, "I have no husband." (John 4:16,17.)

If we read: "The Doctrine of the Church is to be drawn
from the sense of the letter of the Word, and is to be confirmed by it," what idea do we have? Do we think this is
just a matter of the understanding, or do we realize that
it is primarily a matter of the love and the life? The sense
of the letter of the Word is not the sense of the letter of
the Word *in us* unless we have lived it. If we do not live
according to the sense of the letter, the sense of the letter
with us is mere fallacy, from which no geniuine truth or
teaching can be drawn. The first thing is therefore to live
according to the sense of the letter of the Word. But there
are two ways of living according to the sense of the letter
of the Word. One can, in the first state, live according to
the sense of the letter of the Word out of a state of innocence, humility, and modesty, with a holy feeling that it
is to be obeyed because it is the Lord's Word. Or one may
obey the Word from the opposite spirit, namely, out of

vanity, pride, and a feeling of self-righteousness, regarding oneself as one of a "chosen people." In the latter case the Word, even though literally lived in appearance, is still a dead letter in man, from which man can come to no genuine doctrine or teaching.

If a man strives to live according to the sense of the letter, out of a first innocence, the time comes when the Lord may come to him and open his mind to the light of heaven and give him an understanding of the interiors of the Word. The elevation into such truth is from the Lord from within, although drawn out of the sense of the letter, the man cooperating as if of himself.

Then is fulfilled the saying of the Lord to the woman of Samaria: "But the hour cometh, and now is, when the true worshippers shall worship the Father in spirit and in truth; for the Father seeketh such to worship him. God is a Spirit; and they that worship him must worship him in spirit and in truth." (John 4:23,24.)

If a man has been so elevated, he must again descend and confirm the doctrine by the sense of the letter. But again this confirmation is nothing, if it is only a matter of the understanding and is not a matter of the love and of the life. If a man has been elevated to the Lord in the internal of the Word, and then descends to the sense of the letter, he sees innumerable things in the sense of the letter which he had not seen before—a whole vision of the sense of the letter out of the internal. He sees many truths of natural life which he could not see before; thus he can be brought to a wonderful change of his natural life. But this is true only if, out of a new internal innocence, he obeys the sense of the letter, which now has a new spirit within it. Thus man confirms the doctrine that has been drawn from the sense of the letter. To confirm is to make firm or strong. In the dictionary the word "confirm" is defined as follows: "To make firm, to establish, to strengthen, as in a habit, spiritually or physically."

By living according to the literal sense, seen in the light

of the internal sense, until it becomes a habit, the internal sense is confirmed and strengthened so that it is enduring. If the doctrine is not confirmed by the literal sense, it appears as if man's things are in it and not the Divine of the Lord; and, in fact, if man does not confirm the doctrine by a life according to the literal sense seen in the light of the internal sense, the Lord is not present with man. A man may indeed be temporarily elevated so that he sees the teaching or doctrine which makes one with the internal sense of the Word. But if this is not confirmed by a life according to the sense of the letter, seen in the light of the internal sense, genuine doctrine is not confirmed but is weakened for the man, and in the long run is so dissipated that he no longer acknowledges the truth of doctrine. Internally, if not externally, man comes into a state of opposition to the genuine teaching of the Word. Such states of opposition have often manifested themselves in the church.

Note that when the woman took literally the Lord's words concerning the water which He would give, the Lord did not correct her but told her, "Go, call thy husband." To which she replied, "I have no husband." "Jesus said unto her, Thou hast well said, I have no husband; for thou hast had five husbands; and he that thou now hast is not thy husband; in that saidst thou truly. The woman said, Sir, I perceive that thou art a prophet." (John 4:16–19.)

When one is merely affected or moved by the letter of the Word, the Lord in the internal sense does not correct him but tells this ability to be affected or moved by the truth, represented by the woman, to go and bring the internal love conjoined to the desire for truth, out of which one reads the Word, that is, the husband.

To this the affection or desire for the truth replies, "I have no husband," that is, it needs no internal love. The Lord—that is, the internal sense—replies that she had had five husbands, and the one she now has is not her husband; that is, there had been different non-genuine loves out of which man had read the Word, and the one out of which he now reads is not genuine. Having a husband signifies the desire of the truth conjoined with the love of being actively engaged in the things of wisdom; not having a husband signifies just having the love of knowing truth, apart from the love of wisdom. Wisdom is more than intelligence; wisdom exists only with those who live a spiritual life.

If there is something genuine in the affection or love for the true and if there is humility, this causes the affection for the true, represented by the woman, to recognize the voice of the internal truth as a prophet, that is, as the genuine Doctrine of the Church. When such an affection for the true hears from the internal sense of the Word (that is, from the Lord) the teaching that one has not been in the things of wisdom, out of self-acknowledgment it recognizes this truth as being from the Lord, namely, that there has not been in the affection for the truth the internal things of the wisdom of life.

The woman was expecting the Messiah; that is, she believed that a genuine understanding of the Word would be given in the future. "I know that Messias cometh, which is called Christ: when he is come, he will tell us all things. Jesus said, I that speak unto thee am he." (John 4:25,26.) If the affection or love for the truth in man has acknowledged the genuine doctrine of the Church to be a prophet, that is, genuine doctrine, then he is prepared to acknowledge the truth, that It Itself is the Messias, the Christ.

Baptism and the Holy Supper

In the Writings of Emanuel Swedenborg we read:

Baptism was instituted for a sign that a man is of the Church and for a memorial that he can be regenerated; for the washing of Baptism is a spiritual washing, which is regeneration. . . . Since everyone who is regenerated also undergoes temptations, which are spiritual combats against evils and falsities, these also are signified by the waters of Baptism. Inasmuch as Baptism is a sign and memorial of these things, man may be baptized as an infant, and if not in his infancy, he may be baptized as an adult. Let those, therefore, who are baptized know that baptism confers neither faith or salvation; but that it testifies that they may receive faith and be saved if they are regenerated. (*The New Jerusalem and Its Heavenly Doctrine,* Numbers 202–7)

Infants are introduced by Baptism into the Christian heaven, and there angels are assigned to them to take care of them, . . . by whom they are kept in a state of receiving faith in the Lord; and as they grow up, and come into their own right and reason, the guardian angels leave them, and they associate with such spirits as make one with their life and faith. (*The True Christian Religion,* Number 677)

Baptism signifies the cleansing of man's life by a life according to the truths of faith. Water signifies truth, especially the simple truths of the Ten Commandments and the commandments the Lord gave, as stated in the Gospels. When a man lives according to the commandments in their simple form, he is introduced spiritually into the Church. The first truths, as we stated in an earlier chapter of this book, were also represented by the river Jordan, in which the Lord was baptized. A later inner purifying of the spirit is represented by the words of John the Baptist, "He [the Lord] shall baptize you with the Holy Spirit, and with fire." (Matthew 3:11.)

It is to be noted that the cleansing of one's external life by obedience to the commandments may be entirely different with one person from what it is with another. One person may shun evils from a living faith, because they are sins against God; another may shun evils for the sake of his reputation, or from pride, or from some other worldly end. There also are those of whom the Lord said: "Ye make clean the outside of the cup and of the platter, but within they are full of extortion and excess." (Matthew 23:25.) Note that the Lord spoke these words to the learned in the church. It is the spirit and intentions in the deeds and in obedience to the commandments that are regarded in heaven, and never merely the deeds.

One man may lead an orderly life out of ambition to be regarded as a saint or an outstanding man of the Church. His external may appear to be quite impeccable, and yet he is impure in the sight of heaven; whereas another may strive earnestly to order his life from a love of God and his neighbor, and yet he may at times fall into disorders. He may be among those of whom the Lord said: "The spirit indeed is willing, but the flesh is weak." (Matthew 26:41.) Man cannot therefore judge from the outward appearance as to whether one will go to heaven or hell. Some, however, misuse the above words of the Lord to excuse a lack of striving with all one's might to order one's external life, or they may minimize the importance of keeping the commandments as the means of salvation. They forget the words

of the Lord in reply to the question, "What good thing shall
I do, that I may have eternal life?" To which Jesus replied:
"Keep the commandments: . . . Thou shalt do no murder,
Thou shalt not commit adultery, Thou shalt not steal, Thou
shalt not bear false witness, Honor thy father and thy
mother: and, Thou shalt love thy neighbor as thyself."
(Matthew 19:16–19.)

If a man falls into evil, he must repent, for no one who
is unrepentant can enter heaven; but the repentance must
be an actual repentance of the life, not just a repentance
of the mouth. A confession that one is a sinner, without
a change of life, is of no avail, and the change of life must
be both as to the spirit and, as far as possible, as to the
acts in the world.

The external sacraments of the Church have their significance from their internal meaning. If the internal meaning is lacking, the external observances are of no account. In
the Jewish Church, in place of Baptism and the Holy Supper, circumcision, washings and sacrifices, whole burnt of-
ferings, and feasts were used. Concerning these we read:

> Hear the word of the Lord: . . . To what purpose
> is the multitude of your sacrifices unto me? saith the
> Lord: I am full of the burnt offerings of rams, and the
> fat of fed beasts; and I delight not in the blood of bul-
> locks, or of lambs, or of he goats. . . . Bring no more
> vain oblations. . . . Your new moons and your appointed
> feasts my soul hateth; they are a trouble unto me. . . .
> Your hands are full of blood. (Isaiah 1:10–15)
>
> For I desired mercy, and not sacrifice; and the
> knowledge of God more than burnt offerings. (Hosea
> 6:6)

The external representative act is significant and important if it has an internal spirit in it. To illustrate: The
crowning of a king is significant. But the more important
thing is that a king be a good, wise, and just ruler. How
much better is a wise uncrowned king than a foolish

crowned king! In this connection, the Lord, who was the
Christ, the Anointed, the High Priest Himself, was never
anointed king in this world, nor was He inaugurated as high
priest before men. Surely God will judge according to the
heart, and will not condemn anyone because he was not
baptized.

But what, in particular, is the significance or signification of Baptism and the Holy Supper?

Baptism is a washing with water; the Holy Supper is
a partaking of bread and wine.

As we have said, water stands for truth; for we read:
The Lord said:

> If any man thirst, let him come unto me and drink.
> He that believeth on me, as the scripture hath said,
> out of his belly shall flow rivers of living water. [That
> is, a great abundance of Divine truths.] (But this spake
> he of the Spirit, which they that believe on him should
> receive.) (John 7:37–39)

Again:

> Jesus answered and said unto her, Whosoever drink-
> eth of this water shall thirst again: But whosoever
> drinketh of the water that I shall give him shall never
> thirst; but the water that I shall give him shall be in
> him a well of water springing up into everlasting life.
> (John 4:13,14)

It is remarkable that the Lord's first miracle was the
turning of water into wine, that this took place at a marriage feast, and that the water was for the "purifying of
the Jews."

That the water in the water pots for the purifying of
the Jews has a similar signification to baptism is obvious.
The marriage signifies that of the Lord and the Church,
and also the marriage of love and wisdom, or of the good
and the true. The washing of baptism is the removal of evils
by a life lived according to the Divine Truth, as we read:

"Wash you, make you clean; put away the evil of your doings from before mine eyes; cease to do evil; Learn to do well." (Isaiah 1:16,17.)

We read not only of the washing in water, but also of the washing in blood. "Unto him that loved us, and washed us from our sins in his own blood." (Revelation 1:5.)

Blood and wine also represent the Divine Truth, and by being "washed in the blood of the Lord" is represented being purified from evil by a life lived according to the Divine Truth which proceeds from our Lord. Yet the water we are washed in has a different signification from the blood we are washed in. Water, wine, and the Lord's blood are also said to be drink. In Baptism, water is used; in the Holy Supper, wine and bread. In this lies an arcanum, a hidden thing of great importance. What is the difference between water and wine or blood? Why did the Lord as His first miracle turn water into wine?

We read: "For the law was given by Moses; but grace and truth came by Jesus Christ." (John 1:17.)

Water stands for the Truth of the Divine Word, as we first take it up in the mind from without. This is the Law of our life, by which we regulate our actions. If we obey this truth, shunning all things which are contrary to the truth, because God has so commanded, we are washed with water. The Ten Commandments are often called the Law, or the Law of Moses. Baptism represents the purification by a life lived according to the Divine Law. This is the first thing of reformation, and is represented by Baptism.

At a later state, man comes to that truth which is meant by "Grace and Truth came by Jesus Christ." It is this truth that is represented by the water which the Lord turned into wine. This truth is not so much directed to the acts of the body, but to the mind of man, as can be illustrated by the words of the Lord:

Ye have heard that it was said by them of old time, Thou shalt not kill. . . . but I say unto you, That who-

soever is angry with his brother without a cause shall
be in danger of the judgment. (Matthew 5:21)

Ye have heard that it was said by them of old time,
Thou shalt not commit adultery; But I say unto you,
That whosoever looketh on a woman to lust after her
hath committed adultery with her already in his heart.
(Matthew 5:27,28)

Here the Lord raises the question of evil from the plane
of the body to the plane of the mind and heart. There are
many truths by which the mind and heart can be purified.
The inner truths which the Lord gives us are of the Holy
Spirit, for, apart from the Holy Spirit, these truths cannot
be seen in a living way by man. These truths, if they are
loved and done, make an inner dwelling place for the Lord
in man, so that His words can be fulfilled: "At that day ye
shall know that I am in my Father, and ye in me, and I in
you." (John 14:20.)

This inner purification is the "Baptism with the Holy
Spirit and fire," by which, after an inner repentance of the
mind, the Lord can find a clean dwelling place for Himself
with man.

As we have said, water and blood, for which the wine
stood, are both spoken of in relation to washing and drinking. There are truths of the letter which cleanse and also
are a means for the feeding of man's external life; and
there are inner truths which cleanse and feed the inner
mind of the heart and soul.

In the Holy Supper, bread, which the Lord calls His
body, and wine, which the Lord calls His blood, are eaten
and drunk.

In the Writings of Swedenborg, we read: "Bread . . .
denotes the Divine Good of the Lord's Divine Love. . . and
this received by man. Wine denotes the Divine Truth proceeding out of the Good of the Lord's Divine Love and this
received . . . by man." (*Arcana Coelestia,* Number 9393.)

As we have said, the Lord's body is Divine Love in human form, of which the Divine Truth is the blood. Man's spiritual body in heaven is love and charity in human form in an image and likeness of the Lord. And, as man's spiritual love and wisdom are from the Lord, man's spiritual body is fed from the Lord's Divine Body. This is the significance of the Holy Supper.

The great error of many churches is the idea that by being washed in the blood of the Lamb is meant that man is saved by Christ's death on the cross; and the belief that only by faith in this is man saved, rather than by purification by a life according to the Divine good and truth which proceed from our Lord. The passion of the cross was not redemption; it was the last temptation in which the Lord put off all the weaknesses of the human which still remained from His maternal heredity and returned into the pure Divine of His soul, called the Father.

PART THREE

The Second Coming of the Lord—
Swedenborg and "The Lord's
New Church"

[1]

The Second Coming of the Lord

The Lord said:

And then shall appear the sign of the Son of man in heaven. (Matthew 24:30)
Watch therefore: for ye know not what hour your Lord doth come. (Matthew 24:42)

The Apostles, taking His words literally, expected that the Lord would come during their lifetime, for He had said:

Verily I say unto you, This generation shall not pass, till all these things be fulfilled. (Matthew 24:34)

As many centuries passed and the Coming of the Lord was not seen, the Second Coming of the Lord became less and less a reality to the Christian Church. Most persons nowadays either do not believe in the Second Coming or feel an aversion to thinking about it. Yet the Lord made it an important matter of faith. Those few at the present day who place great importance on this subject for the most part have ideas concerning it, such as the sun and moon becoming dark and the stars falling from heaven, which, to most people, appear fantastic, unreal, or impossible, and such ideas, if taken literally, also appear fantastic, unreal, and impossible to us.

How are we to interpret the Lord's words concerning His Second Coming?

Let us consider the nature of prophecy; and in order to

do this, let us first consider the nature of prophecies in the Old Testament concerning the First Coming of the Lord. We find that they fall into two classes. One class of prophecy was literally fulfilled in a most remarkable way. The other class was spiritually fulfilled, but not literally fulfilled.

Those which were literally fulfilled tell the place of the Lord's birth, say that He would be rejected of men and that He would overcome Satan, that is, the power of evil or of the hells, and give a remarkably detailed description of His final trial and death.

On the other hand, we find these prophecies: that He was to be a King who would sit on the throne of David, that He would be a Priest, that He would deliver Israel from its enemies, that He would be a hero, that blood would be sprinkled on His garments, and that He would tread down the wicked.

When asked concerning the prophecy that He, the Christ, was to be a king, He answered: "My kingdom is not of this world." (John 18:36.) He was the Christ, that is, the anointed king, but He was never anointed king with the oil of this world. He sat on the throne of David, but it was not a throne of this world. He was a Priest, but He was never called a priest by anyone in this world. He overcame the enemies of Israel, but it was not the Israel or the enemies of this world. He waged warfare, but not a natural warfare against any in this world.

We read:

> The earth shall quake before them; the heavens shall tremble; the sun and the moon shall be dark, and the stars shall withdraw their shining: And the Lord shall utter his voice before his army: for his camp is very great: for he is strong that executeth his word; for the day of the Lord is great and very terrible; and who can abide it? (Joel 2:10,11)

Again, we read in Joel:

> And I will shew wonders in the heavens and in the

earth, blood, and fire, and pillars of smoke. The sun
shall be turned into darkness, and the moon into blood,
before the great and the terrible day of the Lord come.
(2:30,31)

It might at first be thought that these words refer to
the Second Coming, because of their similarity to the words
in Matthew 24. Yet, referring to these words of Joel, Peter
said:

> For these are not drunken, as ye suppose. . . . But
> this is that which was spoken by the prophet Joel;
> And it shall come to pass in the last days, saith God,
> I will pour out my Spirit upon all flesh; and your sons
> and your daughters shall prophesy, and your young
> men shall see visions, and your old men shall dream
> dreams: And on my servants and on my handmaidens
> I will pour out in those days of my Spirit; and they
> shall prophesy; And I will shew wonders in heaven
> above, and signs in the earth beneath; blood, and fire,
> and vapour of smoke: The sun shall be turned into
> darkness, and the moon into blood, before that great
> and notable day of the Lord come. (Acts 2:15–20)

Though, indeed, at the crucifixion there was an earth-
quake and darkness for three hours, and the sun was darkened, yet there was no general cosmic convulsion such as
one might expect from the prophecy in Joel. No one not
at Jerusalem knew anything about a cosmic convulsion having taken place. Were not the sun, which was darkened,
and the moon, which was turned into blood, things that
are not of this world?

The Jewish Church did not accept the Messiah when He
came because He did not fulfill many of the prophecies the
way they expected. They expected a great earthly king who
would overcome their enemies in this world. Might not
Christians react in the same way if Christ does not fulfill
His Second Coming in the literal way that many Christians
expect?

Turning now to the prophecies of the Second Coming, we also find two very different classes of prophecy.

We are told that the Lord would "come as a thief" (Revelation 3:3; 16:15), that is, unrecognized; that the kingdom of God would come "not with observation" (Luke 17:20), thus, secretly. Contrast this with the description of "the Son of Man coming in the clouds of heaven with power and great glory." (Matthew 24:30.)

Again, contrast the prophecies that the Lord would "sit on the throne of David" with the statement that "we hid as it were our faces from him; he was despised, and we esteemed him not." (Isaiah 53:3.)

The Lord is described as coming again as the Divine Truth. We read:

> Even the Spirit of truth; whom the world cannot receive, because it seeth him not, neither knoweth him: but ye know him; for he dwelleth with you, and shall be in you. I will not leave you comfortless; I will come to you. (John 14:17–18)
>
> Ye have heard how I said unto you, I go away, and come again unto you. (John 14:28)
>
> I have yet many things to say unto you, but ye cannot bear them now. (John 16:12)
>
> The Spirit of truth . . . will guide you into all truth. . . . A little while, and ye shall not see me, and again, a little while, and ye shall see me. (John 16:13,16)

The difference between the above verses which describe the Lord not coming with observation and coming as the spirit of truth which will lead to all truth, and the passages in Matthew which describe the sun being darkened, the stars falling from heaven, and the powers of heaven being shaken and the Son of man coming in the clouds of heaven with power and great glory (24:29,30) is most striking. This is similar to the contrast in the prophecies of the Old Testament concerning the First Coming. As we have shown, the one series of prophecies of the First Coming was fulfilled literally; the other, such as the Lord's coming in glory as a king, was "not of this world."

We might, therefore, assume that the same would apply to the Second Coming; that the Lord's coming as the spirit of truth would be literally fulfilled, but that His coming in glory would be a thing not of this world. There are now some leaders in the Christian Church who believe that the Lord's Second Coming is a coming in His Divine Truth, a teaching we find in the Writings of Swedenborg, written two hundred years ago; but concerning this Divine Truth in which the Lord comes, they have very little idea. Where is the Divine Truth which, like lightning, illumines the whole mind, as we read: "For as the lightning cometh out of the east, and shineth even unto the west; so shall also the coming of the Son of man be" (Matthew 24:27)?

We read:

> Immediately after the tribulation of those days shall the sun be darkened, and the moon shall not give her light, and the stars shall fall from heaven, and the powers of the heavens shall be shaken. . . . and they shall see the Son of man coming in the clouds of heaven with power and great glory. (Matthew 24:29,30)

What are "the clouds of heaven" here spoken of? Are they the clouds of the sky, or are they the clouds of the spiritual heaven? Is the sun here spoken of the sun of this world? Are not the moon, the stars, and the clouds, as is said of the Lord's Kingdom, not of this world?

We read in the Psalms:

> For the Lord God is a sun and shield. (84:11)
> His seed [David's] shall endure for ever, and his throne as the sun before me. (89:36)
> In them hath he set a tabernacle for the sun. (19:4)
> His face did shine as the sun. (Matthew 17:2)

Here the Lord is called a sun. From the Lord as a sun proceeds the heat of love and the light of wisdom. When it says, concerning the Lord's Second Coming, "The sun shall be darkened," does it mean the sun of this world or the Sun of heaven? Is it not more reasonable to think it means the latter? There is no reason for the sun, moon, and stars of this world to fail.

In a prophecy of the Lord's coming, we read: "The light of the sun shall be sevenfold, as the light of seven days, in the day that the Lord bindeth up the breach of his people." (Isaiah 30:26.) This obviously is not speaking of the sun of the world.

When the Lord says, in predicting the Second Coming, that the sun shall be darkened, what is meant?

When agnosticism prevails, when faith is weak, when doubts and confusion over the interpretation of the Word of God prevail, black clouds of doubt and obscurity gather and darken the Sun of heaven, that is, the Lord as the sun. The Lord's love is then not received in men's hearts; and the moon of heaven, that is, faith in the Lord, does not give light; and the stars fall from heaven, that is, the knowledges which are in the inner man fall into worldly reasonings and are destroyed.

This darkness is nowhere more evident than in regard to the subject of the Second Coming, which was a primary matter of faith in the early Christian Church; but the faith concerning it, and the ideas about it, are now so much in darkness that most persons in the Christian Church have no idea as to what is meant and many feel an aversion even to considering the subject.

> Then shall appear the sign of the Son of man in Heaven. . . . and they shall see the Son of man coming in the clouds of heaven with power and great glory.
> (Matthew 24:30)

That clouds stand for obscurity is evident, but here the clouds stand particularly for the obscure things of the Word of God. Many things in the letter of the Word are obscure, called by the Lord "dark sayings," which are not understood.

The Son of Man, coming in the clouds of heaven with power and great glory, is the Lord as the Divine Truth coming with authority and shedding a wonderful light on the whole of the Word of God.

What are the leading subjects which the Lord will reveal in His Second Coming? They are those things which He spoke of when He said, "I have yet many things to say unto you, but ye cannot bear them now." He indeed tells us, for He says: "At that day ye shall know that I am in my Father, and ye in me, and I in you." (John 14:20.)

"These things have I spoken unto you in proverbs: but the time cometh, when I shall no more speak unto you in proverbs, but I shall shew you plainly of the Father." (John 16:25.) Here we are taught clearly that the Lord will come again to reveal the relation of the Son to the Father, that is, the nature of the Divine Trinity, and how the Lord was glorified; also, the nature of the relation of the Lord and man, and how the Lord is present in man. He would come to reveal the nature of the Divine Love and Wisdom and the manner in which man is born again from the Lord and becomes His son. All the wonders of the relation of the Lord and man, and the nature of man's spiritual development, things which in the Word were given in parables, would then be opened.

Some Christians, when they reflect, might well wonder whether, if they had lived at the time the Lord came into the world, they would have believed in Him or not.

Put yourself in the place of the Jew who listened to the Lord. How would you feel if a young man condemned the respected priests and leaders of your church, calling them hypocrites, saying that they had made the Church a den of thieves, condemned your church and nation—on all of which you prided yourself? Could you have believed in Him as the promised Messiah?

Are you sure you would be any more likely to recognize the Lord, when He came again, "not with observation" but "as a thief in the night"? The Lord said: "When the

Son of man cometh, shall he find faith on the earth?" (Luke 18:8.) Do not these words indicate that at the Lord's Coming, the Christian Church would no more recognize and acknowledge Him than the Jewish Church did when He came to them as their Messiah?

The Jews expected the Messiah to come in a spectacular way and fulfill their ambitions by making them the greatest and most powerful nation, but He did not come in that way. Do not those Christians who await the Second Coming for the most part expect something spectacular which will fulfill their ambitions? But does He come that way?

As we read in the first chapter of John, the Lord is the Word, the Divine Truth, which enlighteneth everyone. He comes again as the Word, the Divine Truth, not now in parables, but plainly.

In *True Christian Religion*, by Emanuel Swedenborg, we read:

The Second Coming of the Lord is not a Coming in Person, but in the Word, which is from Him, and is Himself. (Caption before Number 776, *T.C.R.*)

It is written in many places that the Lord will come in the clouds of heaven. And as no one has hitherto known what is meant by "the clouds of heaven," it has been believed that the Lord would appear to them in Person. Heretofore it has not been known that "the clouds of heaven" mean the Word in the sense of the letter, and that the "glory and power" in which He is then to come, mean the spiritual sense of the Word, because no one as yet has had the least conjecture that there is a spiritual sense in the Word, such as this sense is in itself. But as the Lord has now opened to me the spiritual sense in the Word, and has granted to me to be associated with angels and spirits in their world as one of them, it is disclosed to me that "a cloud of heaven" means the Word in the natural sense, and "glory" the Word in the spiritual sense, and "power"

the Lord's power through the Word." (*T.C.R.*, Number
776)

The Second Coming of the Lord is effected by means
of a man, to whom the Lord has manifested Himself
in Person, and whom He has filled with His Spirit, that
he may teach the Doctrines of the New Church from
the Lord by means of the Word. (Caption before Number 779, *T.C.R.*)

Since the Lord cannot manifest Himself in Person,
as shown just above, and nevertheless has foretold that
He was to come and establish a new church, which is
Nova Hierosolyma [the New Jerusalem], it follows
that He will do this by means of a man, who is able
not only to receive these doctrines in his understanding,
but also to publish them by the press. That the Lord
manifested Himself before me, His servant, and sent me
to this office, and He afterward opened the eyes of my
spirit and thus introduced me into the spiritual world
and granted me to see the heavens and the hells . . .
and this now continually for several years, I affirm in
truth; as also that from the first day of that call I have
not received anything whatever pertaining to the doctrines of that church from any angel, but from the Lord
alone while I have read the Word. (*T.C.R.*, Number
779)

In order that the Lord might be continuously present with me He has unfolded to me the spiritual sense
of His Word, wherein is Divine truth in its very light,
and it is in this light that He is continually present.
For His presence in the Word is by means of the spiritual sense and in no other way; through the light of
this sense He passes into the obscurity of the literal
sense, which is like what takes place when the light of
the sun in day time is passing through an interposing
cloud. That the sense of the letter of the Word is like
a cloud, and the spiritual sense is the glory, the Lord
Himself being the Sun from which the light comes, and

thus that the Lord is the Word, has been shown above.
(*T.C.R.*, Number 780)

When one first reads the above words, they may seem
strange, impossible, and even fantastic. Yet if we consider
the problem, how does the Lord make His promised Second
Coming? What alternative is there to the idea that the Lord
does this through a man who has been filled with His Spirit?
We may discover that there is no other way. Some hold that
the Lord will literally come in the clouds of this world.
We read in the book of Revelation:

> And the sun became black as sackcloth of hair, and
> the moon became as blood; and the stars of heaven fell
> unto the earth, even as a fig tree casteth her untimely
> figs, when she is shaken of a mighty wind. And the
> heaven departed as a scroll when it is rolled together;
> and every mountain and island were moved out of their
> places. (6:12–14)

Few who know the size of the stars, as being immensely
larger than the earth, and their immense distance from
earth, can take this prophecy as being about to take place
literally; besides which, if it were to take place literally,
how could the other prophecies which the Lord made concerning His Second Coming be fulfilled, namely, that He
would come as the "spirit of truth," that He had "many
things to say" unto them; but they could not bear them then.
He would come as "the spirit of truth," which would guide
them into "all truth."

Still, there are very few who will have an open mind
toward what Swedenborg says concerning the Second Coming. They may be impressed by other things said in the
Writings of Swedenborg, but they will find this a "hard
saying."

Many who have followed what is written in this book
with a certain affirmation will here tend to turn away.

This brings to mind what is said about those who followed the Lord, when He said to them:

I am the living bread which came down from heaven: if any man eat of this bread, he shall live for ever: and the bread that I will give is my flesh, which I will give for the life of the world. (John 6:51)

Many therefore of his disciples, when they had heard this, said, This is an hard saying; who can hear it? (John 6:60)

From that time many of his disciples went back, and walked no more with him. (John 6:66)

A friend of Swedenborg wrote to him, saying that if he left out of his work the descriptions of the spiritual world and his conversations with angels and spirits, many would accept his doctrine; to which Swedenborg replied that the Lord had commanded him to include these portions of his works.

We often read in the Old Testament that the Lord appeared to a person and gave him a command, and to some this does not appear impossible. But that He should have done so to a man in relatively modern times appears incredible and even fantastic to nearly everyone. But why is this?

There are some who do not believe in any direct revelation of the Word of God to men or in the possible communication between angels (who are men that have died) and men on earth. Such are apt to regard themselves as having a scientific approach. Yet the true scientific approach is an open-minded approach, an approach without prejudice or preconceived ideas; an approach which takes into account all known facts. The facts are that nearly every people on earth have believed in the communication of the departed with men living on earth. To throw out this immense testimony out of prejudice is certainly not scientific and must therefore come from a decision which has its origin in the will.

Those who are proud and vain hate the idea that anyone can see anything they cannot see. It has been observed that some of those who are color-blind and are not aware of this fact become angry and insist that they can see colors when it is demonstrated that they are color-blind.

If those who see a matter clearly speak to others who are in obscurity on the matter, the latter often intensely resent it and may become angry and wish to persecute the former.

Many Jews resented the fact that "he [Jesus] taught them as one having authority, and not as the scribes." (Matthew 7:29.)

If Swedenborg had said that he spoke from himself, instead of saying that he spoke from God, more would have accepted his teaching. Compare this with the saying of the Lord: "My doctrine is not mine, but his that sent me. If any man will do his will, he shall know of the doctrine, whether it be of God, or whether I speak of myself. He that speaketh of himself seeketh his own glory; but he that seeketh his glory that sent him, the same is true, and no unrighteousness is in him." (John 7:16–18.)

Try to explain with great definiteness to a man who is proud of his learning something which he cannot see, an idea which he cannot grasp, and observe his reactions. As long as one will admit that one's own ideas have certain obscurities in them, and it is a matter of opinion, it is all right; but as soon as one says it is as clear as four times four are sixteen, the other is likely to become angry and react irrationally.

For those who believe that there has been communication with God and with angels, as recounted in the Bible, it is still difficult to believe that a relatively modern man could have such communication, because they think such communication came to an end nearly two thousand years ago. Yet if there is a Divine purpose to be fulfilled, it is obviously prejudice that would say it is impossible for God to revive this communication with a man for the sake of a Divine purpose. Yet in spite of the obvious force of this argument, prejudice is so strong that few can overcome it, and few will consider Swedenborg's claim with an open and unprejudiced mind.

A man who has an open mind will view the Writings of Swedenborg unprejudiced by habits of thought or prevailing opinions; he will carefully weigh what is said as to whether it is in agreement with God's love and His desire to communicate the truths of the spirit to man. The question is, Do they reveal a God of Divine Love and Divine Wisdom, of Divine Mercy and Justice? Do they reveal a life after death, that one can perceive is the only kind of life in which man could be happy to eternity? Do they reveal the kind of communication between God and man that is in accordance with God's love and the nature of man? A man with an open mind will struggle to answer these questions for himself and will not be satisfied until he has found the answer.

The documents concerning Swedenborg's life are contained in three large tomes. There are a number of biographies, two of which have a length of four hundred large pages. The following is a brief sketch of his life.

His father, Jesper Swedberg (the name was changed to Swedenborg when the family was ennobled), was at the time of Swedenborg's birth Court Chaplain at the court of Charles XI. Later, Jesper Swedberg was appointed by the king as first professor of Theology at Upsala University and, shortly afterward, as Rector and Dean of the Cathedral. Later he became Bishop of Skara, and his diocese included "New Sweden" on the Delaware River. Emanuel Swedenborg's mother was the daughter of a wealthy mine owner. She was a modest and lovable person. When Emanuel was eight years old, his mother died. Some time later, Bishop Swedberg married again, and Emanuel had a new mother, who loved him dearly. He had a happy childhood. When he was four years old, the family moved to the university town of Upsala, the seat of the leading university of Sweden. At the age of eleven Swedenborg entered the university. He was bright in his studies and took a very active part in an institution which was somewhat like a fraternity but whose activities were mostly intellectual and included debating. These fraternities were called "nations," and the students joined them according to the part of the country from which they came.

While he was living with his father, he took great delight in listening to the religious discussions which went on in the home when visitors came.

He was born in 1688 and died eighty-four years later in the year 1772.

To convey even a general impression of the remarkable career and eighty-four years of Swedenborg's life in a chapter of a book is not easy. There are few indeed who lived two hundred years ago whose life is so fully documented as Swedenborg's.

2

Swedenborg: Youth and Scientific Period

When Emanuel Swedenborg was fifteen, his father was appointed Bishop of Skara and left Upsala to reside in the episcopal mansion of Brunsbo. The youth remained in Upsala to continue his studies, staying with his sister, Anna, and his brother-in-law, Eric Benzelius, the university librarian.

At the time that Swedenborg was in the university, a controversy was raging between the old school of scholastic education and the new spirit of scientific investigation. Descartes, who had lived the last year of his life in Sweden, had given great impetus to the newer philosophic-scientific point of view. Eric Benzelius, with whom Swedenborg lived, was keenly interested in the new scientific development, and by him Emanuel was fired with enthusiasm and the ambition of advancing Sweden and making it one of the leading countries in culture, philosophy, science, and manufacturing.

Some time after Swedenborg was graduated, he journeyed to England, Holland, and France. He was away for four years, most of which he spent in England. Here he contacted the most learned men of the times and worked with some, for example, Halley, the famous astronomer, after whom Halley's comet was named.

At this time, Swedenborg's center of interest was astronomy, mathematics, and inventions. He worked out a system of finding the longitude of any place by the sighting

of two stars in relation to the moon. The difficulty he en-
countered was that at that time the tables of the stars and
moon were not sufficiently accurate to accomplish this purpose. His proposed inventions included a fixed-wing flying
machine, a submarine, something like a player piano, and
many other inventions. He also wrote Latin poetry. He
sent a list of the most worth-while English authors, including Shakespeare, to his brother-in-law, with the recommen-
dation that they should be studied in Sweden. When in
London, he made a practice of living with various artisans
and picking up their trades. In this way, he learned to
grind lenses, to make scientific instruments, and also the
craft of bookbinding. At this period his enthusiasm was
given to science and its practical application. Although he
was intensely ambitious, his ambition was focused on the
advancement of Sweden rather than being merely personal.

On his return to Sweden, he worked with Polhem, the
great Swedish inventor and engineer. Charles XII, King of
Sweden, took a very active interest in the inventions and
mathematics of Polhem and Swedenborg, and encouraged
Swedenborg in the publication of the first scientific magazine in the Swedish language. With the encouragement of
the king, work was commenced on the great canal linking
Stockholm and Gothenburg, traversing Sweden and having
a length of three hundred miles. Swedenborg was put in
charge of the construction of the locks. About this time he
made a name for himself by transporting naval sloops over
fifteen miles of rugged territory, giving Sweden a naval
advantage in the war with Norway.

At this time, Swedenborg desired to marry Polhem's
daughter; Polhem favored such a union, but as the daughter
preferred someone else, Swedenborg withdrew. He never
married.

Swedenborg contemplated the idea of applying for the
appointment as first professor of Mechanics at the University of Upsala. This subject would have included what are
now called Physics and Engineering. But as there was an

insufficiency of funds for the university, this plan did not materialize. When the opportunity came up at a later date, Swedenborg turned it down in order to accept the position of Assessor on the Board of Mines.

The Board of Mines had broad powers: mining was the chief source of Sweden's wealth. The whole economy of Sweden depended on the success of Swedish mines. The Board of Mines was directly responsible to the Crown. It controlled all mining and allied interests, having every power short of actual ownership. It appointed mining officials and settled industrial disputes involving owners and workers. It regulated prices and imposed or withdrew taxes. It licensed new mines, forges, and all buildings and mapped out the distribution of charcoal—the fuel in those days. It was in charge of metal testing, charts and measurements, and a chemical laboratory. Swedenborg undoubtedly felt that by accepting this position he could be of greater service to the welfare of Sweden than in any other way. He had far more knowledge of mechanics and engineering than anyone else on the Board. In fact, there was scarcely anyone else in Sweden who had such a broad knowledge in this field. On accepting this position, he set about learning everything it was possible to learn about mining. He visited mines all over Europe, and finally wrote the most comprehensive work on iron and copper mining and smelting then extant. This work, which was written in Latin, made him famous throughout Europe. It was, however, a description not merely of applied science and engineering, but also of what we now call pure science, which also involved philosophic principles. Swedenborg was an indefatigable worker. The minutes of the Board of Mines report that he traveled extensively in Sweden, to settle disputes and to oversee the mining; the daily meetings he attended when the Board was in session indicate a labor which with most men would have left little time for other pursuits. But in his spare time he was acquiring a thorough knowledge of all the science and philosophy known in his day. During his travels he made remarkable geological observations, with the result that he is considered by those who are acquainted with the facts one of the fathers of geological science. It would take a large book to enumerate all the contributions Swedenborg made to science and philosophy. In science, he made contributions and sometimes discoveries in Anatomy, Cosmology, Crystallography, Mineralogy, Psychology, and other sciences which were one hundred years or more before his time.

Svante Arrhenius, Nobel prize winner, vouched for Swedenborg's cosmology, which surmised the nebular hypothesis and the existence of galactic universes. Anatomists said that he was the first to localize the mental processes in the cortical cells of the brain. He also stated that different parts of the brain controlled different parts of the body, and that nerves from the upper part of the brain controlled the lowest part of the body and vice versa. Leading modern anatomists have marveled at how Swedenborg came to this knowledge, which has since been verified, from the limited anatomical knowledge of his day. His placing of the seat of consciousness in the cortex or cortical cells of the brain was a discovery which may be compared in importance with Harvey's discovery of the nature of the circulation of the blood in the body.

To give even a general idea of Swedenborg's philosophic and scientific works, which are contained in many large volumes, would require a book in itself. We shall here give only some idea of the purposes he had in mind. In his early manhood his ambition was centered in the advancement of Sweden in science and industry. But as he approached middle age, while still serving Sweden diligently in the practical matters of his official office, his mind turned more and more to Philosophy. He had the strong belief that pihlosophy had to be built not only on a scientific foundation, but also on the Word of God. His aim came to be to see the relation of God to His creation. He never questioned the being of God, for in all things of science he saw an order that must have a source in God, and above all, he had faith in the Bible.

In all his later scientific works his aim was to demonstrate the marvelous laws and order of creation as emanating from a God of Divine Love, Divine Wisdom, and Divine Order. In order to convey as full an idea as possible of this, he felt he must have as broad and deep a knowledge of science and the laws governing it as possible. His first concentration along these lines was in Cosmology, within which he sought to show the relation of Divine Order in God Himself to the things of the created world, and by what order the material world was created from God. He took as his premise that God was Divine Order Itself and that, therefore, everything which He did was necessarily done according to the laws of order, including creation. To give too brief an account of Swedenborg's works on creation would lead rather to confusion than enlightenment, according to the saying: "A little knowledge is a dangerous thing." (Alexander Pope, *Essay on Criticism.*) Really, it is not the little knowledge that is dangerous, but the vast ignorance still remaining!

Swedenborg's objective was to see as clearly as possible the aim and purpose of human life, and the relation of God to man and of man to God. After his large work on Cosmology, he turned to the study of Anatomy. His aim here was to acquire a knowledge of the relation of the soul, the mind, and the body.

The principle that guided him in his studies was a truly scientific one, namely, that before we can make any approach to a subject, we must have a sufficient body of factual knowledge. From this, by contemplation, we discover laws. These laws must then be verified by again checking them with known facts. Swedenborg's faith was not, indeed, dependent on science, but his effort at this time was to strengthen faith, which was being brought into doubt by many philosophers and scientists. A true philosophy and science, he believed, would strengthen and confirm faith in God.

He saw the human body and all the laws governing it

as a vehicle for the soul to express itself. He said that the conscious mind corresponded to the soul, and the body corresponded to the mind. By "correspondence" he meant a relationship such as shown by the fact that when the mind is happy, the face smiles; and when the mind is grieved, the body weeps. When love is stirred, the heart beats more rapidly. These relations are obvious, and of them we are instinctively conscious; but he maintained that this revealed a universal law, and that every least thing of the body, of most of which we are not conscious, corresponds to things of the mind and soul. For example, the heart corresponds to love, and the lungs to thought. Love affects the beating of the heart, and thought the breathing of the lungs. The relation of the two correspond to the relation of the will and understanding. To consider these matters fully would also require a separate book.

Swedenborg has been compared to Leonardo da Vinci as being a universal genius. In the eighteenth century there were a number of persons who were outstanding in various fields: Jefferson was outstanding not only as President, but also as a political philosopher, an architect, and an inventor. Benjamin Franklin was a statesman, economist, moralist, and inventor, besides having practical accomplishments in many fields. Neither of these men was, however, an outstanding theologian as well.

Swedenborg was not only a great scientist and philosopher, but he was also an outstanding administrator, a capable businessman, an economist, a legislator, a judge in mining disputes, an inventor, and, above all, a great theologian—in a word, an outstanding man in nearly all realms of human endeavor.

Most persons have a limited bent of mind. This means that they are attracted to a limited field. When they are, therefore, confronted with the Writings of Swedenborg, they are often repelled. Swedenborg is too idealistic for the realist, and too realistic and matter-of-fact for the idealist. He is too poetical and spiritual for the materialistic scientist, and too matter-of-fact and rationalistic for those who are poetically or mystically inclined. He is too literal for those who seek a vague spiritual interpretation, and too spiritual for the literalist. In a word, the golden mean appeals to few. Most people prefer one extreme or another, according to the bent of their mind. A uniting in a balanced proportion of all aspects of life has, to most people, little appeal.

When the family of Bishop Swedberg was ennobled, Emanuel Swedenborg regularly took his place as head of the family at the sessions of the House of Nobles, which was the most powerful legislative body in Sweden.

Swedenborg's Theological Period

When Swedenborg was fifty-nine years old, one of the councilors on the Board of Mines died, and Swedenborg was unanimously recommended by the Board for advancement to the position of councilor. He, however, petitioned the king that another should be selected and that he should be released from office, as he wished to engage in other important work, the nature of which he did not mention.

For more than thirty years, he reminded King Frederick, he had served as an official on the Board, had made frequent journeys and published many works for which he had never asked any recompense from the country. He therefore requested that His Majesty now grant him the continued use of half his salary in his retirement, but without the customary honorary title of councilor.

This favor the king so much the more gladly granted as he felt sure that the new work on which Swedenborg was then engaged would, like all his other publications, contribute to the welfare of the country. When Swedenborg handed in the royal decree releasing him from

duty, all the members of the Board of Mines expressed
their regret at losing so worthy a colleague, and asked
that the assessor continue to attend the sessions until
all those cases had been settled in which he had partici-
pated. To this he consented and we find him present at
five more sessions. On June 17, 1747, on the eve of his
sixth foreign journey, Swedenborg took leave of the
Royal Board of Mines, thanking all the members for the
favors he had enjoyed at their hands during his connection with the Board and commending himself to their
continued kindly remembrance.

The Royal Board thanked the assessor for the min-
ute care and fidelity with which he had attended to the
duties of his office as an assessor up to the present time,
and wished him a prosperous journey and a happy return; after which he departed. (Tafel, *Documents Concerning Swedenborg*, I, 464 ff., Swedenborg to the
King.)

Swedenborg at Fifty-five Commences a New Work

This important work of Swedenborg's was the exposition
of the Word of God. During the next twenty-five years, he
continued to publish his theological works, at first anony-
mously, no one knowing their authorship.

When he was seventy-one years old, returning to his
native land from England, he stopped at Gothenburg. While
at dinner in company with fifteen others, he suddenly an-
nounced that a fire had broken out in Stockholm, three hundred miles away, and was burning quite a large section of
the town and was approaching his house. He later said that
the fire had been arrested, three houses from his, and gave a
description of the extent and region of the damage. This
caused quite a stir, and the account rapidly spread through
the town. Three days later, a messenger brought from Stockholm the news of the fire, which was just as Swedenborg had
described it. About this time he included his name on one of

his theological works, and it became known that he was the author of his other works.

This caused much excitement in Stockholm. In these works Swedenborg had said that he had been Divinely commissioned by the Lord to unfold the Word and that for many years he had spoken with those who had died, in full wakefulness, as man with man. One can imagine the astonishment at this announcement if we picture in our minds what would happen if Herbert Hoover were to announce that ever since leaving the Presidency, at Divine command, he had been publishing an explication of the Bible and was in daily communication with those who had departed this life. Many thought that Swedenborg must have become demented. Yet during the period he had been writing these books, no one had observed anything strange or unusual in his behavior. He had taken part in the sessions of the House of Nobles. Count Höpken, the Prime Minister, said of him during this period, "He possessed a sound judgment upon all occasions; he saw everything clearly and expressed himself well on every subject. The most solid memorials on finance and the best penned, at the Diet of 1761, were presented by him." As a result of one of these memorials, Swedenborg was asked to sit on the government board in control of the finances of Sweden, but he declined.

As a result of what had taken place, a number of the leading citizens called on Swedenborg, and their testimony was unanimous that he spoke most clearly and rationally on every subject. But we do not need such testimony, for the books which he published are most clear and rational, with nothing to indicate any mental disturbance, if one believes in the possibility of communication with those in the spiritual world.

Swedenborg was such a highly respected, good, and lovable man that no one who knew him intimately or who has studied his life has questioned his honesty or sincerity. The only question was whether he was suffering from delusions.

When Swedenborg was asked by Count Höpken, the

Prime Minister of Sweden, why he included the description of the spiritual world in his writings, "of which ignorance makes jest and derision," Swedenborg replied: "that he was too old to sport with spiritual things, and too much concerned for his eternal welfare to yield to such foolish notions, assuring me on his hope for salvation, that imagination produced in him none of his revelations, which were true, and were from what had been heard and seen." (Tafel, II: 241–242, 239–240, 416; I:66.)

Swedenborg was once asked why the Lord had chosen him instead of one of the clergy to make the new revelation, to which he replied:

> In the same manner that fishermen were made disciples and apostles by the Lord; and that I also from early youth had been a spiritual fisherman. On hearing this the inquirer asked, What is a spiritual fisherman? I replied that a spiritual fisherman in the spiritual sense of the Word, signifies a man who investigates and teaches natural truth, and afterwards, spiritual truths rationally. (*The Intercourse Between the Soul and the Body*, Number 20.)

To investigate spiritual truths rationally is to gather together a sufficient number of facts, and upon these, with an enlightened understanding, to come to a conclusion as to the laws involved. As Swedenborg was a master of this in relation to science, he was well suited to do the same in relation to the phenomena of the spiritual world.

Three weeks before his death, Swedenborg predicted the day of his decease. When he told the maid who looked after his room, and who was very fond of him, the approaching day of his death, she said he was as happy as if he were going to a fair. (Tafel, II: 546)

Mr. Hartley, a friend, visited him when Swedenborg was nearing his end. In the presence of another friend, Mr. Hartley solemnly besought Swedenborg to declare whether all that he had written was strictly true, or whether any part or parts were to be excepted. "I have written nothing but the truth," Swedenborg replied with some warmth, "as you will have more and more confirmed to you all the days of your life, provided you keep close to the Lord and faithfully serve Him alone by shunning evils of all kinds as sins against Him, and diligently searching His Word which from beginning to end bears incontestable witness to the truth of the doctrines I have delivered to the world." (Tafel, II: 579–580)

The afternoon of March twenty-ninth—the predicted day—Mrs. Shearsmith (Swedenborg was living with the Shearsmiths in London at the time) and Elizabeth, the maid, were seated at his bedside. It was the close of a peaceful spring Sabbath. Swedenborg heard the clock strike and asked what time it was. When they answered, "Five o'clock," he said, "That is good. I thank you. God bless you." He heaved a gentle sigh and tranquilly expired. (Sigstedt, *The Swedenborg Epic*, p. 433.)

Skepticism About Swedenborg

The great majority refuse to believe that such communication as Swedenborg had with those who have died is possible, and therefore will not evaluate with an open mind Swedenborg's statements about the spiritual world.

Swedenborg's theological writings contain much that is obviously true—truths that have affected the thinking of the world on many subjects. They would have had a wider acceptance if he had not spoken of his intercourse with angels and if he had omitted the description of the spiritual world.

Why Swedenborg's Declarations Are Not Generally Accepted

Why is it that most persons will not believe that such communication as Swedenborg said he had is possible? The whole evidence of the history of the human race is that communication with the dead has taken place in more ancient times. Why, then, cannot people believe that such communication took place in relatively modern times if the evidence is sufficiently strong? We can see no reason but prejudice. This prejudice is based on many things. There have often been charlatans and fakers who have made fantastic claims, so that reasonable people are naturally wary. Swedenborg himself warned against thoughtless credulity on the part of those who had a tendency toward the fantastic.

There are many who feel an aversion for thinking about the life after death, because they find it disturbing, depressing, and troublesome. They form a mental block as a means of escaping the problem of death so that they can live comfortably in this world.

Others are not willing at heart to "Seek first the Kingdom of God" (Matthew 6:33) because they are eager to seek the good things of this world. There are others who are prejudiced against the Writings of Swedenborg because these do not agree with the habits of thought or the teachings in which they have been brought up from childhood. Most, however, are too lazy to think about matters which require concentration of thought in a field to which they are unaccustomed and in which they see no material profit.

Swedenborg had been an open-minded scientist, and as such he did not expect a proposition to be accepted on the mere statement of anyone, but only on the thing being seen as true by the person accepting it. All he asked for was an open-minded consideration of the matter.

Besides the fire in Stockholm, there were several similar incidents. Of the two most widely known, of which there were many witnesses, the first was the queen's secret. Queen Ulrika Eleanora, having heard of Swedenborg, was curious to speak with him. In order to test him, she asked if he could tell her a secret that only her brother, who had died, and she knew. Some days later, Swedenborg visited the court and, calling the queen aside, told her the secret, at which she nearly fainted.

The second was the account concerning the widow of Monsieur de Marteville, the Dutch ambassador to Sweden. A goldsmith presented Mme. de Marteville with a bill, demanding 2,500 Dutch guilders in payment for a silver service bought by her husband. Mme. de Marteville was sure the bill had been paid but could not find the receipt. She was told that Swedenborg might be able to help her. Shortly afterward, through Swedenborg's aid, she was told that the receipt was in a secret drawer about which she did not know and there she found it. These accounts had wide circulation. When Swedenborg was asked by a friend whether they were true, he said they were but were of little moment, and that his writings were to be judged on their contents and not on the basis of such events.

There are two kinds of proof, one a demonstration to the senses, or scientific demonstration on the basis of material facts; the other, by internal evidence, namely, whether the matter is reasonable and harmonious, is in agreement with the laws of the mind, and strikes one as being obviously true. One does not ask for scientific proof that stealing or cheating is bad and honesty is good.

Swedenborg gave as the criterion of judgment "the self-sounding (or resounding) reason of love." That is, his criterion is whether the idea rings true or not—not merely from a cold judgment devoid of feeling, but from a love of

God and one's neighbor, and from a love of the Kingdom of God. A man who is devoid of such loves has no judgment in spiritual matters, for they have no significance or reality to him.

If we consider the Writings of Swedenborg, there are three aspects from which we can come to a judgment: the unfolding of the Word or Bible; the theology contained; and the description of heaven and hell.

The Spiritual World

We have considered the first two above, but to many the third point appears like a real stumbling block. That Swedenborg should have lived consciously in the spiritual world, speaking with those who have departed this world, as man with man, appears to them incredible.

Why is it that this is so difficult to believe? Is denial of this possibility based on reason or on prejudice? On intellectual or on emotional grounds? Most would say it is based on rational or intellectual grounds. But is this really so?

If we believe that there is a life after death, to have knowledge concerning it would obviously be useful, as it would enable us better to prepare for it, and this the more insofar as it became a greater reality to us. It would also remove the fear of death. Many have said they would like to believe in a spiritual world such as is described by Swedenborg, but are not able to.

We have said it is useful to know the nature of life after death. Why could not God reveal this? And if God wished to reveal it, what other way would be more suitable than to introduce the spirit of a man into it while he was still living on earth? From this it can be seen that the grounds for not considering, with an open mind, the possibility of Swedenborg's being introduced into the spiritual world are not intellectual. They must, therefore, be emotional or from prejudice.

What, then, are these emotional prejudices?

1. Many persons are fearful of being considered naïve and credulous, and of being ridiculed on this ground.

2. The spirit or fashion of the times is scientific materialism, and few have the ability or will to think clearly, apart from the intellectual fashion of their day.

3. Many persons wish to appear up-to-date or modern. These people fear to be considered old-fashioned in their ideas; and a belief in the possibility of open communication with the dead is not considered modern.

4. Whereas many have a vague hope for a life after death, with most there is little living faith in such a life.

5. In the case of many people, their life is contrary to the idea of "seeking first the Kingdom of God and his righteousness" (Matthew 6:33), and they do not wish to be disturbed in the life they are leading.

Because Swedenborg described his experiences in the spiritual world, he has been called a paranoiac. Hardly anyone who has read the Writings of Swedenborg and is acquainted with his life doubts his sincerity. The argument for his mental aberration is based solely on the preconceived idea that such communication is impossible. But those holding such a view, if logical, must necessarily apply this epithet to John the Baptist, the Apostle John, Paul and the other Apostles, and the Lord Himself, all of whom were accused in their time of being mad or possessed by a devil, and the same ban applies to the Old Testament prophets, such as Ezekiel and Daniel.

Swedenborg is said to have suffered from paranoia. This word gives the impression that this is a modern, scientific diagnosis. Many psychologists apply the same term to the above-named religious teachers.

"Paranoia" is defined in *Webster's Dictionary* as being "mental derangement; insanity; especially a chronic form of insanity characterized by a very gradual impairment of the intellect, systematized delusions, and usually by delusions of persecution producing homicidal tendencies. In its

mild form paranoia may consist of well-marked crocheti-
ness in persons commonly called 'cranks.' Paranoiacs usually
show evidence of bodily and nervous degeneration, and
may have hallucinations of sight and hearing."

Swedenborg's writings are very clear, logical, and sys-
tematic. As shown above, as to his person, he was highly respected by all who knew him; moreover, he was cheerful
and friendly. He led a very normal and balanced life, and he
was remarkably vigorous in both mind and body until his
death at the age of eighty-four. All these characteristics are
the opposite of paranoia. A prominent psychologist, puz-
zled by Swedenborg, said he was unique and did not fit
into any known classification.

The sole reason for designating Swedenborg a paranoiac
was his statements that he had open communication with
those who had died. This is based on the hypothesis that such
communication is not possible.

Taking such a hypothesis is totally unscientific. The true
scientist examines evidence with an open and unprejudiced
mind. If we go back in history, there is, as we have said, a
great deal of evidence of the communication of some people
with those who have died. But Swedenborg was the only
man, in nearly two thousand years, who claimed such open
communication and at the same time was a very wise and
learned man and profoundly influenced the thinking of some
of the most famous men and women during the past two
hundred years. The fact that Swedenborg was the only man
of this character during this period is no proof of the im-
possibility of such communication.

Although it might be said that open communication with
those who have died has not been fully proved from a merely
scientific point of view, there is certainly no scientific proof
that it has not taken place and much evidence from the
past favors its possibility. It is, therefore, totally unscientific to call Swedenborg a paranoiac on the basis of an un-
proved hypothesis, as has been done. Although the above
argument is, we believe, unanswerable, most will still cling

to their opinion out of preconceived prejudice which makes one with the fashion of the thought of the day; modern education has so strongly formed the patterns of thought that one who has not an exceptionally independent mind can scarcely escape from the type of scientific thinking that is prevalent.

Swedenborg's Theological Writings

As we have said, the Theological Works of Swedenborg were extensively read during the nineteenth century, and many writers, poets, and philosophers were profoundly influenced by them. The whole religious thinking of the world was directly or indirectly modified by Swedenborg's Writings. As a result of this, in some respects, the theology in the Writings of Swedenborg does not appear to be in such contrast to the prevailing theology of the day as it did in the time when Swedenborg wrote his works. Yet in other respects, there is a greater divergence. Swedenborg's Writings, as to their letter, were accommodated to the thinking and language of his age; yet they have a universal application to all ages. But, on account of their more obvious meaning, they appear more remote to the casual twentieth-century reader than they did to those of the nineteenth century. This accounts for the fact that they have been less studied by eminent men in this century than by those in the last; yet a deeper study manifests their great importance for the present day.

Swedenborg Not a Mystic

Many of those who have heard of Swedenborg have misconceptions and prejudices, based on hearsay or on ideas quoted from the Writings of Swedenborg out of their context. The most common misconception of Swedenborg is that he was a mystic.

In *Webster's Dictionary* the definition of "mystical" includes: "remote or beyond human comprehension; baffling understanding; unknowable, obscure."

The definition of "mysticism," however, includes the following:

> The doctrine that the ultimate nature of reality or the divine essence may be known, in an immediate apprehension, intuition or insight, differing from all ordinary sensation or ratiocination, hence the experience or ecstasy of those mystics who claim to attain this insight in vision, trance or sense of absorption in or union with the divine spirit or ultimate being . . . a knowledge of God or spiritual things, unattainable by the natural intellect, and incapable of being analysed or explained.

Leading ideas in the Writings of Swedenborg are that Divine Spiritual or theological ideas can be understood and explained and grasped by the mind, that the rational mind is capable of receiving inmost truths, and this not in ecstasy but in wakefulness and in the clear light of the intellect. His Writings also oppose the idea of absorption in the Divine Spirit.

In the *Encyclopaedia Britannica* under "mysticism," we read:

> Swedenborg, though selected by Emerson in his "Representative Men" as the typical mystic, belongs rather to the history of spiritualism than to that of mysticism as understood in this article. He possesses the cool temperament of the man of science rather than the fervid Godward aspiration of the mystic proper; and the speculative impulse which lies at the root of this form of thought is almost entirely absent from his writings. Accordingly, his supernatural revelations resemble a course of lessons in celestial geography more than a description of the beatific vision.

Although Swedenborg rightly does not belong in a class

with the mystics, still less does he belong in a class with the spiritualists. The above quotation manifests another common misconception concerning Swedenborg's Writings.

His Writings treat throughout of man's knowledge of God and the orderly steps by which man can advance to conjunction with God and charity toward one's neighbor. Swedenborg revealed many things about the spiritual world, yet all things seen in the spiritual world, called by the writer "celestial geography," are not understood unless it is realized that every appearance in the spiritual world is representative or an appearance of some idea, thought, or affection of the inhabitants of that world. If the things seen in the spiritual world are not seen as images of the minds or spirits of those dwelling there, they have no significance.

According to the Writings of Swedenborg, the things seen in the life after death appear so similar to those seen in this world, and the life appears so much like that of this world that those who have died, if not told otherwise, believe they are still living on earth. Yet the things of the spiritual world are not material or spatial as they are in this world. For example, if one has a desire to see someone, that person is immediately present.

The spiritual world is not a material world, but a world of the mind—the most real world we can know. But the mind includes all sensations as we know them. This is illustrated by dreams, in which things appear to the mind exactly as if they were in space, namely, in appearances similar to those of the physical world. So fully is this the case that when dreaming one is not aware of the difference, although the things sensated in a dream are not material things bounded by space. In this respect the spiritual world is like a dream. But the spiritual world in other respects is opposite to a dream. In the other life, a man's mind is more alert and wide-awake than it is on earth. Contrary to what occurs in dreams, things seen in the life after death have a greater order than the things on earth, and the thinking is clearer.

In the Most Ancient Church, represented by Adam, it was common for men to have visions and dreams which were in order and in which they were instructed concerning God and heaven. But after men cast themselves out of Paradise, the mind was no longer in its primitive order, and dreams became confused and disordered. Then only occasionally were divine visions and dreams given which were of spiritual significance. The fullest descriptions of the spiritual world are recounted in Ezekiel and in the book of Revelation.

All primitive peoples, however, feel a contact with the spiritual world. Although their relation to that world is confused and mixed with superstitions it is very real to them and affects their lives, as is portrayed in their literature, their dances, and all things of their daily life. A leading Basuto chief told me I should do well in his country because I, like the Basutos, believe in the spiritual world. He said Christians say that they believe in the spiritual world, but they really do not. Now most Christians think they believe in a life after death and a spiritual world, but it is a thing very unreal to most of them, having little effect on their lives.

Primitive people have a feeling of the reality of the spiritual world which gives life to their arts and a living meaning to life which the scientifically inclined often lack. Not only primitive people, but also the wisest men of antiquity, all had a strong belief in the spiritual world—not only those we read about in the Word of God, but also the great philosophers, such as Socrates, Plato, and Cicero.

Considering the great testimony of the whole human race as to the reality of the spiritual world, does not the lack of the perception of the reality of the spiritual world in this scientific age testify to the fact that, owing to an overdevelopment of the scientific faculty of the mind, the region of the mind that is sensitive to the reality of the spiritual world has become atrophied? Surely, to throw out the whole body of testimony of the past is neither rational nor truly scientific.

Imagine the human race so changed that no one would have dreamed for two thousand years. If a man then recounted a dream, scarcely anyone would believe him, no matter how truthful, reliable, and well-balanced the man was known to be; and those who believed his report would be considered unscientific. Is it not reasonable to believe that when the human race concentrated on the things of the material world and science, this would make such a change in the mind that communication with those who had died would cease?

Swedenborg was different from the prophets, like John and Ezekiel, who recounted what they saw and heard in vision, in this: that he not only saw and heard the things of the spiritual world, but understood them in a state of full wakefulness. He had a clear idea of the thoughts and states of mind of those whom he saw and spoke with in the spiritual world; and he saw how these states of their mind were represented in the things which appeared around them.

To have a clear idea of the spiritual world, as something which we can prepare for by our life in this world, is evidently of great value; and if the Lord wished to give such an idea to men, the natural way to do it would be to open a man's spiritual eyes and introduce him to that world, and it would be a man well prepared to describe not only the appearances of that world, but also the minds and lives of those there. Is it not irrational to deny that God could do this? Cannot a wise man see the logic of this? The sophisticated, however, either deny the possibility of a life after death, or they have an idea so abstract, so lacking in normal human appearances, that, if we are the same persons after death that we are here, we would be most miserable in the kind of life they envision.

The life of those who go to heaven, as described in the Writings of Swedenborg, however, though in appearance so similar to life on earth that apart from reflection it seems the same, is still far superior to life on earth, for the faculties of the mind become purer, clearer, and more

awake, and those living there are not distressed by the material problems of this world. Nevertheless they have the
same mind, with its loves and desires; the essential person-
ality does not change. Is not any other idea one can form
of the spiritual world necessarily a fantastic and unreal
idea? Yet, strange to say, very few are even willing with
an open and unprejudiced mind to consider the possibility
that what Swedenborg said is true. By far the greater part
of the theological Writings of Swedenborg are an explication of the Old and New Testaments. From his experiences
in the spiritual world, he knew what things in the mind were
represented by the things which are recounted in the Word.
He tells us that words in the Word of God have their significance according to the appearances of the spiritual world.
To illustrate: When those in the life after death are con-
versing about the understanding of the Word, horses appear.
A horse therefore in the Word signifies the understanding
of the Word. A white horse, as described by John in the
book of Revelation, means the genuine understanding of
the Word, and a red or pale horse, a false understanding
of the Word. Again, when a man is meditating on the Word
in heaven, and drawing doctrine therefrom, at a distance
he may appear to be drawing water from a well, wherefore
in the Word the drawing of water from a well is frequently
spoken of.

The Style of the Theological Writings
of Swedenborg

Turning now to the Writings of Swedenborg, we find
them written in a style that is most exact, without poetic
or literary effect. The reading of them requires careful attention, and one is not carried along easily by the beauty
of the style. This is purposeful, for Swedenborg in his earlier writings at times wrote with a powerful poetic imagery.

In the *Doctrine of the Holy Scripture*, by Emanuel Swedenborg, we read:

> It is in everybody's mouth that the Word is from God, is Divinely inspired, and is therefore holy; and yet hitherto no one has known wherein it is Divine. For in the letter, the Word appears like a common writing, in a style that is strange and neither so sublime or brilliant as apparently are the writings of the day. A man . . . who thinks from himself . . . and not from heaven from the Lord, may easily fall into error in respect to the Word, and into contempt for it, and while reading it may say to himself, What is this? can this be Divine? could God, whose wisdom is infinite, speak in this manner?

> Yet the style of the Word is the Divine Style Itself, with which no other style, however sublime and excellent it may seem, is at all to be compared. . . . The style of the Word is such that there is holiness in every sentence, and in every word, and some places even in the very letters. (Numbers 1 and 3)

What is here said about the style of the Old and New Testaments is equally true of the Writings of Swedenborg. In fact, the Old and New Testaments are often written in a more poetic style than the Writings of Swedenborg.

In this connection, what is said in prophecy in Isaiah concerning the Lord's Coming applies, like many prophecies, also to His Second Coming: "He hath no form nor comeliness; and when we shall see him, there is no beauty that we should desire him. He is despised and rejected of men. . . . We hid as it were our faces from him; he was despised, and we esteemed him not." (53:2,3.)

Being one of the most learned men of his age and in intimate contact with other learned men, and living in a sophisticated and skeptical age, Swedenborg was well aware of the attitude of the sophisticated of his day. He knew that they would regard his Writings as visionary, reflecting a mental aberration. He also expected, as frequently declared in his Writings, that few would accept them for what they were. At the age of sixty he had nothing to gain and much to lose in reputation by publishing his theological works. He had independent means, and he ordered that any profit that might come from the sale of his theological works was to be given to a society for the distribution of the Bible. He made no attempt during his lifetime to organize a following or to form a church, although he foretold that a church would be formed on the basis of the Writings given through him.

3

Beginning of the New Church and Its
Spiritual Development

It is recommended that the reader, if he has not already done so, make a study of at least some of the Writings of Swedenborg in order to understand better what follows. In the meantime we suggest that he skip to the Epilogue of this book.

In the New Testament the word translated "Jerusalem" in the English Bible is often "Hierosolyma" in the original Greek.

In the *True Christian Religion*, by Emanuel Swedenborg, we read:

> By the Nova Hierosolyma [or the New Jerusalem] coming down from God out of heaven [Revelation 21] a new church is meant for the reason that Hierosolyma [or Jerusalem] was the metropolis in the land of Canaan and the temple and altar were there, and the sacrifices were offered there, thus the Divine worship itself . . . and also for the reason that the Lord was in Hierosolyma [or Jerusalem], and taught in its temple, and afterwards glorified His Human there. This is why "Hierosolyma" [or Jerusalem] signifies the Church . . .
>
> Behold, I create a new heaven and a new earth, and the former shall not be remembered. . . . Behold, I create Hierosolyma a rejoicing and her people a glad-

ness; that I may rejoice over Hierosolyma and be glad
over my people. (Isaiah 65:17–19)

That Hierosolyma [or Jerusalem] here means a
church about to be established by the Lord, and not the
Jerusalem inhabited by the Jews, is evident from . . .
its description . . . that Jehovah God was to create a
new heaven and a new earth. (Number 782)

Apart from publishing the books written through him,
Swedenborg did nothing toward organizing a new church.
When asked when the New Church spoken of in his writings
would come, he replied that the Lord alone knew this. He
also foretold that the Church would grow very slowly in
Christian lands.

During Swedenborg's lifetime, there were about fifty
who accepted his Writings as Divine Truth. These were
mainly in England and Sweden, with a few in Germany and
Holland. Two leading ministers, who were members of the
consistory of Gothenburg, were tried for heresy during
Swedenborg's lifetime for teaching the doctrines of the
New Church and as a result of the trial were forbidden to
teach theology. Later a minister of the State Church of
Sweden, the Reverend Sven Schmitt, was even less fortu-
nate: he was declared insane, deprived of his office, and
imprisoned on account of teaching the new doctrine.

As there was no freedom of religion in Sweden, it was
many years before the New Church could be organized
there; but in 1788, sixteen years after Swedenborg's death,
the first New Church Society was organized in London.

From the beginning of the New Church, there were two
points of view concerning the nature of Swedenborg's writings. This difference was expressed in a letter published
in 1794 in *The Aurora*, the first New Church magazine.
To quote:

I have in my journeys from place to place, lately
met with different classes of readers of Honourable
Baron Swedenborg's works: One class holding it as a

fixed principle with them that the Baron's writings are really the Word of the Lord, as positively as the Writings of any of the evangelists, Matthew, Mark, Luke or John in his Revelation. The other class allow the Baron to be a person highly illuminated by the Lord; and that his writings are highly useful in opening the spiritual sense of the Word, and thereby the true nature of the New Jerusalem church state; but still they cannot allow his writings to be upon an equal footing with the Word Itself.

In this difference of ideas we may note a similarity to a controversy which took place in the early Christian Church when the question arose as to whether the Gospels were the Word of God and were the Scriptures, and were therefore equal to the Old Testament Scriptures. In time, those holding that they were not lost out, and this position ceased to exist in the Christian Church.

What the Writings of Swedenborg Say About Themselves

The important question is: What do the Writings of Swedenborg say concerning themselves?

Swedenborg, in a conversation with Carl Christopher Gjörwell, said:

> When I think of what I am about to write, and while I am in the act of writing, I enjoy a perfect inspiration, for otherwise it would be my own; but now I know for certain that what I write is the living truth of God. (Tafel, *Documents Concerning Swedenborg*, II, 1404–405)

> Every one can see that the *Apocalypse* can by no means be explained but by the Lord alone. . . . Wherefore it has pleased the Lord to open the sight of my

spirit and to teach me. Do not believe, therefore, that
I have taken anything therein from myself, nor from
any angel, but from the Lord alone. (*Apocalypse Revealed*, by Emanuel Swedenborg, preface)

What has come from the Lord has been written.
(*Apocalypse Explained*, Number 1183)

The books are to be enumerated which were written, . . . by the Lord through me. (*Ecclesiastical History*, Number 3; *Post. Theol. Works*, I, p. 305)

But that the internal sense is such as has been set
forth, is evident from all the details that have been
unfolded, and especially from the fact that it has been
dictated to me from heaven. (*Arcana Coelestia*, Number 6597)

It is not my work but the Lord's, who wished to
reveal the nature of heaven and hell, and of man's life
after death. . . . This (Revelation) is the male child
whom the woman brought forth, and whom the dragon
wished to devour. (*Spiritual Diary*, Number 6101)

On the flyleaf of the small work, the *Summary Exposition*, Swedenborg wrote, "This book is the Advent of the
Lord, written by command."

Swedenborg states: "In the spiritual world there was
inscribed on all these books: 'The Lord's Advent.' The same
I also wrote by command on two copies in Holland." (*Ecclesiastical History*, Number 8.) One of those copies has
been found and is now in the British Museum.

Without the Lord's coming again into the world in
Divine Truth, which is the Word, no one can be saved.
(*True Christian Religion*, Number 3)

The Coming of the Lord in the clouds of heaven
with power and glory [signifies] His presence in the
Word, and revelation. . . . Such immediate revelation is
granted at this day because this is what is meant by the
Coming of the Lord. (*Heaven and Hell*, Number 1)

We read: "And Pilate wrote a title, and put it on the cross. And the writing was, JESUS OF NAZARETH, THE KING OF THE JEWS . . . and it was written in Hebrew, and Greek, and Latin." (John 19:19.)

The Old Testament is written in Hebrew, the New Testament in Greek, and the Writings of Swedenborg were written in Latin. That the two Testaments were not complete, but looked to a Third Testament, thus to a trine, is indicated by the Lord's words: "I have yet many things to say unto you, but ye cannot bear them now." (John 16:12.)

> These things have I spoken unto you in proverbs: but the time cometh, when I shall no more speak unto you in proverbs, but I shall shew you plainly of the Father. (John 16:25)

Most Protestants at this day doubt that the Bible is the Word of God, inspired as to every word. These, even if they are impressed by many things in the Writings of Swedenborg, will still not accept them as the Word of God.

As we have pointed out, there are two reasons why the Bible is not accepted by many as the Word of God, one intellectual and the other emotional. The intellectual reason is that many things in the Bible treat of history, of wars, and of dynasties, which do not appear to differ much from other history; and there are other things in the Bible which appear to be of little importance; and some things appear to be impossible, as, for example, the sun standing still. The emotional reason is, that a man—a sophisticated man— does not like to submit or humble himself before a written Revelation from God.

There are some, indeed, who are conceited, vain, and proud, and who accept the Bible but are proud of their own interpretation of it, and they are therefore unwilling to accept any interpretation that is superior to their own, especially the revelation that speaks with divine authority. This was the case with the Jews, who resented the fact that the Lord spoke to them with authority and not as the scribes.

Those who have such a pride will seldom accept the Writings of Swedenborg, and especially will they not accept them as the Word of God. They may indeed accept certain things in them, because they appear more rational than the usual interpretations of the Bible, provided they feel they have an equal right to interpret the Scriptures and to judge for themselves in all matters. A man indeed must judge for himself whether the Lord has made His Second Coming in the Writings of Swedenborg or not. If, however, he comes to see that in them the Lord has made His Second Coming, if he is not proud, he will then humble himself before these Writings as the Word of God.

Every religion, to begin with, thinks the books which it regards as holy are of God. Otherwise it is not a religion but a philosophy. A church not based on Divine Truth can be based only on the shifting sands of human opinion. Such a church cannot long stand. In its beginnings, the Protestant Churches were founded on the idea that the Bible was the Word of God and was of divine authority. This faith, to a large extent, has been lost, and with this loss the Protestant Churches have become internally so weak that some, even in these churches, have asked the question, "Can Protestantism be saved?" The confusion even to insanity has become so great that some theologians, who call themselves Christian, inspired by Nietzsche, have proclaimed that God is dead.

Much of what the Lord said was a rebuke to hypocrisy, the counterfeit, and the false—especially those who were leaders of the church. "Woe unto you scribes and pharisees, hypocrites." (Matthew 23:13.) Pride, clothing itself with the appearance of humility; vanity in the guise of piety; ambition masquerading as brotherly love and service; and sophistication pretending to be erudition, were rebuked.

If the hypocrisy of the world of today were denounced in the very words of our Lord, which were most sharp, the denouncer would be charged by most so-called Christians with lacking Christian charity. He would be called intolerant and arrogant. This clearly illustrates the hypocrisy so prevalent in what are called Christian lands.

No wonder that they who say God is dead think so, for haven't they killed God already in their hearts?

If there is no belief that there is a foundation of eternal truths in a written revelation, and if men think, therefore, that all is a matter of human opinion, they soon lose interest in religion and turn to something which has a solid foundation, namely, to science or nature.

Many think that scientific knowledge is relative and uncertain, yet there are few who do not believe that eternal laws govern nature, and most think that science has discovered at least some of these laws. And though it may be felt that some of these laws, as formulated, may have to be modified, it is seldom doubted that nature has its own order and laws, whether man has discovered and knows them or not.

It is the nature of the mind to wish to deal with something that has a solid foundation, as science has in nature. For this reason the intellectual development which has taken place in modern times has been mostly scientific. Unless the Bible is regarded as a Divine basis containing all spiritual laws, as nature is a basis containing all natural laws, theology becomes a vague guesswork, unable to satisfy the mind of man.

Can We Surely Know Truth?

It is widely thought that in matters of religion, philosophy, and the arts, all is opinion and there is nothing certain. It is a common saying that "a man has a right to his own opinion"; yet if a man is of the opinion that he is Napoleon, he belongs in a mental institution.

Is there any sense in saying that a man has a right to the opinion that 2 times 2 equals 5? Indeed, no one can stop him from holding such a notion; but is this what is meant when it is said that "a man has a right to his own opinion"?

There are laws which protect the right of freedom of speech and of the press, within bounds, for the freedom of expression can be unjustly taken away; but there are no laws in regard to the freedom of opinion, because no one can, by force, take away another's opinions. Wherefore the expression, "every man has a right to his own opinion," can refer only to a legal right, not a moral right.

For does a man have a moral right to the opinion that it is permissible to cheat or do harm to others? A man has a moral duty to weigh opinions freely and seek for the truth, but does he have a moral right to believe what is false?

When someone repeats this phrase, he usually means that no one has a right to say, or even think, that his (the speaker's) opinions are not as good as anyone else's. Thus what he says is the opposite of what he means; and yet the above saying he regards as an expression of charity.

When this saying is used, it is also usually implied that truth cannot be ascertained beyond a doubt, or that a man cannot grasp the truth in its completeness. The latter of these statements is true; but it is obvious that because a man's knowledge of mathematics is very limited, this does not prevent him from being certain that he has solved a problem in mathematics. Cannot such certainty exist in other fields of thought?

It is self-evident that to kill or harm one's neighbor is evil, and that to steal from or cheat the neighbor is evil; one who doubts this is not sane. But when it comes to theology, men are for the most part blind and therefore think that everything is a matter of opinion. They therefore doubt the words of the Lord: "I am the light of the world." (John 8:12.) If the Lord heals our blindness so that we see, then we know for a certainty that we have been given sight. This is just as true of the sight of the mind as of physical sight.

Few are willing to make the struggle needed to become able to distinguish between holding an opinion and seeing a thing clearly in light. Many of our thoughts are opinions, because we have no light on the subject or because our knowledge of the subject is too limited; still, we should realize that a clear light is possible. Many people sacrifice and labor industriously to find the answer to scientific problems, with the conviction that they can find out the truth of the matter. But few will labor with all their might to find the answer to spiritual problems. The reason for this often is that coming to the truth of a scientific matter brings a reward of this world, whereas coming to a spiritual truth brings the inner reward of a closer conjunction with God.

As the majority of the Protestant Churches no longer have faith in the Bible as a solid foundation, their faith has become weak. In the same way, many of those in the New Church, called Swedenborgians, do not believe in the Writings of Swedenborg as the Word of God, the Rock of Truth upon which the New Church is founded, and such have tended to become weak in their faith.

With those in the New Church who believed in the Writings of Swedenborg as the Word of God, the question arose as to what was the nature of these Writings as the Word of God.

The Understanding of the Word

According to the Writings of Swedenborg, the Word, like a man, has a soul and a body. The inner or spiritual sense or meaning is its soul, and the sense of the letter is its body, in order that it may live in the world. The inner or spiritual sense forms the letter of the Word, in order that it may manifest itself in the world. Divine Truth, in the sense of the letter of the Word, is in its fullness, holiness, and power, for in this it rests upon its divine foundation.

The Word of the Lord, as we have said, treats of nothing but the things of the spirit. It does not in its spiritual sense treat of the history of nations, of science, or of the things of the world. Because the facts of science and history do not appear to agree with the Word of God, when seen in its letter, many have come to deny the importance of the letter, not knowing that every word, every jot and tittle, has a spiritual significance. Such may try to find the spirit of the Word, but, as we have said, the spirit without the body of the Word—that is, without the letter—is a ghost or phantom. The learned in the New Church (Swedenborgian) have been faced with the same problem in relation to the Writings of Swedenborg as Christians have in relation to the Bible. Some, like the fundamentalists in the Christian Church, cling to the unopened letter; others, not seeing that every word has a spiritual signification, look for the spirit or rational idea—which, apart from the letter, is a phantom.

Some held that the Writings were the internal sense of the Word. Others maintained that, although they were indeed the internal sense of the Word, they were also clothed with a letter and were therefore part of the letter of the Word.

The question later arose as to how the Word of the Lord becomes Divine Truth in the mind of man. Is it Divine Truth with man merely because man has read it and has it in his memory?

In the *Doctrine of the Sacred Scripture,* by Emanuel Swedenborg, it is said:

> The Church is from the Word, and is such as is its understanding of the Word. That the church is from the Word does not admit of doubt, for the Word is Divine truth itself. The doctrine of the church is from the Word, and through the Word there is conjunction

with the Lord. But doubt may arise as to whether the understanding of the Word is what makes the church, for there are those who believe they are of the church because they have the Word, read it or hear it from a preacher, and know something of its sense of the letter, yet how this or that in the Word is to be understood they do not know, and some of them little care. It shall therefore be proved that it is not the Word that makes the church, but the understanding of it, and that such as is the understanding of the Word among those who are in the church, such is the church itself. (Number 76)

The Word is the Word according to the understanding of it in a man, that is, as it is understood. If it is not understood, the Word is indeed called the Word, but it is not the Word with the man. The Word is the truth according to the understanding of it, for it may not be the truth, because it may be falsified. The Word is spirit and life according to the understanding of it, for its letter if not understood is dead. And as a man has truth according to his understanding of the Word, so has he faith and love according thereto, for truth is of faith and love is of life. Now as the church exists by means of faith and love, and according to them, it follows that the church is the church through the understanding of the Word and according thereto; a noble church if in genuine truths, an ignoble church if not in genuine truths, and a destroyed church if in falsified truths. (Number 77)

Further: it is through the Word that the Lord is present with a man and is conjoined with him, for the Lord is the Word, and as it were speaks with the man in it. The Lord is also Divine truth itself, as likewise is the Word. From this it is evident that the Lord is present with a man and is at the same time conjoined with him, according to his understanding of the Word, for according to this the man has truth and the deriva-

tive faith, and also love and the derivative life. The
Lord is indeed present with a man through the reading
of the Word, but He is conjoined with him through the
understanding of truth from the Word, and according
thereto; and in proportion as the Lord has been conjoined with a man, in the same proportion the church
is in him. . . . The church that is outside of him is the
church with a number of men who have the church
within them. This is meant by the Lord's words to the
Pharisees who asked when the kingdom of God would
come:—

"The Kingdom of God is within you." (Luke 17:21)

Here "the Kingdom of God" means the Lord, and
from Him, the church. (Number 78)

The Lord said: "Abide in me, and I in you. As the
branch cannot bear fruit of itself, except it abide in the
vine; no more can ye, except ye abide in me." (John 15:4.)
If the Lord does not abide in us and we do not abide in
the Lord, we can have no genuine understanding of the
Word, no matter how many knowledges from the Word
we have in the memory.

To understand anything, there must be three things:
There must be an objective world outside of ourselves.
Furthermore, there must be a sound eye and there must be
light. In relation to spiritual things, we have the Word outside of ourselves. This is of no use unless we have light.

The Lord said: "I am the light of the world: he that
followeth me shall not walk in darkness, but shall have the
light of life." (John 8:12.)

To follow the Lord is to keep His commandments not
only in the letter, but also in the spirit. The light which
the Lord said He was, is the Holy Spirit which those receive
who live in the Lord and the Lord in them. Apart from
such a dwelling and such a life, the man is in darkness as
to all things of the Word. He may know many things from
the Word; but if his understanding of them is not genuine,

he indeed has the Word, "but it is not the Word" with the man.

The third thing which a man must have to see is a sound or healthy eye. If a man is blind, he cannot see; or if his eye is badly defective, he sees all things distorted. The spiritual eye is the understanding, for by the understanding man can see truths as they really are. Man, to begin with, is either spiritually blind or he has a very imperfect understanding which distorts the things which he sees. If a man is humble, he comes to the Lord acknowledging his blindness and asks the Lord to heal his blindness. If a man is proud, he thinks he sees very well and does not need to be cured of his blindness. This is the meaning of the Words of the Lord:

> And Jesus said, For judgment I am come into this world, that they which see not might see; and that they which see might be made blind. And some of the Pharisees . . . said unto him, Are we blind also? Jesus said unto them, If ye were blind, ye should have no sin: but now ye say, We see; therefore your sin remaineth. (John 9:39–41)

The Lord comes to those who acknowledge their lack of understanding of the Word, that such may see. But at His Coming those who are in the pride of their understanding of the Word are made blind. If men acknowledge their blindness, that is, their lack of understanding of the Word, "they have no sin"; but if from pride in their own intelligence, they insist that they understand the Word, then their "sin remaineth."

The Lord said, "If thine eye offend thee, pluck it out, and cast it from thee; it is better for thee to enter into life with one eye, rather than having two eyes to be cast into hell fire." (Matthew 18:9.) How many are willing to acknowledge that their eye offends them, that is, that they falsely interpret the Word of God? or that they are blind and cannot see the true meaning of the Word for themselves

unless the Lord heals their blindness? Yet it was just this
for which the Lord came—"for judgment I am come into
this world, that they which see not might see, and that they
which see might be made blind." (John 9:39.)

Our Lord said, "Ye must be born again." (John 3:7.)
It is the new eye which man has from being born again that
alone sees the inner truth of the Word. The old eye can see
the things of the letter of the Word, but it is blind to the
inner truth or spirit of the Word. This regeneration and
rebirth cannot take place quickly. A man must again enter
into the womb of the Church and be gestated for a long time
before he can be born again with a new eye which can see
clearly; and even when he is born again, like a new infant,
he cannot at first see the internal things of the Word, for
this takes time. The spiritual eye, or understanding of
spiritual things, must first be formed and then be perfected
as to sight by the use of the spiritual eye.

Many in the Christian churches think that merely because they read the Bible they are in the spirit of the
Gospels. Yet, as we have said before, without struggling
with all one's mind and strength to obey the Ten Commandments and the Lord's Commandments, both in spirit and
according to the letter, one remains in his old life. One who
remains in his old life does not receive a new heart and a
new spirit; that is, he is not born again. To believe that
one can be born again in a moment, by a miracle, without
his cooperation, is a fallacy.

In the same way, there is the danger that those in the
New Church (Swedenborgian) may think they are in the
Spirit of the Writings of Swedenborg, which are the Third
Testament, merely because they read these Writings and
have them in their memory and outer understanding, apart
from giving much consideration to the light in which they
are, or the state of their eye, that is, to their spiritual understanding. They may not realize that it is only the new eye,
which belongs to the new body when man is born again,
which has an inner sight of the Word.

The Lord said:

> Where your treasure is, there will your heart be also. The light of the body is the eye: if therefore thine eye be single, thy whole body shall be full of light. But if thine eye be evil, thy whole body shall be full of darkness. If therefore the light that is in thee be darkness, how great is that darkness! (Matthew 6:21–23)

This teaching applies to all reading of the Word. No matter how wonderful the Lord's Word is, no matter if we have only one or two or three Testaments of the Word, if our eye is evil, our whole body is full of darkness; and if we are not proud and conceited, we shall acknowledge that we are first in such darkness, that is, until the Lord has opened our eyes and given us sight.

To come to an understanding of the Word, our minds must be active, not just in a state of passive receptivity. That is, we must work to come to a real understanding of the teaching of the Word. For this reason, the Church and the men of the Church must make a doctrine.

We read in the *Arcana Coelestia*, by Swedenborg:

> Those are said to "see the back parts of Jehovah and not the faces," who believe and adore the Word; but only its external, which is the sense of the letter, and do not penetrate more interiorly, as do those who have been enlightened, and who make for themselves doctrine from the Word, by which they may see its genuine sense, thus its interior sense. (Number 10584)

The Words which the Lord spoke, He called Spirit and Life, and so they are. But a man who only remains passively in the sense of the letter and whose mind is not opened to the Lord in heaven does not see the Lord's face, but only His back.

In the Writings of Swedenborg, or the Third Testament, the Lord has come again and unfolded the Word in an infinite way, and this Testament is again Spirit and Life; it is in itself the internal sense of the Word. But if a man receives the Third Testament only passively, and if he is not enlightened by the Holy Spirit, he remains only in the sense of the letter of this Testament. All Three Testaments necessarily have a soul and a body, and apart from the presence of the Holy Spirit and the cooperation of the Church and the men of the Church in making doctrine, man sees only the body and not the soul. A man when he reads the Word can be in no truth unless the truth flows into his mind from the Lord through heaven above while he is reading or meditating on the Word. This is expressed in the *Arcana Coelestia* as follows:

> When a man is in truth, as is the case before he has been regenerated, he knows scarcely anything about good; for truth flows in by an external or sensual way [that is, by the bodily senses], but good by an internal way [that is, from the soul]. Man is sensible of that which flows in by an external way, but not, until he has been regenerated of that which flows in by an internal way. (Number 4977)
>
> When the state with a man who is being regenerated is inverted, that is when good takes the first place, then come temptations. . . . When good is taking the prior place and subordinating truths to itself, which takes place when man is undergoing spiritual temptations, the good which then flows in from within is attended with very many truths that have been stored up in his interior man. . . . For while a man is living in the body, and does not believe that all things flow in, he supposes that the things which come forth interiorly are not produced by causes outside of him, but that all the causes are within him, and are his very own. Yet such is not the case. For whatever a man thinks and whatever he wills (that is, his every thought and his every affection) are either from hell or from heaven. (Numbers 4248 and 4249)

The celestial are in such a state, [that] they are able to acknowledge that all good and truth flow in from the Lord; and also that there is a perceptive power of good and truth that is communicated and appropriated to them by the Lord, and that constitutes their delight, bliss and happiness. (Number 3394)

The Divine that proceeds from the Lord, when received by the angels, makes heaven. Thus in respect to what is their own the angels themselves do not make heaven; but in respect to the Divine which they receive from the Lord. . . . That the Divine of the Lord makes His Kingdom with man, that is, heaven and the church with him, the Lord also teaches in John: "The Spirit of truth shall abide with you, and shall be in you, and ye shall know that I am in My Father and ye in Me, and I in you." (14:17,20)

The "Spirit of truth" denotes the Divine truth that proceeds from the Lord, of which it is said that it "shall abide in you"; and afterward that "He is in the Father, and they in Him, and He in them" whereby is signified that they would be in what is Divine of the Lord, and that what is Divine of the Lord should be in them. (Number 10151)

In the *Arcana Coelestia*, Number 1807, it is said: "They who are in Divine ideas never come to a stand [stop] in the objects of the external sight; but from them and in them constantly see internal things."

Those who are in "Divine ideas" never remain in the letter of the Word, which is the chief object of the external sight in the Church, but constantly see the internal things which belong to the spiritual sense of the Word.

From the above it is clearly evident that to be in the Divine Truth does not come merely from reading the Word, apart from the reception of the "Divine Truth which proceeds from the Lord."

It is also evident from the above that it is not only the

individual who should receive the Divine Truth proceeding
from the Lord, but also the Church, as is evident from the
number in the *Doctrine of the Sacred Scripture* quoted
above. "The church is the church through the understanding of the Word and according thereto; a noble church if
in genuine truths, an ignoble church if not in genuine
truths, and a destroyed church if in falsified truths."
(Number 77.)

The importance of man's taking an active part in coming to an understanding of the Word is described as follows:

> *The genuine truth which must be of doctrine ap-*
> *pears in the sense of the letter to none but those who*
> *are in enlightenment from the Lord.* Enlightenment is
> from the Lord alone, and exists with those who love
> truths because they are truths and make them of use
> for life. With others there is no enlightenment in the
> Word. The reason why enlightenment is from the Lord
> alone is that the Lord is in all things of the Word. The
> reason why enlightenment exists with those who love
> truths because they are truths and make them of use
> for life, is that such are in the Lord and the Lord in
> them. For the Lord is His own Divine truth, and when
> this is loved because it is Divine truth (and it is loved
> when it is made of use) [or when lived] the Lord is in
> it with the man. This the Lord teaches in John: "In
> that day ye shall know that ye are in Me and I in you.
> He that hath My commandments, and doeth them, he
> loveth Me, and I will love him, and will manifest My-
> self to him; and I will come unto him, and make My
> abode with him." (John 14:20,21,23)
>
> And in Matthew: "Blessed are the pure in heart, for
> they shall see God." (5:8)
>
> These are they who are in enlightenment when they
> are reading the Word, and to whom the Word shines
> and is translucent.
>
> The reason why the Word shines and is translucent

with such, is that there is a spiritual and celestial sense in every particular of the Word, and these senses are in the light of heaven, so that through these senses and by their light the Lord flows into the natural sense, and into the light of it with a man. This causes the man to acknowledge the truth from an interior perception, and afterwards to see it in his own thought. . . .

With such men the first thing is to get for themselves doctrine from the sense of the letter of the Word, and thus light a lamp for their further advance. Then after doctrine has been procured, and a lamp thus lighted, they see the Word by its means. (*Doctrine of the Sacred Scripture*, Numbers 57–59.)

We read in *Arcana Coelestia*:

The Lord does these [good and truth] through man's heaven, that is, through his internal; for all good and truth are from the Lord, insomuch that good and truth with man are the Lord Himself. (Number 9776)

"No man hath ascended into heaven, but He that came down from heaven, the Son of man who is in the heavens," (John 3:13) . . . for this [Divine truth] comes down, and therefore ascends, because no one can ascend into heaven unless Divine truth comes down into him from heaven. (Number 9807 [9])

From this it can be known what is meant by "Spirit" when said of the Lord, namely, the Divine truth that proceeds from His Divine good, and that when this Divine truth flows in with man, and is received by him, it is "the Spirit of Truth," "the Spirit of God," and "the Holy Spirit"; for it flows in immediately from the Lord, and also mediately through angels and spirits. (Number 9818 [3])

The sense of the Word is circumstanced in accordance with the heavens: the supreme sense . . . is for the inmost or third heaven; its internal sense . . . for the middle or second heaven; but the lower sense . . .

for the lowest or first heaven . . . and the lowest . . .
sense is for man while living in the world, and who is
nevertheless of such a nature that the interior sense,
and even the internal and supreme senses can be communicated to him. For man has communication with
the three heavens. . . . Hence it is that within man is
the Lord's kingdom, as the Lord Himself teaches in
Luke: "Behold, the Kingdom of God is within you."
(17:21) (Number 4279 [2])

Angels, all of whom have at one time lived on earth as
men, are in the inner sense of the Word from the Lord and
not from themselves; wherefore, the internal sense which
is communicated to man is from the Lord and is indeed the
Lord with man.

In the two quotations above there is an apparent paradox. One passage treats of the teaching or doctrine drawn
from the sense of the letter of the Word, by reading or hearing, that is, by physical influx, through the bodily senses.
In this, by study, man works as if from himself. The other
treats of the actual spiritual influx, an influx of the Holy
Spirit, that comes to man from within.

In order to live an actual spiritual life, man must be
prepared so that he can receive the spiritual influx and communication from the Lord, and at the same time in the apparent physical influx from without, in which he acts as if of
himself. Thus a man draws teaching or doctrine from the
sense of the letter of the Word as if of himself, but acknowledges that every genuine truth of doctrine with him is from
the Lord, who is the internal of the Word. Thus he believes
the words, "A man can receive nothing, except it be given
him from heaven." (John 3:27.)

From the above, it is evident that whereas the Lord de-
scended and made His Second Coming in the Writings of
Emanuel Swedenborg which are in their essence the Internal
Sense of the Word, but clothed on earth with a letter, the
Truths which are set forth in the literal sense of this Testa-

ment are not spiritual and celestial truths with a man unless they at the same time flow into man from the Lord from within.

For we read:

> The natural [mind] of man sees things in the light of the world, which light is called natural light. Man procures for himself this light by means of the objects which enter through the sight and hearing. . . . When light from heaven flows into these things, the man begins to see them spiritually. . . . This insight increases according to the influx of the light of heaven . . . for the light of heaven inflows from the Lord through the internal man into the external man. From this then man has perception. . . . There must be an influx of living light through the internal man from the Lord. (*Arcana Coelestia*, Number 9103 [3], [5])

To illustrate the above in a somewhat crude way: All laws of nature exist in the created world whether man knows them or not. In the same way, all Divine Truth exists in the Word of the Lord whether or not it is known by man. In fact, the truths which men know, compared to those that are unknown, are as a cup of water is to the ocean.

There are things which man knows directly by his five senses, things which are often better known by a primitive man than by an educated man. The laws of science are arrived at by an intellectual process. These laws are sometimes quite contrary to the direct evidence of the senses: for example, that the sun stands still relative to the solar system and does not traverse the sky from east to west. That objects which appear inert, as to their particles, are in a high state of activity. In the same way, there are appearances in the letter of the Word, as seen in the light of the world, which appear very differently when seen in the light of heaven.

Every revelation of the Word is clothed in a letter. There are those who cling to the letter and ignore the Spirit, that is, the inner sense, and those who would seek the Spirit and lose faith in the letter.

It is said in the Writings of Swedenborg that John the Baptist represents the Word in the external sense.

We read:

> John only inaugurated them into the knowledges from the Word respecting the Lord, and thus prepared them to receive Him; but . . . the Lord Himself regenerates man by means of the Divine Truth and Divine Good proceeding from Him. . . ."The waters" with which John baptized signified introductory truths, which are knowledges from the Word respecting the Lord. (*Apocalypse Explained*, Number 475:20)

In relation to the Lord's First Coming, there had to be one who would go before and prepare the way by preaching repentance and proclaiming the Coming of the Lord. In the same way, in relation to the Second Coming, the understanding of the literal sense of the Writings of Swedenborg has to come first; and again, this sense calls to repentance and prepares the way for the Lord's Coming in the Divine Truth of the Holy Spirit and the fire of His Love, which proceed from Him.

That Swedenborg teaches that the Writings have a literal sense is evident from the following quotation:

> They [certain spirits] said . . . that those things which I have written are so rude and gross, that they suppose nothing which is interior could be understood from these words or the mere sense of the words. I also perceived by a spiritual idea that it was so, that my expressions were very rude, wherefore it was given me to reply that my words are only vessels into which purer, better and interior things might be infused, as if the literal sense [thereof]; that such vessels, as it were, are the many literal senses of the prophets. (*Spiritual Diary*, Number 2185)

There are four characteristics of the Word of the Lord, in which it differs from all other writings.

One: It is written in a continuous and perfect Divine series from beginning to end. (See *Arcana Coelestia*, Number 7933.)

Two: In this series as to its inmost sense, it treats solely of the Lord and His glorification; in its inner sense, it treats of His Kingdom or the Church and the man of the Church and his regeneration. (See *Arcana Coelestia*, 3540)

Three: Every word in the Word of the Lord is from the Lord and can be opened to infinity. (See *Arcana Coelestia*, 771, 1936)

Four: The Word is perfect in ultimates or as to its letter, for every least thing therein is holy. Seen merely as to its letter, it indeed appears imperfect; but seen from within, or seen in the light of heaven, its perfection appears. (See *Doctrine of the Sacred Scripture*, Numbers 6 and 28.)

If a sophisticated man views the Word from his unregenerated mind, he will not accept these statements as true. For the Word as seen from without does not appear to be perfect; rather, it appears to contain errors, things contrary to scientific knowledge and many things that are crude and apparently unworthy of God.

If one believes that the Old and New Testaments are the Word of God, one can see how this applies to these books.

If one believes the Writings of Emanuel Swedenborg are the Word of the Lord, one can see that this also applies to these Writings, for we are told in these Writings that books not having these four characteristics are not the Word of the Lord; yet viewed only from without, the Writings of Swedenborg do not appear to have the above four characteristics.

If the Writings are the Word of the Lord, they are open to a continuous unfolding. The explication of the Word may be true or false. The true explication of the Word is from the presence of the Lord in the Church, that is, it is

the work of the Lord's Holy Spirit, although man does this
unfolding, in appearance, as of himself.

The genuine Truths drawn from the Word in the Church
are the doctrine of the Church or its teachings. This doctrine is from the Lord and is open to indefinite expansion
even to eternity.

To illustrate how a man may be enlightened when he
reads the Word, consider the following quotation:

"Certain spirits . . . were in unbelief concerning the
Word of the Lord, as to there being such [sublime]
things stored up in its bosom, or within it; for in the
other life spirits are in unbelief like that in which they
had been in the life of the body; and this is not dissipated except by means provided by the Lord, and by living
experiences. On this account, while I was reading some
of the Psalms of David, the deeper insight or mind of
these spirits was opened, . . . and being amazed at them
[they] said that they had never believed such things.
The same portion of the Word was then heard by many
other spirits; but they all apprehended it in different
ways. With some it filled the ideas of their thought with
many pleasant and delightful things, thus with a kind
of life in accordance with the capacity of each one, and
at the same time with an efficacy that penetrated to
their inmosts, and this to such a degree with some that
they seemed to be uplifted toward the interiors of heaven, and nearer and nearer to the Lord, according to
the degree in which they were affected by the truths
and the goods therewith injoined.

The Word was then at the same time brought to
some who had no apprehension of its internal sense,
but only of the external or literal sense; and to them
the letter appeared to have no life. From all this it was
manifest what the Word of the Lord is when the Lord
fills it with life—that it is of such efficacy that it pene-
trates to the inmosts; also what it is when He does not

fill it with life—that it is then the letter only, with scarcely any life.

Of the Lord's Divine mercy I too have been permitted in the same way to see the Lord's Word in its beauty in the internal sense, and this many times; not as it is while the words are being explained as to the internal sense in detail, but with all things both in general and particular brought together into a single series or connection, which may be said to be the seeing of a celestial paradise from an earthly one. (*Arcana Coelestia,* Numbers 1771 and 1772)

A certain spirit . . . was suddenly taken up on high. . . . He then spoke with me from thence, saying that he saw things more sublime than human minds could possibly apprehend . . . . Soon others also were taken up into the same heaven, . . . one . . . testified to the same effect, saying . . . that he was too much amazed to describe the glory of the Word in its internal sense. Then, speaking from a kind of pity, he said that it was strange that men knew nothing at all of such things. (*Arcana Coelestia,* Number 3474 [1],[3])

A man so far as his spirit is concerned may also be raised into heaven; only then can he see the Word of the Lord in its beauty as a celestial paradise. A man in this world may not be conscious of having been so taken up into heaven, but he can know it from the fact that he has been given to see the Word in its glory and beauty as a heavenly paradise. A man who has not been so elevated has never seen the beauty and glory of the Word, no matter how diligently he has studied it, and no matter how extensive his knowledge of it is, or how well he can appear to explain it.

The Genuine Church

The genuine Church is the Word made flesh in an image of the Lord, who was the Word made flesh in an infinite way. Anything in the Church which is not the Word made flesh is not the genuine Church. A wise man, therefore, in giving his loyalty to the Church, gives his loyalty to what he sees in the Church to be the Word become flesh. To anything which he sees has crept into the Church from any other source, he does not give his loyalty. The simple who are not wise in the things of the Word can only with difficulty make this distinction. Still, all should strive for this ability. A man should feel loyalty to the Church and a desire to protect it, as long as he perceives that the Church's dominant love is loyalty to the Word of the Lord. If a man comes to perceive that the Church is not giving its first loyalty to the Word, but rather to itself and its own traditions, then he should eagerly seek for a Church which gives its first loyalty to the Word of the Lord.

Those who are genuinely of the Church have the Kingdom of the Lord within them—of these the Church is constituted. Others who may be in the Church are not of the Church. Even with those who have received something of the beginning of the implantation of the Church, there are great regions of the mind which are outside the Lord's Kingdom, and as to those regions they are not of the Church.

The Kingdom of Heaven is a Divine man. It is said, in the *Divine Providence*, by Emanuel Swedenborg:

Its inmost [the Divine Providence] is that man may be in this or that place in heaven, or in this or that place in the Divine celestial man; for thus he is in the Lord. (Number 67)

Each one from infancy is introduced into this Divine Man; whose soul and life is the Lord. . . . [That is] those who receive are carried to their places through infinite turnings. (Number 164)

In heaven the Divine of the Lord is love to Him and charity toward the neighbor. (*Heaven and Hell*, Number 13 heading)

Man, so far as his mind and body are concerned, however, is not Divine, but only a vessel which may receive the Divine. Man is no more Divine than a candle is light or an electric light filament is light. Nevertheless, the Kingdom of Heaven which is Divine can be received by man, but it is never man's, for man of himself apart from reception is spiritually dead.

The Lord, however, is life, for He made the very vessels of His body Divine and therefore rose with the body unlike any man.

The Divine of the Lord received by man, compared to the Divine of the Lord Himself, is in the ratio of the light of a candle compared to the sun.

There are some who think that the Divine, being Infinite, is far above the Church and the man of the Church and cannot be in the Church and in man.

Although the Infinite Divine cannot be in man unaccommodated, yet it is the teaching of the Writings of Swedenborg that the Divine can be so accommodated that it can be in the Church and in the man of the Church, as in the following quotation:

The "candlestick" [signifies] the Divine Spiritual in heaven and in the Church. . . . The Divine Celestial in the good of love, and the Divine spiritual in the truth of faith thence; both proceeding from the Lord. (*Arcana Coelestia*, Number 9548)

Confusion may arise from failure to distinguish between the Divine Itself of the Lord and of His Word, the Infinite source of all good and truth, and the Divine as received by the Church and the man of the Church. This Divine is called above, the celestial and spiritual Divine. Concerning this distinction, we read:

> In the case of the angels, the Divine is not in them, but is present with them, because they are only forms recipient of the Divine from the Lord. (*Arcana Coelestia*, Number 4971)

The great importance of acknowledging that the Divine is received by man is evident from the following passage:

> Man is above the beasts, in such a state as to be able to understand what pertains to the Divine Wisdom, and to will what pertains to the Divine Love, thus to receive the Divine; and a being that is capable of so receiving the Divine as to see and perceive it in himself cannot but be conjoined with the Lord and by that conjunction live forever. What would the Lord be in relation to the entire creation of the universe if He had not also created images and likenesses of Himself, to whom He could communicate His Divine? . . . What of the Divine would there be in all these things, unless they had as their end to be serviceable to subjects that could receive the Divine more nearly, and see it and feel it? And as the Divine is of glory inexhaustible, would He keep it to Himself alone, or would it be possible for Him to do so? (*Divine Providence*, Number 324)

We read in the *Arcana Coelestia*, Number 8328:

> Frequent mention is made [in the Word] of *"the Father who is in the heavens"*. . . . Regarded in Itself the Divine is above the heavens; but the Divine in the heavens is the Good that is in the Truth that proceeds from the Divine. This is meant by "the Father in the heavens," as in Matthew:
> "That ye may be the sons of the Father who is in the heavens; that ye may be perfect, as your Father who is in the heavens is perfect." (5:45,48; 6:1)

"Our Father who art in the heavens, hallowed be Thy name." (6:9)

"He that doeth the will of the Father who is in the heavens." (7:21)

The Divine that is in the heavens is the Good which is in the Divine Truth that proceeds from the Lord; but the Divine above the heavens is the Divine Good Itself. . . . How the case is with the Divine Truth that proceeds from the Lord, that it is in heaven good, may be illustrated by comparison with the sun, and with the light that is from the sun. In the sun is fire, but from the sun proceeds light, which light has within itself heat, from which gardens sprout forth and become like paradises. The very fire of the sun does not pass to the earth (for it would burn up and consume all things), but the light wherein is heat from the fire of the sun. In the spiritual sense this light is the Divine Truth; the heat is the good in the Truth from the Divine Good; and the resultant paradise is heaven.

There are those who think they have in them a spark of the Divine Itself, a spark of the Sun of Heaven. Such may desire to approach the Infinite Divine Itself. Like Daedalus, they fly toward the sun with wax wings, until the wings melt and they fall to earth. Such regard themselves as little gods.

At the other extreme are those who regard all the truths they have as human and uncertain, who deny that the Lord, Who is the light of the world, can dwell in their heaven or inner mind and form a paradise from the Divine Truth received in which is the Lord's love.

To approach the Divine Itself is to approach the invisible Father, God, whom "no man hath seen at any time," rather than the Lord, our Father in the Kingdom of God which is within. The true believers acknowledge the Lord present in the light of Divine Truth, within which is good. The Lord forms a paradise of the Church within them.

Such see the Divine Human of the Lord, the visible God-
man. Those who deny that the Divine Truth can be seen
and received in the mind and life worship an invisible God
with whom there can be no conjunction by love.

A man may enter the Church for many reasons. He may
do so because he wishes to feel or appear spiritually more
important than others. He may do so because he wishes to
belong to the wave of the future. He may do so because he
has a rebellious spirit, and out of such a spirit he may resent the Church he is in and express this resentment by
joining another Church. There are also other nongenuine
reasons for joining a Church. Such, however, are not true
members of the Church. Nor are those true members of the
Church who have been brought up in a church and remain
in it from habit, from natural affections, and from a personal
love for those with whom one has associated from childhood,
such as parents and companions. There are many who love
the external of the church, its services and customs, from
attachment to childhood memories. Such think they have
a faith, though many of them have little love of the truth
for the sake of the truth and for the sake of the good of
life and, apart from such personal attachments, would care
little for the Kingdom of Heaven. Others who lack a living
faith remain in the Church out of fear and the distress it
would cause them to break away from their family and
friends.

The genuine Church consists only of those who cleave
to the Church in order that they may lose their old life and
receive new life from the Lord by means of the Word.

Those who are truly of a genuine Church do not believe
that its members are necessarily better than those of other
churches—far from it. The characteristic of those in the
Lord's Church is this: that there is a continuous call for
repentance and for humiliation before the Lord in order that
it may continually become more and more the Lord's Church
on earth; but as few have the desire to give up the life they
are in, a true Church expects to grow slowly.

EPILOGUE

The spirit of the Church was powerfully expressed by Bishop W. F. Pendleton in an address to the assembly of the General Church of the New Jerusalem on June 30, 1899. In this address he said:

It is clear, however, that what makes the Church is not so much its doctrine as its spirit; for the essential of doctrine, the essential of faith, the essential of law, is the spirit that is in it; and while it may be said that doctrine makes the Church yet it is not the doctrine itself, but the spirit and life within it, that makes the Church. . . .

The most important principle of all the truth that is within the doctrine is;—*the love of truth for its own sake.*

The love of truth for its own sake is the love of truth for the sake of the truth itself, and thus for the sake of the Lord, who is in the truth, and not for the sake of self and the world; a love that will lead a man to sacrifice himself for the sake of truth, and not the truth for the sake of himself; a love that makes him willing to give up fame, reputation, gain, friends, even his own life, for the sake of the truth; that causes him to be regardless of consequences to himself, where it is necessary to uphold the standard of the truth. This is what is meant by the words of the Lord, "He that findeth his life shall lose it, and he that loseth his life for my sake shall find it." (Matthew 10:39)

If this love is in the Church, and continues in it as

its ruling principle, as its spirit and life, the Church
will have a spiritual internal from heaven, by which it
will be enlightened and guided in the performance of its
uses, and by which it will be protected from the spheres
in which the spirit of the world rules; for then no man
will come to it, or remain in it, who is not willing to
sacrifice himself for the sake of the truth, who is
not willing to die that the truth may live and prosper.
"Then said Jesus unto His disciples, If any man will
come after me, let him deny himself and take up his
cross and follow me."

By "losing one's life" in the above is not meant primarily
losing the life of the body, or even giving up one's life in
the world.

There are those who gladly give up their lives out of the
ambition to be heroes or saints, who will sacrifice everything
for the sake of glory. There are those who gladly become
martyrs, in order to become renowned or gain a pre-eminent
place in heaven, and there are those who care little
for their life and may even have a tendency toward suicide.
Even animals will fight to the death to protect their kind,
particularly their young. It is a kind of animal instinct to
defend one's country or church to the death when it is at-
tacked.

By this we do not mean to minimize the virtue of those
who give their life for the defense of their country, for the
church, or for the sake of their belief, if it is done from a
genuine love of country or church. But the essential giving
up of one's life is the giving up of one's life that exists in
the love of one's self and of one's own intelligence, one's
life of worldly ambition; a giving up of one's life secretly
and without the knowledge of anyone; a giving up with no
ambition to receive a martyr's crown.

To give up the life existing in one's love of self and of
one's own intelligence, to give up one's false ideals, with no

thought of glory in heaven or earth, is a greater sacrifice than the yielding up of the life of the body.

To sacrifice one's loves solely for a love of God is the giving up of one's life that the Lord meant when He said, "He that loseth his life shall find it."

Those who sacrifice wealth, position, and reputation, and put on the greatest appearance of humility, may do so out of mere egotism, whereas internally they are often the proudest and most vain members of the human race.

The hope is that there may be some who, from love of our Lord as the way, the truth, and the life, and having lost their soul in secret, may find it, for of such is the Kingdom of Heaven.

POSTSCRIPT

The Religious Turmoil of the Mid-Nineteen-Sixties

Since this book was written, the leading weekly magazines have come out with a description of what is regarded
by some as the greatest religious revolution since the time of
Luther.

We shall not here treat further of the lunatic fringe,
who, considering themselves to be Christian, say that "God
is dead" and speak of Christian Atheism, but shall analyze
the ideas of a present line of thought concerning the question
"Who was Jesus?" held by many of those who have departed
from the traditional Christian faith.

There are many who consider themselves Christian who
deny the Virgin Birth, the Resurrection of Christ, and miracles; they deny or question the life after death in the Kingdom of Heaven; they question or deny the Deity of Christ.
Thus they deny ninety-five per cent of the verses of the
Gospel and still consider themselves Christians. Many of
them put the emphasis on what they call "the Social Gospel."

Christianity without God is nonsense, but Christianity
without Christ is more obviously nonsense. A member of a
church who is not eager to know who Christ was and to
know His teaching is not a Christian. Neither is one a
Christian who searches to know Christ and His teachings
but does not live according to them. The higher, the purer,
and the nobler a religion, the worse are they who are in it
and do not live according to its precepts. A bad heathen is
not nearly as bad as a bad Christian. As the Lord said,

"That servant, which knew his lord's will, and prepared not himself, neither did according to his will, shall be beaten with many stripes. But he that knew not, and did commit things worthy of stripes, shall be beaten with few stripes." (Luke 12:47,48.)

A nonreligious agnostic is not nearly as bad as a bad so-called Christian; whereas a Christian who lives contrary to the Lord's Commandments, and feels certain he is saved, is the worst of all, for to his other sins he adds the worst form of pride.

What is called the Social Gospel can be found in the Old Testament as well as the New. The two great commandments are in the Old Testament, as is also the teaching that one is to regard others as one's brothers. The eternal mercy of God and the importance of mercy on the part of man are frequently taught in the Old Testament, and also that love should extend not only to one's brethren by race, but to all. The Old Testament also speaks of the duty of charity toward the poor, the miserable, and the afflicted. The teachings which are most distinctly new in the New Testament and are not found in the Old are particularly a totally new idea of the nature of Christ, the Messiah; and the Kingdom of Heaven as the all-important goal of life.

Those who regard the belief in one God and in love to one's neighbor as the only things of importance are not distinctly Christian, for the Jewish faith includes this, as also does Islam. As to what is called the Social Gospel, much of this is included in the teaching of Confucius.

Those who would do away with most of what is said in the Gospels are apt to accept the Crucifixion and to regard this as important. But why was Christ crucified? If Christ was a wonderful, gentle, and loving man who taught the social gospel, as many think, why was He crucified? There is no record in history of a man being put to death for being a gentle and loving man and for teaching love toward one's neighbor.

According to the Gospels, the Jews stated the reason

for the crucifixion: "Jesus answered them, Many good works have I shewed you from my Father; for which of those works do ye stone me? The Jews answered him, saying, For a good work we stone thee not; but for blasphemy: and because that thou, being a man, makest thyself God." (John 10:32, 33.)

According to the account in the Gospels, the Lord said, of the leaders of the Jews, that their father was the devil, that they were hypocrites, whited sepulchres full of dead men's bones and all uncleanness. Such statements by most so-called Christians would be called very unchristianlike. If we believe the Lord made them, it is understandable why they crucified Him. But if it is thought that He did not claim to be one with the Father, and did not make the above statements about the leaders of the Jews, then His crucifixion is inexplicable.

The idea of a gentle and lovable man preaching the social gospel and getting crucified for it does not make sense. Who would wish to crucify the late Pope John?

If one does not believe in the possibility of miracles, he may in one sense believe in a God, but is he really a Christian?

It is said that science has proved that miracles are impossible. A true scientist would never make such an omniscient, dogmatic statement, for he would have a feeling for the truth in the words of Hamlet, "There are more things in heaven and earth, Horatio, than are dreamt of in your philosophy."

To regard oneself as a Christian and to regard Jesus as only a lovable man, contrary to all the records we have concerning Him, is nonsense.

Note that no one has been able to explain away the miracle of how a man born in a despised nation, with no formal education and with a few fishermen as followers, was accepted as God by all the nations of Europe.

The Lord's New Church, Nova Hierosolyma

(The New Jerusalem)

at

Bryn Athyn, Pennsylvania

A PICTORIAL ESSAY

by

Richard Yardumian

A PICTORIAL ESSAY

The Lord's New Church, Nova Hierosolyma, at Bryn Athyn, Pennsylvania

Emanuel Swedenborg (1688-1772). A portrait that hangs in Gripsholm Castle in Sweden

Theodore Pitcairn

The Tower beyond the Church Hall buildings houses administrative offices

The Church entrance, with the Right Rev. Philip N. Odhner (*left*), and the Rev. Theodore Pitcairn

The Church Hall used for social events

A closer view of the Chapel

A Greek fragment expressing the tenderness of a sister's love for her baby brother (in the Chapel of the Lord's New Church, Bryn Athyn, Pennsylvania)

Bust of Egyptian woman, Eighteenth Dynasty

An Egyptian princess of the Eighteenth Dynasty

A Greek Tanagra (terra cotta), *ca.* third century B.C.

In the Chapel

View from the balcony, looking north, showing twelfth-century columns and an Assyrian plaque on the north wall

View of the Chapel across the lawn from the southeast

View from the balcony, looking south over the lawn toward the Church Hall

The Council Room

Twelfth-century wooden French sculpture of the Lord or one of the twelve Apostles, in the Chapel (purportedly from Chartres)

Pablo Picasso (1881-   ) *Femme et Enfants,* 1961

EMANUEL SWEDENBORG

(1688–1772)

A portrait that hangs in Gripsholm Castle in Sweden

Theodore Pitcairn

**The Tower beyond the Church Hall buildings
houses administrative offices**

The Church entrance, with the Right Rev. Philip N. Odhner *(left)*, and the Rev. Theodore Pitcairn

The Church Hall
Used for social events

A closer view of the Chapel

A Greek fragment expressing the tenderness of
a sister's love for her baby brother

*(In the chapel of the Lord's New Church,
Bryn Athyn, Pennsylvania)*

Bust of Egyptian woman, Eighteenth Dynasty

An Egyptian princess
of the Eighteenth Dynasty

A Greek Tanagra (terra cotta), ca. third century B.C.

In the Chapel

View from the balcony, looking north, showing twelfth-century
columns and an Assyrian plaque on the north wall

View of the Chapel
across the lawn from the southeast

View from the balcony, looking south over the lawn
toward the Church Hall

The Council Room

Twelfth-century wooden French sculpture of the Lord or one of the twelve Apostles, in the Chapel (purportedly from Chartres)

Pablo Picasso (1881-   ) *Femme et Enfants,* 1961